TEXTBO

Women and Law

JUDITH BOURNE
LLB, LLM, Barrister,
Senior Law Lecturer at London Metropolitan University
CAROLINE DERRY
MA (Hons), LLM, Barrister,
Senior Law Lecturer at London Metropolitan University

OLD BAILEY PRESS

OLD BAILEY PRESS
at Holborn College, Woolwich Road,
Charlton, London, SE7 8LN

First published 2005

© Holborn College Ltd 2005

ISBN 1 85836 526 0

British Library Cataloguing-in-Publication.
A CIP Catalogue record for this book is
available from the British Library.

Acknowledgement
The publishers and author would
like to thank the Incorporated
Council of Law Reporting for
England and Wales for kind
permission to reproduce extracts
from the Weekly Law Reports, and
Butterworths for their kind
permission to reproduce extracts
from the All England Law Reports.

Printed and bound in Great Britain

Contents

Preface

This book grew out of materials designed to accompany our Women and Law module for the London Metropolitan University LLB. It is therefore an appropriate textbook for undergraduate students of law or women's studies undertaking similar modules. Although (sadly) women and the law remains an optional rather than compulsory subject, feminist perspectives are increasingly integrated into other legal modules, so this book would benefit all undergraduate and CPE law students as a companion text.

At first sight the law appears to apply in exactly the same way to women and men, and our legal system appears to be gender neutral. However, this book illustrates that this is by no means the case. It sets out many of the leading issues and the debates that surround them, aiming to highlight both controversies and common themes in a way which is accessible without over-simplification.

We would like to thank our families, friends and colleagues for their help and encouragement whilst writing this book, in particular: Angela Derry, Esther Shickle, Janet Loveless and Paresh Mistry. We would also like to thank our colleagues Jicca Smith, Jill Sheppard and Connie Ostmann for their support in starting up the Women and Law module that led to this book, and our students for their feedback, ideas and debates. We owe a huge debt of gratitude to Dr Rosemary Auchmuty (University of Westminster), our original teacher and mentor in this subject. Our final thank you is to Adam Mistry for his patience.

To our parents
with love and thanks.

Table of Cases

Table of Statutes and Other Materials

1

Introduction

1.1 Why a book on women and law?

1.2 Methods of study of women and law

1.1 Why a book on women and law?

If you've studied other legal subjects, they've probably talked about the law with the presumption that it applies in exactly the same way to both women and men. Our common sense tells us that women obey the same laws as men, which are applied by the courts in the same way as to men.

However, you may have picked up some hints that things aren't quite so black and white. In criminal law, you might have noticed that most of the recent provocation cases concerned battered women who killed their abusers. In tort and land law, you probably came across cases discussing how to value women's unpaid work in the home. Employment law has had to grapple with the issue of pregnancy. But all of these might have seemed like small parts of a bigger, gender-neutral legal system.

This book analyses those issues, and many more, but more importantly, it shows that they are not isolated examples. Instead, the position of women in the legal system of England and Wales is different to that of men in both obvious and very subtle ways, and has a long legal history as well as very contemporary importance. This book will introduce you to the issues, the debates and the wider theories on women and law.

1.2 Methods of study of women and law

One of the most important points to note about this subject is that the law cannot be studied in a vacuum. Our laws have been made by people who shared or responded to the attitudes and prejudices of the society in which they lived. The effect of those laws depends partly upon social and economic issues, as well as the interpretation of the legal words themselves. Changing the law alone cannot transform society, while changes in society can alter the law.

However, interpreting the way the law affects women is not uncontroversial.

There are fierce debates among feminists, as well as between feminists and other legal critics. One way to appreciate some of these debates is to understand the different kinds of feminist theories which exist, and we discuss these in Chapter 3. Following chapters will show you how the different theories have been applied to various areas of the law, and set them in a wider context (economic, political and sociological).

Before that, we will begin by explaining how women's legal position has changed in the last 200 years. Understanding how much things have altered, and how very recent some of those changes are, will help you to understand why this is such an important subject today.

2

Women's Legal History

2.1 Background

Women have criticised their treatment by society and the law since the Middle Ages. In 1405, a lady of the French court called Christine de Pisan wrote *The Book of the City of Ladies*, which supported women and answered men's claims that women were morally and intellectually inferior to men. A number of women followed her example, writing books in support of women's rights. In England, such writing became particularly popular in the second half of the sixteenth century, when Queen Elizabeth I provided a powerful role model for women. Pamphlets were often published anonymously under pseudonyms ('Jane Anger' is just one example).

While the ideas in these books were not necessarily ones we would recognise as feminist today, they were nevertheless important in criticising women's position in society and promoting women's abilities and aspirations. To understand their importance, as well as why ideas of women's rights and feminism have changed over time, it is crucial to look at the historical context in which these early advocates of women's rights were writing.

The Middle Ages

Medieval society was feudal. This meant that there was a rigid class structure, with the royal family at the top and serfs (peasants) at the bottom. In between were vassals who controlled land in return for giving their allegiance to the king. Serfs were the largest class, and had few rights. They worked on the king's or vassals' land, with women working alongside men. Thus for the majority of British people, there was little difference between women's and men's work.

However, things were very different for the upper classes. While men were frequently involved in politics, women were generally prevented from participating. The public sphere (eg politics, business, religious leadership, etc) was seen as a male domain, with inherited wealth and privileges passing down the male line. Upper class and middle class women were encouraged to stay within the private sphere (that is, at home pursuing female activities: managing the household; bringing up children; and behaving piously to provide a moral example). Wealth and power were protected and passed on through suitable marriages and through inheritance. This system depended upon arranged marriages and upon women's chastity (to ensure legitimate offspring).

Nonetheless, women often achieved a great deal in their own right. Some did so when widowhood or lack of a male heir left them in possession of lands and influence: Ela, Countess of Lacock, even rose to the very public position of Sheriff of Wiltshire in 1231. By the fifteenth century, widows of London businessmen were able to carry on their late husbands' businesses, inheriting their position as freemen of the city. Others were intellectuals or poets (as early as the twelfth century, Marie de France was not only writing poetry but actively criticising men who would plagiarise her work). Thus despite the general lack of opportunities, many women proved resourceful at making contributions to public and cultural life.

After the Protestant Reformation

An important way for wealthy mediaeval women to gain some independence was by becoming nuns, either instead of marrying or after being widowed. However, as society changed, so did women's options. First, Britain became Protestant in the sixteenth century (an event known as the Reformation) and nunneries were no longer widely available. Second, the class structure became less rigid, especially as a new middle class (who made their wealth through trade) developed. However, women of this new class tended to be bound by many restrictions similar to those of aristocratic ladies.

The limited ideas of women's rights at this time are well illustrated by the views of Thomas More (later executed by Henry VIII). He was considered to be a progressive because he believed that women should be educated. However, he was not advocating equality: he thought women should have just enough education to enable them to be pious, bring up their children and carry out their domestic chores.

Many women from this new middle class were very critical of their expected role and of their inferior education. One such critic was Mary Astell, a coal merchant's daughter who received some education from her uncle. She left home in her 20s and lived independently in London until her death during an operation for breast cancer in 1731. In 1694, she published *A Serious Proposal to the Ladies*. This controversial book suggested that wealthy women should use their dowries to set up colleges for middle and upper class single women. These residential institutions would enable women to receive a wide education and to live independently without husbands. In her next book, *Some Reflections on Marriage* (1706) Astell criticised marriage as tyrannical, asking 'If all men are born free, why are women born slaves?'. However, despite these radical opinions, Astell's views on other issues were very typical for an upper middle class woman: the colleges were not for lower class women, and she was both a royalist and a Tory.

2.2 The eighteenth century: liberalism

The eighteenth century saw the rise of a very important political philosophy which is still influential today: liberalism. Declaring that 'all men are created equal', it was opposed to the old feudal system and inspired historical events like the French Revolution and the US Constitution, but originally had little to say directly to women. Nonetheless, many women were inspired by liberal philosophy and used it as the basis of feminist writing and campaigns (see Chapter 3).

Perhaps the best known eighteenth century liberal feminist was Mary Wollstonecraft, often described as the 'mother of feminism'. The daughter of a small farmer, she had to earn her own living. Initially she worked as a governess and in 1783 she opened a school which subsequently failed; she returned to being a governess until she eventually made a living from her writing. Inspired by the French Revolution, she went to France in 1793 where she further developed her liberal views. She later lived with the philosopher William Godwin whom she married upon becoming pregnant. She died in 1797 after giving birth to Mary Wollstonecraft Shelley, who would become famous in her own right as the author of *Frankenstein*.

Her most famous book was *A Vindication of the Rights of Women*. This work was very radical at that time, although it accepted the idea of different roles for women and men. It criticised women's education and their position in the family as condemning them to ignorance, 'headstrong passions and grovelling vices': she argued that they were trained to outwardly obey men while obtaining male protection by cunning.

Wollstonecraft believed that only through education could women develop solid virtues. However, such virtues were to be judged by their conduct as 'daughters, wives and mothers': emancipation would make them better in their allocated role rather than take them out of the private sphere.

2.3 Victorian feminism: introduction

The Reform Act 1832 extended the vote to a large number of men but women were excluded from electing MPs or standing for Parliament themselves. They also faced a number of other legal disabilities: women were excluded from universities and professions; when married, they lost control over their property; if a marriage ended, they had no rights over their children and virtually no access to divorce.

The growing feminist movement (often referred to as the 'first wave' of feminism) campaigned on all these issues. Many such campaigns were based on the liberal philosophy that we are all born equal, and sought women's equality with men, concentrating upon rights in the public sphere of paid employment and politics. However, other feminists looked beyond these issues to ones such as prostitution, child abuse and the double standard which overlooked men's sexual activity outside marriage but condemned women for the same behaviour. Their campaigns can be called 'radical' because they suggested that men as well as women needed to change – in private as well as in public – and that removing women's legal disabilities alone was not enough.

Women's legal position in the nineteenth century

Imagine that you are a woman in 1837, when Victoria becomes queen. If you are middle class, your male relatives will be able to vote in parliamentary elections but you will not. Your brothers will be able to go to university and enter professions such as law and medicine, but you will not. You will be expected to marry, but by marrying you will become a feme covert. This means that legally, you and your husband are one person – and that person is your husband. The consequences affect every part of your life.

1. You cannot have your own money or property (even the clothes you are wearing belong to your husband).
2. Your husband can chastise you, ie physically punish you for disobedience.
3. Your husband has the right to sexual intercourse with you whenever he chooses: legally, he cannot be guilty of raping you.
4. You have no rights over your children: even a baby you are breastfeeding is not in your guardianship.
5. You can only divorce your husband by Act of Parliament, a very expensive and difficult process which will leave you a social outcast.
6. If you and your husband separate or divorce, you have no right even to see your children.

As a working class woman, you would be even worse off. The same laws would apply to you, but some would have a harsher effect on you.

1. Neither you nor your male relatives would have the vote.

2. You will probably work outside the home, perhaps in a factory, as an agricultural labourer, or in domestic service, but can be paid much less than a man for doing the same work.
3. If you are married, your wages will legally belong to your husband.

That your legal position today is very different is mainly due to feminist campaigns. Many important changes to the law happened in the nineteenth century, and we will now examine these in more detail.

2.4 Victorian feminism in the public sphere

The struggle for the vote

We have already seen that the French and American revolutions, with their idea that all men are created equal, inspired British feminists. Importantly, it also encouraged both men and women to seek universal suffrage, ie the right to vote for all adults, not just those who owned property.

The first major campaigns were for the extension of the vote to more men. At the beginning of the century, the vote was only available to male property owners. The electoral system was also seen as very corrupt. Some men had more than one vote, because they qualified in several different ways or places. Constituencies were of very different sizes, with the smallest known as 'rotten boroughs'. These had only a few voters left, but still sent an MP to Parliament, giving one or two landowners in those constituencies complete power over which MP was elected.

Important changes were made by the Representation of the People Act 1832, which abolished rotten boroughs and made small extensions to the categories of men entitled to vote. Some campaigners for the Act sought universal male suffrage, although almost no attention was paid to votes for women. The campaigns continued and further changes were made by the Reform Act 1867, which extended the vote to all men living in cities and to men in the country who had property with a rateable value of over £12.

In the few years before the passing of the 1867 Act, the campaign for votes for women also began in earnest. The liberal philosopher and MP John Stuart Mill put forward an amendment to include qualifying women householders (ie heads of household: only single or widowed women) in the Act; it failed, but over a quarter of MPs had voted in favour of it, an important encouragement to feminist campaigners. These campaigners included the 1,499 women of all classes who signed the women's suffrage petition in 1866.

The next step was to appeal to the courts: see *Chorlton* v *Lings* (1886) LR 4 CP 374. Mary Abbott attempted to register to vote but was refused; she challenged this refusal in court. She argued that women were incorporated into the 1867 Act because the earlier Lord Brougham's Act 1851 said 'words importing the masculine gender shall be deemed and taken to include females, unless the contrary is expressly provided'. In other words, because the 1867 Act did not specifically say that women were excluded, its references to men should be deemed to include women. Had the court agreed, women would have had the right to vote. However, this argument was rejected. The court said that women could be excluded not only where this was expressly stated, but also where it could be 'properly implied'.

The judge, Bovill CJ, went on to explain why women's exclusion should be implied in this instance. He said that women were denied the vote because of 'the respect and honour in which [they] are held', and that, rather than a disadvantage, it was 'a privilege of the sex' because it upheld female decorum. In other words, the oppression of women was disguised as protection and male chivalry. We will see throughout this chapter that similar arguments have been used to deny all sorts of rights to women, while the law often failed to protect women when they most needed its help.

Despite these setbacks, the campaign for votes for women continued. Women's suffrage societies had been set up throughout Britain, and they presented petitions and supported Bills placed before parliament.

In 1894, the movement entered a new phase when the National Union of Women's Suffrage Societies (NUWSS) was formed. This was an organisation of suffragists, ie women seeking to win the vote by constitutional means, working within the existing political system. They were led by Millicent Fawcett, who moved in political circles and was married to an MP. The NUWSS was significant because it was the first such national union, uniting many women's groups within one political organisation.

However, some women became disillusioned with conventional politics when, by the end of the century, women had still not gained the vote. Emmeline Pankhurst, an established suffragist, formed the Women's Social and Political Union (WSPU) in 1903. The WSPU felt that conventional, ladylike methods had achieved little: it was pointless to produce petitions which were frequently ignored, and rely upon sympathetic men to put their case in parliament. The women of the new organisation used demonstrations, parades, plays and literature, and even a chain of shops selling WSPU merchandise, to promote their cause. They heckled meetings, chained themselves to railings, set fire to post boxes and broke windows to gain publicity. The *Daily Mail* used the derogative term 'suffragettes' to describe them, and this is the name by which they are best known.

The two factions became more and more distant from one another. Millicent Fawcett believed that the criminal activities of the WSPU, such as causing property damage, were harmful to the cause. She and the NUWSS preferred working through committees and democratic structures, while the WSPU had a very different structure centred upon the charismatic leadership of Emmeline Pankhurst and her daughters.

The campaigns, and particularly the activities of the suffragettes, attracted a great deal of public hostility – from both women and men. The women had to be protected by the police when they spoke in public, as their listeners threw missiles at them and pulled away the chairs on which they stood: for their own safety, they replaced these with soap boxes from grocers' shops. We still use the phrase 'getting on your soap box' today, a phrase that originates from an Edwardian feminist campaign.

Although the best known campaigners were middle class women, the membership of the organisations came from all sections of society. Many working class women were active in the movement, and there were also important male supporters (Mark Wilks went to prison, Bowman Watson Clark funded many of their activities). The high profile activities of the WSPU attracted increasing numbers of women to the cause, although most of these new recruits actually joined the less radical NUWSS.

By 1913, as a result of the government's continued refusal to allow female suffrage, the suffragettes were provoked to more militant action, including the arson of churches. When convicted of criminal activities, the suffragettes carried on their activism within prison by going on hunger strike. At first, the official response was to force-feed them (a brutal and very dangerous procedure). The government then passed the Prisoner's Temporary Discharge of Ill Health Act 1913, which became known as the 'Cat and Mouse Act'. Women were released when dangerously undernourished, then brought back into prison to complete their sentences when their health had improved.

The split within the movement became worse as the WSPU concentrated increasingly upon dramatic public gestures. Not only the NUWSS, but also other radical women, were critical of their approach. Working class campaigners saw tactics inviting arrest as reliant upon class privilege: being in prison was an option for middle class women with servants, but not for working class women with families to support and care for. However, all of this became academic in 1914, when the First World War broke out. Suffrage campaigning was put on hold for the duration of the war as women played a central role in the war effort.

The campaigns were not resumed as before: at the end of the war, the Representation of the People Act 1918 gave all men over the age of 21 the vote, along with women over the age of 30. This was largely a result of the pre-war campaigning, as well as a recognition of the work (for example, munitions manufacturing) which women had done during the war. The Parliament (Qualification of Women) Act 1918 enabled women to stand for election – ironically, with no such discriminatory age restriction. Constance Markiewicz was elected at the next election to become the first female MP, but as a member of Sinn Fein she did not recognise the Westminster parliament and so did not take her seat. In 1919, Nancy Astor became the first woman to actually sit in parliament. Only in 1928 did a further Franchise Act give women the vote on the same terms as men.

Medicine and law

It was not only in respect of the vote that the law had denied women were 'persons'.

They were also excluded, following the same reasoning, from many professions including medicine and the law. Although women could be nurses, they were barred from qualifying as doctors or as solicitors and barristers.

However, women did not meekly accept these prohibitions. Some women campaigned vigorously to be allowed to qualify in professions for which they had the necessary skills and abilities. Sophia Jex-Blake was one such woman. She wanted to follow the example of two women who had managed to qualify as doctors in the United States of America and who had then returned to Britain to practise. The first such woman was Elizabeth Blackwell, who had grown up and qualified in America but came to Britain to practise as a Professor of Gynaecology in 1858. Blackwell inspired Elizabeth Garrett Anderson, who qualified as an apothecary in 1865 and went on to establish the New Hospital for Women in north London (now the Elizabeth Garrett Anderson Hospital). By 1867, women were barred from following Garrett Anderson's route and qualifying medically as apothecaries.

Attempting to follow in these doctors' footsteps, Sophia Jex-Blake and six other women went to study medicine at Edinburgh University. Initially the University admitted them, although their male fellow students demonstrated against them and tried to bar them from lectures. At the end of their course, however, the University refused to let the women sit their exams. Jex-Blake brought a case against Edinburgh University, which defended it by arguing that they had breached their own statutes by allowing the women to study there.

Giving his judgment in the case (*Jex-Blake* v *Senatus of Edinburgh University* (1873) 11 M 784), Lord Neaves argued that women and men have a different mental, as well as physical, constitution:

> 'The general mass of an army cannot move more rapidly than its weakest and slowest portion ... Add to this the special acquirements and accomplishments at which women must aim, but from which men may easily remain exempt ... Much time must or ought to be, given by women to the acquisition of a knowledge of household affairs and family duties, as well as to those ornamental parts of education which tend so much to social refinement and domestic happiness ... we are apt to get a false view of the question by comparing extraordinary women with ordinary men.'

Women's rightful place, Lord Neaves went on to say, was as 'absolute mistresses of their houses', although he conceded that they could be midwives, a fitting and noble profession. This seemingly chivalrous attitude did not extend to all women. Whilst those in the middle classes were to ornament their homes, working class women were struggling to improve appalling conditions and long hours in the factories and sweatshops where they had no choice but to work.

Meanwhile, middle class women found it no easier to enter the legal profession. During the nineteenth century women had attempted to sit the Law Society's examinations but the Law Society had not allowed them to do so. In 1913, four women graduates took the Law Society to court: *Bebb* v *Law Society* [1914] 1 Ch 286. They argued that s1 Interpretation Act 1889 stated that the masculine provision included the feminine, so the Attorneys and Solicitors Act 1729 ought to apply to women as well as men, enabling them to qualify. However, as in *Jex-Blake*, the Court rejected this argument. The Court and the Law Society relied upon a mediaeval treatise, *The Mirror of Justices*, which stated that 'the law will not suffer women to be attorneys, nor infants nor serfs'. Since women could not qualify as lawyers, they would not be allowed to take the exams.

In the same year, the Legal Profession (Admission of Women) Bill was put before parliament: it was opposed by the Law Society and failed. As with the campaign for the vote, little was done during the war years (1914–1918) but in 1919 a very important piece of legislation was passed. The Sex Disqualification (Removal) Act 1919 made it unlawful to disqualify women (by reason of their sex or marriage) from holding a civil or judicial office or entering or carrying on a civil profession or vocation. It also allowed universities to admit women and enabled women to sit on juries. Section 2 specifically permitted women to be admitted as solicitors, even when the universities at which they had studied refused to grant degrees to women.

The first female solicitor, Carrie Morrison, was not admitted until 1922; in 1923, nine women qualified. In 1922 Helena Normanton (1882–1957) became the first woman to practice at the bar of England and Wales (Ivy Williams was the first woman to be called to the bar, but she then pursued a career in academia). The daughter of a pianoforte manufacturer, Helena Normanton became a teacher, history graduate and linguist, but she was determined from childhood to be a barrister:

> 'Indeed, I have a most vivid recollection of accompanying my own mother, at the ripe age of 12, to her solicitor and most eagerly drinking in all his remarks anent some mortgage house property. My mother evidently failed to understand their purport, and the kindly old man said, "I am sure your little girl quite understands what I have told you, from the look on her face". And turning to me: "Do you?" he asked. And he then and there made me repeat his observations. After I had shyly survived the ordeal, he then remarked, "Quite the little lawyer!"... "Well" I thought to myself, "so I will be when I grow up". I did not like to see my mother nonplussed in that way, and I still do not like to see women getting the worst end of any deal for lack of a little elementary legal knowledge which is almost common form amongst men.' (Everyday Law For Women, 1st ed, (Helena Normanton) Richard Clay & Sons, 1932.)

The 1917 Annual General Meeting of the Bar Council refused to allow women to enter the profession. However, after the enfranchisement of women in 1918 Normanton applied to be admitted to the Bar and was refused. Within 48 hours of the 1919 Act being passed she made a second application and was admitted as a student at Middle Temple. She passed all three exams on her first attempt while supporting herself by writing. In 1922, Helena was called to the Bar of England and Wales. She was the first woman to lead the prosecution in a murder trial, the first woman to conduct a trial in America and the first female counsel in the High Court and the Old Bailey. Her career was not a smooth one, however: in both 1922 and 1933 she was accused of advertising (barristers are not allowed to advertise), charges of which she was cleared; and (probably because of her sex?) her practice never really took off. She supplemented her income with journalism, public speaking and as a landlady.

Why did women gain these rights?

There are many possible reasons why attitudes changed after the end of the First World War with respect to women entering public life, having the vote and entering certain professions.

1. By the time the First World War began, women's campaigns had already made important progress and gained increasing support. Many of the rights campaigned for might even have been gained sooner had the war not intervened.
2. Women had carried out typically male work to assist the war effort. Although they were encouraged back into the home after the war, there was some feeling that they had earned new rights by their efforts.
3. Many professions had lost large numbers of their younger men in the war. Women were able to help to fill those gaps.

However, these new rights did not go far enough.

1. Only women over the age of 30 were initially given the vote, while men qualified at the age of 21. Many of the women whose war work had helped change public opinion were therefore still unable to vote. Women under the age of 30 only gained the vote in 1928.
2. Many universities did not take the opportunity to admit women and award them degrees. Although they had female students, Oxford University first let women actually graduate in 1923; those who studied at Cambridge University had to wait until 1948.
3. Although the Sex Disqualification (Removal) Act 1919 appeared to prevent women being barred from professions because of marriage, there were important exceptions. Women could be excluded by regulation from any post within the civil service or foreign service. This exception was used to require women to resign from the civil service if they married. In *Price* v *Rhondda UDC* [1923] 1 Ch 372, the courts also upheld a similar 'marriage bar' preventing married women from working as teachers.
4. Even when they were able to work in new jobs and professions, women had no right to equal pay. In fact, in *Roberts* v *Hopwood* [1925] AC 578, the House of Lords went further and declared that Poplar Borough Council acted ultra vires when it decided to give male and female workers equal pay. Lord Atkinson referred to the Council's policy as 'eccentric principles of socialistic philanthropy or … feminist ambition'.
5. The idea that women had somehow 'earned' their rights during the First World War was patronising. Why did women have to 'earn' equal status with men?

2.5 What about working class women?

While middle class women struggled for the right to obtain a university education and to work in professions such as medicine and law, many working class women were already working outside the home. This had little to do with equal rights. Employers would employ women – and children – because they provided cheap labour. Women took paid work because it was essential for economic survival. Their employment was often in dangerous and unpleasant conditions (notorious examples of women's work in the first half of the nineteenth century include jobs in coal mines and cotton mills), which endangered women's health and safety but paid poor wages.

One of the principal issues for such women was protective legislation. Such legislation would limit the work women could do and the hours they could labour for. While the law's 'protection' for middle class women was clearly a pretence for discrimination, excluding them from certain professions, the position for working class women was more complicated. The women themselves, their male colleagues, employers and middle class reformers all had their own perspectives on the issue and, to some extent, pursued their own agendas. Female workers had divided views on protective legislation.

1. Working conditions were awful, and protective legislation was many women's best hope of relief.
2. Unlike men, they had a double workload: paid employment outside the home, and domestic work and childcare within it.
3. Many women were unable to bargain collectively for better conditions as men did. Some were home workers, who were too isolated from each other to organise together; women were often not welcome in men's trade unions.
4. If they were excluded from their workplaces, many women feared for how they and their families would survive.

Male workers shared these concerns, and many felt that protective legislation could further men's interests too.

1. Social attitudes made it politically easier to get legislation to protect women enacted. It was hoped that once women had such protection, it would be extended to men too. For example, where men and women worked alongside each other, it might not be practical to have part of the workforce work longer hours than the other part.
2. Once the principle of state interference in the economy was accepted to help women, political opinion might change to allow similar legislation for all workers.
3. Some male workers believed their jobs and conditions were threatened by cheap female labour. Legislation restricting or excluding women workers could remove that threat.
4. Like middle class men, many working class men believed that the home was

women's proper sphere. Factory work, unlike domestic or agricultural work, could not be seen as an extension of women's domestic role.

Middle class male and female campaigners had their own reasons for supporting protective legislation.

1. There was concern for the health of children borne by working mothers, and for the standard of their upbringing when both parents were out at work.
2. Industrialists who had improved hours and conditions favoured other employers being made to do the same, so that they were not at a competitive disadvantage.
3. Many people felt moral outrage at the idea of women doing manual work. In particular, the Report of the Committee on the Employment of Women and Children in Mines and Collieries (1842) emphasised the way women worked partially naked, and alongside men.
4. However, some middle class feminists were concerned at the lack of formal equality if protective legislation applied only to women. Particularly where arguments were based upon women's greater weakness, they mirrored the discriminatory approach which excluded middle class women from certain professions.

The legislation which was produced achieved few of the aims of any of these groups. Powerful opposition from industrialists meant that the measures were diluted, brought in at times when they had limited impact and poorly enforced. For example, one of the first major Acts, the Ten Hours Act 1847, which reduced women's working hours, was introduced when a recession had already led to shortened working hours. It resulted in women having to work shifts, so that men's unrestricted working hours were unaffected. The Mines Act 1842 banned women from working underground, but was poorly enforced.

Progress was slow. For example, on working hours, it was not until the 1850s that women's start and finish times were required to be standardised. There was little further progress until the following century. Even then, the British government refused to ratify the International Labour Organisation's Hours of Work Industry Convention 1919, which called for an eight-hour working day. Only with the Factories Act 1937 was women's working day reduced to nine hours, with no more than six hours' overtime a week. However, this legislation applied only to women working in industry, and there were various exceptions and exemptions.

It is important to remember that while these legislative changes were significant for large numbers of women, many others were excluded from protection. Home-workers (in trades such as sewing and glove-making, where they were often paid by the piece rather than by the hour), sweatshop employees, and domestic servants were generally outside the scope of legislation. Women who worked in homes (their own or their employers') were seen as being in the private sphere and so outside the proper realm of state legislation. Their often isolated working conditions also made it difficult for them to contact and organise with other workers.

2.6 Victorian feminism and the private sphere

Marriage

While female children were kept within the private sphere by paternal authority, many adult women continued to be under male authority in the home through the institution of marriage. The law gave men power over women in the home, sometimes explicitly and sometimes by lack of regulation. For example, the doctrine of coverture (a woman's existence being legally 'covered' by her husband's) gave men legal rights while depriving women of theirs; at the same time, the law did little to protect women from abuses by their husbands.

In his *Commentaries on the Laws of England 1765–69*, the legal writer Sir William Blackstone described coverture as making husband and wife legally one person, the husband 'the very being or legal existence of the woman is suspended during the marriage, or at least is incorporated into that of the husband: under whose wing, protection, and cover she performs everything'. The practical effects of coverture were that women could not make contracts or bring legal actions in their own name, could not bring cases against their husbands (because legally, that would be the same as bringing a case against themselves), did not have rights over their children or even their own bodies, and could not control their own property. A man who raped or committed adultery with a wife would be offending against the husband's property rights.

Married women and property

Upon marriage, all of a woman's property became her husband's. Although he had control of her real property (land) only during his lifetime and so could not sell it, he was entitled to all the income, rents and interest earned from it and could even mortgage it. He had some control over what happened to it after her death too, because she could not make a will without his consent. Her personal property (jewellery, clothes, books, cash, etc) became his absolutely: he could do what he wanted with it. Even any savings from the housekeeping money which he had allowed her belonged to him.

Wealthy women did have a little legal protection. The equity courts devised the marriage settlement, which allowed a woman's property to be held on trust for 'her sole and separate use' by a third party (the trustee). The income from the trust belonged to her, and her husband had no access to the capital so he could not spend the money or mortgage the land. However, such trusts were of no use to a working class woman who would not have property to place in trust, and even for a wealthy woman they were aimed as much at protecting her children's inheritance as at providing her with a measure of financial independence.

Women without a settlement (ie most married women) had no financial independence. Their earnings and the clothes they wore belonged to their husband, who could take them and dispose of them at any time. It is not surprising, then, that many women were angry about these laws and sought to change them.

Reform first came in the Married Women's Property Act 1870, which allowed women to keep their income (but not other property) for their own use. However, this reform was motivated less by the ideology of promoting sexual equality than by the wish to save taxes. There were concerns that feckless, spendthrift, working class men were spending their wives' earnings, leaving the women to be supported by poor relief at the parish's expense. In other words, communities wanted to reduce the amount of money they were paying to these women by allowing them to keep their own earnings.

Greater progress came 12 years later with the Married Women's Property Act 1882. This enabled a married woman to keep separate property in a statutory trust, to use and dispose of it as she wished, and to enter contracts in relation to that property. She could both sue and be sued in her own right over disputes relating to her separate property.

The need for a statutory trust only disappeared with the enactment of the Law Reform (Married Women and Tortfeasors) Act 1935, which gave married women the same rights over their property as single women and men. However, although a married women could now sue and be sued as if she were a single woman, she and her husband could not sue each other until the Law Reform (Husband and Wife) Act 1962.

Married women and divorce

For much of the nineteenth century the only way a couple could divorce was by private Act of Parliament. The only ground for divorce was adultery, but while a man could divorce his wife simply by proving that she had been unfaithful, a woman had to prove her husband had committed 'aggravated adultery', ie bigamy, incest or unnatural vice. This double standard was based upon a man's need to be confident that he was the biological father of his wife's children, and to ensure that inheritances passed along the blood line. A husband's adultery, by contrast, did not confuse issues of paternity for children of the marriage.

Acts of Parliament were very difficult, time consuming and expensive to obtain, meaning that only the wealthy had any access to divorce. In addition, there was huge social stigma, especially for an adulterous woman. When divorce became a matter for the courts, with the Matrimonial Causes Act 1857, the grounds for divorce remained almost unchanged, although 'aggravated adultery' was expanded to include adultery with desertion for two years, adultery with cruelty, or rape (of a woman other than the wife). Importantly, divorce was now quicker and cheaper, although it was still out of the reach of most people because of legal costs and the need to travel to the court in London. It also continued to carry enormous social stigma.

The Matrimonial Causes Act 1923 finally equalised the grounds for divorce. It created one single ground of simple adultery by husband or wife. This reform was important, but still prevented people from divorcing where neither party had committed adultery. The later Matrimonial Causes Act 1937 finally increased the grounds to include cruelty or three years' desertion.

2.7 Victorian mothers and child custody

The mothers of illegitimate children were their legal guardians. If the father's identity could be proved, he would have a duty to support the mother financially so that she was not dependent upon parish poor relief. The identity of the father was often known because of his relationship with the woman, and by making him pay for their child's upkeep, the burden on the ratepayers of the parish was reduced. However, he generally had no rights or duties beyond that financial one. Since an illegitimate child was not usually heir to the father's property, there was no perceived need for the father to have control over the child's upbringing. Further, the imposition of the burden of bringing up a baby upon the mother reflected the sexual double standard which condemned women for sexual activity outside marriage, but condoned it in men. The mother had to pay the social, practical and emotional price of her sin; the father only paid a financial price.

However, as we have seen, married women were entirely subject to their husbands' control, and this was as true with regard to what happened to their children as with their money and property. Men's rights over their legitimate children were absolute: a mother had no legal right to bring up, or even see, her own daughters and sons. Thus in an 1824 case, a father who was in prison with his mistress retained custody of his child, while the innocent mother had no rights at all (*Ex parte Skinner* (1824) 9 Moore 278; (1824) 27 Rev Rep 710). A father even retained his rights after death: he was legally entitled to appoint guardians for the children in his will, regardless of the mother's wishes. The effect of these laws was not only to deny women who separated from their husbands any rights over their children, but also to prevent women from leaving unhappy, abusive or adulterous marriages for fear of losing their children.

A clear example of the courts' attitudes can be seen in *R v De Manneville* [1804] 5 East 221 (discussed in detail by Danaya C Wright, '*De Manneville v De Manneville*: Rethinking the Birth of Custody Law Under Patriarchy' (1999) 17(2) *Law and History Review* 247). Mr and Mrs De Manneville had separated shortly after their marriage as a result of his ill treatment of her. However, Mr De Manneville was much poorer than his wife, and threatened to prevent her from seeing her child again if she did not sign over property and make a will in his favour. In 1804, Mr De Manneville snatched the baby while his wife was breast-feeding it, and carried it off almost naked in an open carriage during bad weather. Mrs De Manneville applied to the court to have the baby returned to her. Britain was at war with France, and she was especially concerned that her French husband might take the baby abroad either by choice or because he was deported as an enemy alien. However, despite his nationality and his utter failure to take account of the child's needs, Mr De Manneville's right to custody of the baby was upheld. The court said that only if he abused his rights over the child to the detriment of that child would they take those rights from him. However, they did not accept that the father's treatment in this case had injured the baby.

Mrs De Manneville did not let the matter rest there, and appealed to the chancery court. This court applied the law of equity. She argued both that her husband was unsuitable to care for the child, especially given his irreligious views and ill treatment of her, and that the very young age of the child meant that it needed to stay with her. Lord Eldon was sympathetic to her, but ruled against her because the doctrine of coverture meant that first, she was not legally entitled to live separately from her husband and second, she was not a separate legal person from him and so could not bring a case against him (*De Manneville* v *De Manneville* [1804] 10 Ves 51). However, he did make an order forbidding Mr De Manneville from removing the child abroad.

At the same time, the court referred to a case involving Sir W Murray, who wanted custody of a child born to his wife during their marriage. The court accepted that there was no reason to believe Sir W Murray was in fact the child's father, but even that was not a sufficient ground for denying him custody.

Likewise, the husband's misbehaviour was not a ground for refusing him custody of the children, as Mrs Greenhill discovered when her husband sought the return of their children in *R* v *Greenhill* (1836) 4 A & E 624. She had left him when she discovered that he was openly living in an adulterous relationship with a Mrs Graham. However, despite his adultery, the fact that at least one of his children did not even know him by sight, and his admission that he would not look after the children himself but would place them in the care of his mother (with whom both he and his wife had quarreled), the court ordered them to be returned to his custody. They emphasised that only where there was danger to the child would the father not be given custody, and claimed that the court did not even have the right to order that Mrs Greenhill should see her children. Lord Denman claimed that this ruling was in the best interests of children: 'any doubts left on the minds of the public as to the right to claim the custody of children might lead to dreadful disputes, and even endanger the lives of persons at the most helpless age'. Rather than lose her children, Mrs Greenhill defied the court order by fleeing abroad with them.

Perhaps the most famous child custody case, and one which launched a campaign for law reform, was that of Caroline Norton. Her husband Richard was violent and their marriage was an unhappy one. When Caroline left the marital home after a row, her husband used the opportunity to place the children in his cousin's care, and refused to let Caroline see them. She found that she had no legal rights to access, and was separated from them for some time; permanently in the case of one child, who died before she saw him again.

Although she had no legal remedy, Caroline was a published author and campaigned publicly against the law. Working with an MP, Sargeant Talfourd (who ironically had been Mr Greenhill's barrister in his custody case), she saw the Infants' Custody Act 1839 passed – despite the arguments of some MPs that no woman of 'delicate mind' would go to court to enforce her rights, and so there was no point in granting them. Married women now had some very limited rights: they could seek custody of a child under the age of seven and access to a child over seven years old, although whether such petitions were granted was a decision for the courts, who applied strict moral standards to women applicants in a way they had refused to do for men.

In particular, a woman's adultery was considered an absolute bar to her obtaining custody, as Mrs Seddon found to her cost in 1862 (*Seddon* v *Seddon and Doyle* (1862) 2 Sw & Tr 640). She had committed adultery, but the court recognised that her husband's own adultery and neglect had driven her to this: he was very far from blameless himself. Nonetheless, her conduct removed her right to access to her children. The judge opined that 'it will probably have a salutary effect on the interest of the public morality, that it should be known that a woman, if found guilty of adultery, will forfeit as far as this court is concerned, all rights to the custody of or access to her children'. One could assume, however, that the effect on public male morality was far from salutary.

The Custody of Infants Act 1873 increased the age limit so that mothers could petition for custody of children under the age of 16. However, there was still no equality between men and women, since women had to show that they were of good character. These Acts were limited and unsatisfactory: they were only available to those women rich enough to bring a court case, and 'pure' enough to show that they had not committed adultery or otherwise behaved in a way of which the court did not approve.

One of the most prominent women to have her morality examined by the court was Annie Besant. A lifelong activist, she had married a Church of England vicar but became atheist and the marriage ended. She then worked with Charles Bradlaugh to promote birth control among the poor, publishing a book for which they were prosecuted (but acquitted) in 1877. She subsequently became a socialist, and famously led the match girls' strike. Young women working at Bryant & May's factory in London were exposed to high levels of phosphorous, and developed 'phossy jaw', a kind of cancer. Annie led their successful strike for better pay and conditions. Finally, she converted to theosophism, a religion which claimed that all religions share a fundamental truth, and was heavily influenced by Asian mysticism. She devoted much of the rest of her life to promoting theosophy and working for India.

However, it was atheism and her campaigning on birth control which came under court scrutiny. When their marriage ended, the Reverend and Mrs Besant had agreed that she would have custody of their daughter Mabel for 11 months each year. Mrs Besant did not allow Mabel to receive religious instruction, and the

Reverend sought to have his daughter removed from her custody. The Court of Appeal considered her prosecution for the 'obscene book' and her atheism, and held that these were sufficient grounds for removing Mabel from her custody (*In Re Besant* [1879] 11 Ch 508 (CA)). The deed of separation originally agreed between the couple had no effect upon the Court's decision: they felt that the duty to ensure that the child was brought up in her father's religion was more important.

The Guardianship of Infants Act 1886 brought further advances in the law. Section 3 gave a mother the power to appoint a guardian to act after her death. The courts were also specifically allowed to take into account the wishes of the mother as well as those of the father when making custody and access orders (s5).

Section 7 of the Act allowed the court to refuse custody to the parent whose behaviour caused the divorce. Although this now meant that fathers' behaviour could be considered too, the sexual double standard still applied since men had to commit aggravated adultery in order to be divorced, while a woman's adultery alone sufficed. It was easier for a man to show that his wife was the guilty party than vice versa.

Not until the Guardianship of Infants Act 1925 did the law give equal rights on divorce to both parents. It did so by emphasising the best interests of the child as the 'paramount consideration' for the courts. However, there was not yet full equality between parents: while they were married, fathers remained the legal guardian of the children until the Guardianship Act 1973.

2.8 The Contagious Diseases Acts

Many of the campaigns we have considered so far were largely based upon liberal ideas of equality before the law. However, a number of Victorian feminists went further, and developed radical theories about the relationships between men and women. They saw the need for more fundamental changes than simply legislation which appeared to give women equal rights. In particular, they attacked the double standards which ensured that women's behaviour was judged differently, and more severely, than men's.

We have already seen that the double standard reduced the effectiveness of laws such as the Guardianship of Infants Act 1886, which allowed the courts to take into account whose behaviour had led to the divorce. On its face, this Act appeared to treat women and men in the same way, but in fact the different grounds for divorce meant that women were still treated more harshly.

However, the double standard did not only affect middle and upper class women who could afford to bring or defend cases before the civil courts. It operated in a particularly punitive way against certain working class women, thanks to the Contagious Diseases Acts of 1864–1869. Despite their ambiguous name, these were Acts aimed at limiting the spread of sexually transmitted diseases among soldiers and sailors.

Sexually transmitted diseases were of enormous concern in the Victorian period.

Preventative measures such as condoms were not widely available, and not always terribly effective. Once a person was infected, there was often no cure for them as antibiotics had not yet been discovered. The result was that a large proportion of the population suffered from diseases such as syphilis, which could eventually cause insanity and death, and could also infect the unborn children of syphilitic parents.

There was particular concern in the 1860s that high rates of venereal diseases were affecting the health and effectiveness of the army and navy. One out of every three cases of sickness among the armed forces was caused by sexually transmitted diseases (see Paula Bartley, *The Changing Role of Women 1815–1914*, Hodder and Stoughton, 1996, p85). Since most soldiers and sailors were unmarried, much of their sexual activity took place with prostitutes. Senior officers and doctors therefore believed that the way to stop the spread of these diseases was to ensure that the men had access to healthy, uninfected prostitutes.

The Acts provided that any woman in named garrison towns could be stopped and taken for medical examination. If the examination showed that she had a sexually transmitted disease, she could be detained in a lock-hospital and forcibly treated. If she refused the examination, she could be imprisoned until she did agree.

A huge campaign against the Acts was launched, with Josephine Butler its most prominent leader. The Contagious Diseases Acts were objected to for many reasons.

1. The first Act was passed late at night by only a handful of MPs, many of whom thought it applied to animals (as earlier Acts of the same name had).
2. Not all the women taken and forcibly examined were prostitutes. Any working class women could be targeted: it was enough that the police said they suspected them of being common prostitutes.
3. The examinations were invasive, rough and unpleasant. Conditions of hygiene were generally poor, and diagnosis was unreliable.
4. The doctors were male, and often unsympathetic, making an internal examination a humiliating and degrading experience.
5. There was no due process: a woman wrongly suspected of being a prostitute or wrongly diagnosed had no way of challenging this.
6. There was no effective cure for sexually transmitted diseases. The most common remedy, mercury, was toxic and unpleasant.
7. Being held in lock-hospitals with hardened prostitutes was felt to coarsen non-prostitute women.
8. Nothing was done to examine men or prevent them from visiting prostitutes: women were made to carry all the blame and responsibility for spreading disease. Officers believed that forcing the men to submit to examination would damage morale.
9. The Acts therefore enshrined the double standard: men used prostitutes and spread disease both among prostitutes and to their wives and children, yet it was women who had to suffer the worst consequences.
10. Radically, many feminists identified themselves with prostitutes: they argued that

'respectable' women sold their bodies through marriage just as these prostitutes more directly sold their bodies on the streets.

11. Josephine Butler drew parallels to the abolition of slavery, arguing that the Contagious Diseases Acts were a 'slave code'.

12. She also argued that prostitution symbolised women's wider oppression, particularly their lack of opportunities for education and employment.

13. She claimed that the magistrates sentencing women to lock-hospitals were often themselves also clients.

14. The Acts appeared to legalise prostitution, since they aimed to provide safe, regulated access to prostitutes.

15. Vice was encouraged since the use of prostitutes was made safer for men.

16. The Acts were considered to be based on class since they affected the poorest prostitutes (those who worked on the streets) rather than the more expensive, higher class courtesans.

The opposition to the Acts included large numbers of women. Over a hundred women (including the famous nursing reformer Florence Nightingale) signed a 'Women's Protest' which was published in the national press. It took courage for women to publicly oppose the Acts since respectable ladies were not supposed to be aware of such matters, let alone to discuss them in public. They often faced threats and abuse. Nonetheless, the movement grew and attracted increasing support from women and men. However, it was not until 1886 that a Repeal Act was finally passed. (For further discussion of the Contagious Diseases Acts, see Chapter 9.)

The campaigns against the Contagious Diseases Acts are just one example, albeit a powerful and high profile one, of radical feminist campaigning in the nineteenth century. Although the largely liberal reforms (such as votes for women) are perhaps better known now, the radical challenge to the sexual double standard and the institution of marriage show that a sustained and far reaching critique of women's position in society was also being developed.

3

Feminist Legal Theory

3.1 Introduction

Feminists have not simply criticised and campaigned for or against particular laws. We have developed various legal theories which address how the law treats women, how it ought to be changed and the ways in which those changes might be achieved.

There are many different theories, and many (probably most) feminists don't fall precisely within any of the categories. Even those who broadly agree with one theory or another will disagree about some aspects of it. This diversity of views is one of the great strengths of feminism, ensuring that an enormous range of issues are debated from a wide range of viewpoints. Thus a single definition of feminism is neither necessary nor desirable (see for example Rosemary Auchmuty, 'Agenda for a Feminist Legal Curriculum' (2003) 3 *Legal Studies* 1).

However, to help make sense of the different ideas concerning law, we will concentrate here upon four broad types of feminism: liberal, socialist, radical, and postmodern feminism. The ideas discussed in this chapter will be referred to again in other chapters: indeed, liberal and radical feminism have already been mentioned in the historical context.

3.2 Liberal feminism

History

We have seen that liberalism developed in the eighteenth century, and inspired both the American and the French Revolutions. Liberalism emphasised the equality of all men, and it was therefore unsurprising that women began to ask why they couldn't have equal rights too. Many men responded by repeating the theory of an ancient Greek philosopher, Aristotle, that equal rights were based upon the capacity for reasoned thought, and that women were biologically incapable of this. The French philosopher Jean-Jacques Rousseau (1712–1778) argued that rights were not general human rights, but were specific to men:

> 'Men and women are made for each other, but their mutual dependence is not equal. We could survive without them better than they could without us … Thus women's entire education should be planned in relation to men.'

We have seen that in 1792, Mary Wollstonecraft responded to such arguments by arguing that it was only women's education, not their biology, which failed to develop their ability to reason.

However, it was in the nineteenth century that liberal feminism really developed as an important force for law reform. One of the most prominent theorists was in fact a man: the philosopher and politician John Stuart Mill. He stated:

> 'What is now called the nature of women is an eminently artificial thing – the result of forced repression in some directions, unnatural stimulation in others … men, with that inability to recognise their own work which distinguishes the unanalytical mind, indolently believe that the tree grows of itself in the way they have made it grow, and that it would die if one half of it were not kept in a vapour bath and the other half in the snow' (*The Subjection of Women*, London, 1869).

Equality in marriage, education and, in particular, women's right to the vote were seen as the answer to this problem. If women were treated in the same way as men, then they would reason in the same way, and thus they deserved the same rights to develop themselves and to participate in society.

Liberal feminist campaigns have therefore focused upon obtaining equal rights for women, so that they have the same political rights, education and employment rights as men. We have seen how women campaigned for, and achieved, the right to vote and the right to higher education and professional careers. However, liberal feminism did not end with the achievement of those rights. (Nor was liberal feminism solely responsible for them.) Instead, liberal feminist ideas were developed throughout the twentieth century, with particular focus upon women's employment. Female bodily autonomy was also seen as an important example of the general liberal principle of personal autonomy and minimal state interference. For example, liberal feminists based their arguments concerning the right to abortion on this principle.

Key points of liberal feminism

1. Entitlement to various rights is based upon rationality (the ability to reason). Because women are as rational as men, they are entitled to the same rights.
2. These are individual rights, such as the right to personal autonomy, the right to equal representation (one person, one vote) and the right to equal treatment before the law.
3. Equality means that everybody is free to compete on equal terms. Thus the focus is on eradicating prejudice.
4. The state should not interfere unnecessarily with its citizens, for example by unwarranted intrusion into people's private lives.

Who is involved?

Liberal feminists believe in working within existing systems, using methods such as political campaigning and lobbying. The approach is often seen as one of 'common sense' rather than confrontation and challenge: liberal feminism is seen as 'moderate' and 'sensible'.

Campaign – the Equal Pay Act 1970

Until 1970, women had no right to equal pay with men: in other words, it was perfectly legal for a man to be paid more than a woman for doing exactly the same job. However, the campaign against such discrimination began long before the 1970s. As early as 1888 the Trades Union Congress (TUC) passed a resolution in favour of equal pay for women (although their main concern was to prevent women from undercutting men in the labour market).

In the 1940s an amendment to the Education Bill 1944 which would have given equal pay for women teachers was introduced. However, there was a campaign against this led by Winston Churchill and Ernest Bevin, which culminated with Churchill declaring that supporting the amendment amounted to a vote of no confidence in the government. Supporters therefore felt unable to vote in favour of the amendment, and it failed. That same year, a Royal Commission on Equal Pay was set up but was allowed only to describe the existing situation, not to recommend changes.

Equal pay for women was seen not only as a danger to the economy, but also as a potential disaster for women (who were assumed to keep their jobs only because their labour was cheap). There was also an attitude that men worked to support their families, and should be paid accordingly, while women had men to support them and worked only for 'pin money'.

Nonetheless, women continued to campaign for equal pay. In the 1960s the National Joint Action Campaign Committee for Women's Equal Rights was set up, and organised a large rally in London in 1969. In 1970, the Equal Pay Act 1970 was passed.

It is important to realise that the same campaign can be supported by different types of feminists for different reasons. Many of those involved in the campaign for equal pay were not liberal feminists. Socialist feminists, in particular, supported equal pay legislation as a vital tool for improving the position of working class women. They were strongly involved in the campaign and played a leading role through industrial disputes and the trade union movement.

However, the seeking of formal equality in the public sphere of employment is a typically liberal feminist aim. Katherine O'Donovan notes that '[t]he aim was to eliminate women's differences as a source of subordination so far as possible by opening up the public sphere and assimilating women to men' (*Sexual Divisions in Law*, Weidenfeld & Nicolson, 1984). To do this through a political campaign for law reform is also characteristic of the liberal feminist approach.

Ironically, the campaign may have been liberal feminist but it was not necessarily one which all liberals would support. In particular, one prominent strand of contemporary liberal theory emphasises the importance of economic liberalism (not necessarily coupled with a liberal approach to other areas of life). This type of liberalism influenced the policies of Margaret Thatcher's Conservative government, for example. It argues that the liberal principles of equal competition, individualism and minimal state interference mean that the government should impose very few rules or restrictions upon business, and that the free market will work in everyone's best interests if left to operate with little regulation. On this view, equal pay legislation is an unjustified interference with the free market, and stops wages being set in the way they should be: that is to say, according to the market value of the particular employee.

Liberal feminists emphasise different aspects of liberal theory, and in particular concentrate upon how individual equal rights have been limited by discrimination. Thus there can only be equal competition if the law creates a 'level playing field' by preventing unjustified discrimination on the grounds of sex. In other words, the law is not interfering with the free market, but is rather enforcing fundamental liberal principles by outlawing such discrimination.

However, the Equal Pay Act 1970 has not been an unqualified success. Women's pay remains significantly lower than that of men. In 2002, women's hourly full-time earnings were 81 per cent of men's, while women's part-time earnings were only 59 per cent of men's full-time hourly earnings (Equal Opportunities Commission, cited in Malcolm Sargeant (ed), *Discrimination Law*, Pearson Longman, 2004). Because women do not always work in the same jobs or on the same terms as men, comparisons can be difficult and progress is therefore slow. For example, some types of job are done almost entirely by women or by men; some types of working (such as part-time jobs) are far more common among women than men. Even the later, more sophisticated approach of European Community law has not brought women's pay into parity with men's.

The concept of equality is also inadequate to deal with the situation where different pay is justified, but the degree of difference is not. For example, if two jobs are not of equal value, then equal pay in not appropriate. However, what if one job is of only slightly less value but the pay is much lower? That difference would be unfair, but not unequal.

Should the public sphere alone be the focus of campaigning in any event? Katherine O'Donovan points out that the equal pay campaign 'seemed to forget the analysis of difference that identified the private sphere as the location of women's oppression' (*Sexual Divisions in Law*). Equal pay is discussed in further detail in Chapter 11.

Criticisms and shortcomings

1. The law now states that women have equal rights, but in practice women are disadvantaged (for example by their unequal domestic and caring responsibilities and by more subtle forms of discrimination).
2. Male standards and values are accepted without criticism. For example, 'equality' is largely defined by a comparison with men – but do we want everyone to be in the same position as men are now, or do we want deeper social changes? Even more fundamentally, which men are we talking about? Liberal feminism can seem to be aimed at achieving the rights and advantages of the most privileged men for the benefit of the most privileged women, ignoring many issues vital to poor, working class, black, disabled and other disadvantaged women and men.
3. There is an emphasis upon individualism, but this neglects social relationships. For example, many women have responsibilities for children, elderly relatives, etc; they cannot treat themselves as detached individuals, nor would they probably want to: these friendships and relationships are an important and enriching part of life. At the same time, much of men's ability to think and behave individualistically exists only because of women's support (for example, by bearing the main burden of childcare, housekeeping and cooking).
4. Rationality is emphasised at the expense of other qualities traditionally viewed as feminine, such as co-operation and empathy.
5. The emphasis is upon the public sphere, for example through the right to equal competition in the workplace. However, many of these rights are irrelevant to domestic life and caring responsibilities, and liberalism can therefore fail to value these adequately.
6. Liberalism opposes state interference in the private sphere, yet this (the home and family) is the site of much of women's oppression. Women's responsibilities in the home, as well as issues such as domestic violence, all affect their ability to compete on equal terms in the public sphere.
7. While working within the system has historically brought enormous gains for women, can it be taken any further? Is a more radical approach needed?
8. A liberal approach to economics can operate against women's interests, as it

opposes state interference with the economy. This type of liberalism (sometimes called neo-liberalism or Thatcherism) became particularly prominent in the 1980s. Neo-liberalism views equal rights policies, equal pay legislation and maternity pay as examples of unjustified state interference. While most liberal feminists would disagree, they can find it more difficult to resist such arguments since they use similar principles in other contexts.

3.3 Socialist feminism

History

One of the most influential political theories of the last two centuries is socialism. It covers a huge range of different approaches, but what they all have in common is an opposition to unrestricted capitalism and a belief in greater economic equality. Although socialism can emphasise paid employment and thus ignore much of women's contribution through unpaid work, many feminists quickly saw its potential for improving women's as well as men's position in society.

One of the first socialist feminists was the Frenchwoman Flora Tristan (1803–1844), author of *The Workers' Union*, Imprimerie Lacour et Maistrasse Fils, (1843). In it, she wrote: 'I am demanding rights for women because I am convinced that all the world's misfortunes originate from the neglect and contempt with which the natural and imprescriptible rights of a woman have been treated until now'. She advocated the self-emancipation of workers through communal facilities including hospitals, old people's homes and schools to emancipate women as well as men. Her ideas influenced Marx and Engels, authors of the *Communist Manifesto*, Communist League (1848).

Friedrich Engels (1820–1895) later wrote about women's oppression, which he described as rooted in women's exclusion from social production (ie work outside the home) and in the private ownership of property. One consequence of this was monogamous marriage: 'Monogamy arose from the concentration of considerable wealth in the hands of a single individual – a man – and from the need to bequeath this wealth to the children of that man and of no other' (*The Origin of the Family, Private Property and the State*, Hottingen-Zurich (1884)).

Socialist feminism grew out of both an acceptance of socialist principles and frustration at the labour movement's failure to accept feminist principles. The relationship between feminists and the mainstream (male dominated) labour movement has therefore not always been a straightforward or happy one. However, there have been important alliances, and women have always been actively involved in socialist activism – from the Bryant & May matchgirls' strike in the late nineteenth century to industrial action for equal pay by women machinists at Ford in 1968 and Women Against Pit Closures in the 1980s.

Key points of socialist feminism

1. Capitalism depends upon the subordination of women, particularly through their unpaid work in the home which keeps male workers productive, and their unpaid reproductive labour producing the next generation of workers.
2. Issues such as the adequate provision of childcare are therefore public issues, not just private ones.
3. Because of the nuclear family's central role in capitalism, it is supported by ideology which favours women's principal role being motherhood and men's their career. It supports marriage while condemning single parenthood and lesbianism. Socialist feminism therefore criticises this ideology and supports measures which help liberate women from it, such as sexual autonomy and reproductive rights.
4. Equal rights include freedom from exploitation and economic and social rights.
5. These may be achieved in a variety of ways, from expansion of the welfare state to the revolutionary overthrow of capitalism.
6. Socialist feminism prioritises the interests of the working class (unlike liberal feminism, which often seems more concerned with the middle class).
7. The focus is upon class interests rather than individualism, and collectivism rather than competition.
8. The shared interests of working class women and men are recognised, and may be seen as stronger than the shared interests of working class and middle class women. However, relations between socialist feminists and the wider socialist movement has not been unproblematic. Many socialist and working class men have seen feminist aims as diversions from the real struggle, or even as opposed to working class interests.
9. Although women are divided by class (as well as race, politics, etc), socialist feminism recognises that they share a common oppression as women.
10. The emphasis upon human fulfilment through work can open the way to reducing the division of labour into 'men's' and 'women's' work: everyone does the work they find most rewarding, instead of conforming to stereotypes.
11. Technology is often seen as a liberating force, freeing women from housework and even from reproductive labour.

Who is involved?

Socialism emphasises working through coalitions of the oppressed. Thus women will work with men, and members of many disadvantaged groups can campaign together in their mutual interests.

Campaign – abortion

As with the other campaigns considered, not only one type of feminist took part in the campaign for abortion rights. Radical feminists and liberal feminists were also very much involved. However, here we are going to examine the socialist feminist role in the campaign for the legalisation of abortion.

We have seen that socialist feminists are critical of the ideology of the nuclear family, which sustains capitalism. One way to oppose this is to give women control over their own fertility, rather than forcing them into the mothering role the patriarchal state demands of them. Victorian socialist and feminist Annie Besant campaigned for birth control, arguing that it would increase opportunities for working class women. Feminists such as Stella Browne, who campaigned for abortion rights before the First World War, also advocated 'free love' (sexual freedom) and contraception. She argued that women could not be liberated by the end of capitalism alone: abortion was part of a wider transformation in women's situation, and in particular in their relationships with men.

In 1936 Stella Browne became one of the founder members of the Abortion Law Reform Association. This was a group of socialist feminist women who worked with the labour movement including the Labour Party and the Co-operative Society (usually through local and women's groups, since the Labour Party itself gave little support). There were a number of reasons why socialist feminists in the 1930s supported abortion rights.

1. Middle class women had access to safe, clinical abortions through private doctors. However, working class women had to rely on more dangerous pills (which were effectively poisons with miscarriage as one of the side effects) or procedures carried out by medically unqualified people who often used non-surgical implements such as knitting needles.
2. Repeated pregnancies had an often devastating effect upon the health of working class women.
3. Large families could put an unbearable strain upon family finances, especially in the economic depression and high unemployment of the 1930s.
4. Many working class families depended upon the woman's wages, but childbirth would prevent her from working.
5. Freedom of choice about pregnancy was vital for women to make the most of growing opportunities in the public sphere.

Despite campaigning, abortion remained illegal (with one narrow exception: see the discussion in Chapter 6) until the Abortion Act 1967 legalised it in certain circumstances. Abortion is still not available upon demand: specific criteria have to be met, and in particular the approval of two doctors is needed. Additionally, access to abortion under the NHS remains limited in many areas.

The law remains under attack from anti-abortion campaigners and MPs. One such attack prompted the formation of the National Abortion Campaign (NAC) in 1975. The NAC was predominantly socialist feminist in its approach. It formed alliances with the labour movement (particularly trade unions and the Labour Party) to defend the Abortion Act 1967, and played an important role in defeating bills seeking to limit abortion rights. However, working through such alliances made it difficult to pursue the more radical aims of the organisation, especially free abortion on demand, since the wider socialist movement is far from universally accepting of such feminist principles. Radical feminists in particular were uncomfortable with such compromises and coalitions; socialist feminists were generally cautious but more pragmatic about them.

Criticisms and shortcomings

1. Socialist feminism depends upon accepting socialism: many people disagree with socialist theory.
2. While socialism may support women's liberation in principle, many socialist men still expect women to do the housework, the secretarial work and the cooking.
3. Many male workers do not even support feminism in principle. For example, during the twentieth century many trade union campaigns in male dominated industries were aimed at keeping women out so that they did not undercut male wages.
4. Not only the capitalist system, but also individual men (of all classes) benefit from female subordination.
5. It is difficult to adequately explain women's oppression in economic and class terms alone (and most socialist feminists no longer seek to do so).
6. Like liberalism, socialism is a political theory devised largely by men, which women have had to fit themselves into.
7. Socialist feminism may have relatively little to say about women who do not live with men within the nuclear family, such as childless single women and lesbians.

3.4 Radical feminism

History

Feminists have taken a radical, rather than liberal or socialist feminist, approach since the nineteenth century (if not earlier). For example, Josephine Butler in her campaign against the Contagious Diseases Acts recognised that the problem was one of attitudes to sexuality, particularly the double standard which condemned female prostitutes but endorsed and protected their male clients.

However, the term 'radical feminism' came into wider use in the 1970s and 1980s. Although it is less dominant now, and in particular has been the focus of postmodernist attacks, radical feminism is still an important strand of the women's movement and has in turn provided its own critiques of postmodernism. Like the other types of feminist theory, there are many different strands within radical feminism; the most extreme form is lesbian separatism, which advocates a complete withdrawal of women's energies from men and male institutions as the only way to allow women to develop our own theories and change society. Since lesbian separatists would avoid any involvement with the patriarchal institution of the courts, they have had perhaps the least influence upon feminist legal theory, although their criticisms of involvement in the legal system are reflected in the cautious approach of many other radical feminists. As Audre Lorde stated: 'the master's tools will never dismantle the master's house' (*Sister Outsider: Essays and Speeches*, Crossing Press, (1984)).

Key points of radical feminism

1. Radical feminism sees patriarchy (the system of male domination) as the central oppressive force for women, and sexuality as the central site of that oppression. Important issues therefore include sexual violence, pornography, the sexual double standard, and 'compulsory heterosexuality'.

2. Adrienne Rich identified the political institution of 'compulsory heterosexuality': the way that society does not allow women a free choice between heterosexuality and lesbianism, but instead forces women into heterosexuality and thus into servicing the needs of men ('Compulsory Heterosexuality and Lesbian Existence', (1980) *5 Signs: Journal of Women in Culture and Society* 631).

3. Radical feminism represented a move away from adapting male theories to feminism; instead, it takes women and their experiences as the starting point.

4. The problem is identified as patriarchy, ie a whole system of male power over women. This is apparent in education, religion, the family, literature, economic exploitation and other forms of oppression such as racism and class, state power and violence against women (including sexual violence).

5. All women share a common oppression (though it may take very different forms for different women) and can unite around this. Their common interests are more important than the differences between them (contrast this with the socialist feminist emphasis upon the importance of class).

6. The idea of separate public and private spheres is criticised and rejected. The radical feminist slogan 'the personal is political' summarises the idea that we must examine our personal lives and relationships as well as traditionally political issues. Treating the private sphere as outside our politics means that we ignore the site where much of women's oppression happens (eg domestic violence, acquaintance rape and most of women's unpaid and unvalued work).

7. In examining the personal, we must recognise our own role in oppressive structures: for example, no matter how repugnant we as individuals may find racism and classism, white women as a group benefit from racism; middle class women as a group benefit from the exploitation of working class women.

8. Relationships based upon domination of one person or group by another are to be avoided in all aspects of life, from personal relationships to radical feminist organisations (which should ideally be collective and non-hierarchical in form, ie without 'leaders' or structures which place some members above others).

Who is involved?

Radical feminism emphasises the importance of women-only space and women-only campaigns. Alliances with mixed or male groups are entered into only occasionally, with caution. For example, many radical feminists had already experienced the sexist attitudes of male 'comrades' in socialist organisations, and were aware of the dangers in mixed-sex campaigns of women being silenced and expected to do the stereotypically feminine work.

Campaign – against sexual violence

Radical feminists have identified sexual violence against women as a crucial area in which they are oppressed. It can affect all aspects of a woman's life, including when and where she will go out (alone? At night? Through an unlit short cut? Past a building site with cat-calling builders?), how safe her home and family life feel, whether work is bearable or an intolerable place of sexual harassment, whether she dreads answering the phone to another obscene caller.

The campaign has focused upon three main areas. First, rape crisis centres were set up and continue to provide a vital service to women who have suffered sexual violence. The first such centre opened in London in the 1970s. Second, campaigns have attempted to change public attitudes. An important first step towards changing attitudes was raising awareness of sexual violence against women. 'Reclaim the night' marches in numerous British towns, and an international tribunal on crimes against women held in Brussels in 1976 were among the activities which helped achieve this. Third, criticisms of the law have aimed (and to some extent succeeded) at making the criminal justice system's treatment of rape victims more appropriate, from police report to eventual trial.

Radical feminists led the outcry over the decision in *DPP* v *Morgan* (1975) 61 Crim App R 136, which ruled that a man's honest belief that a woman consented to sexual intercourse, however unreasonable, meant that he would not be guilty of rape. One result of such campaigning was the Heilbron Report (1975) which recommended changes to the law, some of which were enacted in the Sexual Offences (Amendment) Act 1976. While the Act left the *Morgan* principle unchanged, it did introduce more positive measures such as restrictions on the questioning of complainants about their previous sexual history.

Further impetus to the campaign was provided by the killing of a number of women in Yorkshire by Peter Sutcliffe (the 'Yorkshire Ripper') and the police response to these crimes. In particular, women were advised to stay at home after dark, and the first non-prostitute woman to be killed was described as an 'innocent victim', implying that the other women were not. Feminists asked why there should be a curfew on women, who had done nothing wrong, rather than upon men, some of whom were to blame for such violence. They criticised the assumptions that women were safe at home, that women always had a choice about going out at night, and above all, that women should be forced to restrict their own movements (Dusty Rhodes and Sandra McNeill (eds), *Women Against Violence Against Women*, Onlywomen Press (1980)). The feminist response included a series of Reclaim the Night marches.

The division of victims into 'innocent' (chaste, virginal) and not innocent (promiscuous or prostitute women) has also been strongly challenged. In the legal context, attention has focused upon limiting the cross-examination of complainants regarding their sexual history, while non-legal campaigns have aimed to challenge and change these attitudes among the public and those who work in the criminal justice system. The campaigns for changes in the law have had real results. From the Sexual Offences (Amendment) Act 1976, which introduced the first limits upon the cross-examination of complainants regarding their previous sexual history, to the Sexual Offences Act 2003 which has changed the definition of rape in several significant ways (see Chapter 8), the campaign for legal reform has had a significant impact.

Sexual violence has not decreased, but the conviction rate has dropped. This did not come as a complete surprise to radical feminists, who argue that legal reform alone cannot be enough (contrast this with the liberal feminist approach). Nonetheless, the fact that rape is so firmly on the legal agenda at all is a tribute to the effectiveness of campaigns by radical feminists and others. While the criminal justice system remains under scrutiny, work on the other two areas – changing attitudes and supporting victims of sexual violence – also continues. As with other campaigns, such work is not done by one type of feminist alone: all feminist approaches have developed critiques of the law on sexual violence.

The law on rape is discussed in detail in Chapter 8.

Criticisms and shortcomings

1. The principle that the personal is political can seem to result in being accountable to the sisterhood for everything that a woman does. This may mean that instead of an attempt to change the world, the focus turns to putting one's own life in order. This is perhaps one of the most contentious criticisms of radical feminism: radical feminists would dispute it, and point to the huge amounts of positive, outward-directed work done by them, including rape crisis centres, awareness of domestic violence, etc. However, a lot of recent feminist writing by young writers does reflect a perception of radical feminism as judgmental.

2. A focus upon male oppression can encourage women to identify only with their bad experiences of men. As a result, women can be seen as passive, complaining victims.

3. At the same time, radical feminists have also been criticised as dogmatic, forceful and unfeminine!

4. The emphasis upon the system of patriarchy can turn into an argument that all

men are bad, all women good. What about oppressed men? What about caring men? What about unpleasant women? In reality, the radical-feminist position is more complex than this: while individual men all benefit from patriarchy, they do not all choose to do so, or benefit to the same extent and in the same ways.

5. Some women feel that radical feminism forces them to choose between their feminism on the one hand, and their commitment to other aspects of their identity such as their ethnicity or their heterosexuality on the other.

6. Collective, non-hierarchical working has often proved difficult in practice. Sometimes, particular women come to dominate the groups they work in; at other times, differing views within a group make it very difficult to reach any kind of agreement – how can disagreements be resolved without anyone feeling that they have been dominated in some way by other group members?

3.5 Postmodern feminism

History

Postmodernism is a difficult theory and one that needs careful thought and further reading. The term identifies it as coming after modernism: modernist philosophy emphasises rationality, the idea of humanity as progressing and the importance of science in understanding the world and achieving that progress. Liberalism is one example of a modernist theory.

However, from the 1970s there was a reaction against modernism, producing the theories known as 'postmodernist'. The postmodern movement covers art, philosophy, architecture, music and literature.

One of the best known writers on postmodernism is Jean-Francois Lyotard (1924–1998), a professor from Paris. In *The Postmodern Condition*, Manchester University Press (1979) Lyotard wrote that there was no one, 'grand' theory or truth about anything. There is no universal truth, rather many other smaller, local stories. He wrote that postmodernism means the collapse of the grand or meta-narratives (those which claim to be applicable in all times and places) which have legitimised the truth of history and science. He asks: 'What proof is there that my truth is true?'. This is the central question of postmodernism and can be applied to anything. So postmodernism rejects the idea of any 'grand' theory and admits that there may be doubts about everything.

Many feminists have questioned the usefulness of postmodernism, particularly because it rejects the idea of an essential commonality between women (Patricia Cain, 'Feminist Jurisprudence' [1989] *Berkley Women's Law Journal* 191). Postmodernism challenges what we understand by 'man', 'woman', 'sex' and 'gender'. It argues that, like other concepts, these have no universal truth. Instead, these terms are socially constructed, not based upon biological realities. They have no fixed, settled meaning. Our understanding of them (and even the existence of the terms themselves) are created by society, and vary from time to time and from place to place.

This idea that nothing has a fixed, ahistorical meaning is applied to the legal system too. It is not seen as a unitary system with a single set of principles and interests, but as something growing out of particular and changeable circumstances. The legal system therefore acts in different, even contradictory, ways on different issues and at different periods. Postmodern feminism rejects any suggestion that the law works in a single way to further patriarchal interests, or that it affects all its subjects in the same way. Ngaire Naffine (*Law and the Sexes*, Allen & Unwin (1990)) writes that the postmodernist feminist believes that although the law is male-dominated, this is not in an organised or uniform way, because the law is not as coherent or logical as it makes itself out to be. Hilaire Barnett (*Introduction to Feminist Jurisprudence*, Cavendish (1998)) suggests that a postmodernist feminist must focus on the specificities of women's lives, rather than assuming the commonality of all women's experiences. This focus upon, and celebration of, difference is an important feature of postmodernism.

Postmodernist feminism's rejection of fixed categories and meanings is controversial. Leslie Bender ('From Gender Difference to Feminist Solidarity' [1990] *Vermont Law Review* 1) struggles with postmodernist feminism because it would make us unable to speak of women as a category for theorising and for political and legal struggle. Mary Joe Frug (*Postmodern Legal Feminism*, Routledge (1992)) agrees that 'women' cannot be erased from the dictionary yet.

Key points of postmodern feminism

This is not a clearly defined theory, but rather a loose body of thought (and indeed a rejection of the idea of a single, defined theory) which draws on interconnected ideas. Some of the most important of these ideas include the following.

1. The meaning of something is not inherent in it. Its meaning is called into being by words alone, and can therefore change (or be changed). Terms such as 'woman' are not biological truths firmly based upon a 'female body', but constructions given a certain meaning by a certain society at a certain time.
2. Any text is capable of multiple readings. We cannot assume that our own interpretation of words, images or actions is the only or 'correct' one.
3. Difference and diversity are to be celebrated.
4. Objectivity is impossible: we cannot be neutral, we always bring our own ideas and attitudes to our interpretation of texts and events.
5. Understanding can never be complete and truth is only partial.
6. There can be no universal ideals or principles, no fundamental values, no 'common good'.
7. No single theory can explain something for all people, at all times. Instead, our

theories should be specific in time and place, and emphasise differences as much as common features.

8. This uncertainty operates at a personal as well as societal level. Identity is fluid and shifting: when someone says 'I' they do not mean the same 'me' throughout their lives, regardless of the times, places and circumstances.

Who is involved?

Postmodern feminism is largely an academic movement. It has been developed by feminists in universities rather than activists in the wider community. Its origins in philosophy and literary theory, its rejection of 'common sense' understandings of the world around us, and its often difficult concepts and language, mean that it is not easily accessible to many non-academic feminists. However, some of its ideas have had a broader influence, particularly through 'queer theory'.

Because it rejects the idea of fixed identities such as 'woman', emphasises working on a local level, recognising that aims are contingent (ie no single aim is valid at all times and in all places), and celebrates the idea of difference, postmodernism emphasises loose alliances of different people. Since the idea of a fixed identity is rejected, those alliances tend not to be around particular personal identities such as 'woman', but rather about more general, less defined concepts such as 'queer' (defined as including an enormous range of sexual identities, not simply lesbian and gay). In a feminist context, the emphasis is upon 'gender' rather than upon 'women'.

Campaign

Postmodernist feminism deliberately avoids association with any particular campaign. Instead, it could be said to be campaigning for the end of the 'grand theory'. Feminism is often seen as one such grand theory, because it attempts to explain the position of all women through one set of ideas and principles.

Postmodernist feminists essentially say that there is no physical woman. Sex identification has been socially produced rather than being inevitable through our biology. Society attaches too much significance to the label 'woman' and to the female anatomy. Postmodern feminists such as Judith Grant (*Fundamental Feminism*, Routledge (1993)) believe that identity should be fluid and multiple. She sees the aim of feminism as being the end of gender and the creation of human beings who are self-determining.

Judith Butler argues in *Bodies That Matter: On the Discursive Limits of 'Sex'* (Routledge (1993)) that gender is 'performative'. It is a set of behaviours which we repeat and which are then assumed to be natural. In other words, there is no set meaning to 'male' or 'female'. Instead, they are called into being by our behaviour. Every time we behave in a way which is 'masculine' or 'feminine' we are performing gender (although we do not usually realise that we are doing so, and tend to think of our behaviour as natural). The reiteration of such behaviour effectively creates the 'masculine' and 'feminine'. In other words, gender is not a biological given: it is being constantly created.

This approach can lead to the view that there are many genders, each with their own behaviours and norms. Postmodernists argue that by making visible and recognising these different genders, we challenge the idea that 'femininity' is natural and thus liberate ourselves from the construction 'woman' (and from 'masculinity' and 'man'). For example, transvestism, drag, transsexuality, butchness, etc, can all be seen as distinct genders. The result is to give us an ever-shifting continuum of genders to choose from, rather than our being allocated to one of just two, which we are then compelled to perform.

Criticisms and shortcomings

1. It is largely an academic theory, in contrast to others such as socialist feminism and radical feminism which were based upon many women's own understanding of their experiences.
2. The language used by postmodernists is difficult to understand. It contains not only jargon, but also familiar words used in unfamiliar ways (eg 'texts' are not simply written words). Many postmodern ideas are not new: radical feminists have also argued that gender roles are socially constructed rather than dictated by biology. Black feminists have been aware of the lack of a fixed meaning for 'black', the fact that it is defined politically rather than biologically, for decades.
3. Many of the ideas and principles of postmodernism contradict our understandings of the world. While this challenge to fixed ideas can be stimulating and exhilarating, it can also be frustrating and limiting. For example, when society treats us very differently according to the gender we are deemed to belong to, how can it be useful to act as if the concepts of male and female have no meaning?
4. How can we make any meaningful attempt to improve women's position if we don't accept 'woman' as a meaningful term? Some postmodernist feminists have responded to these difficulties by accepting that 'woman' is a useful concept to organise around, even if they believe it is fundamentally meaningless.

3.6 Black feminism

Black feminism arguably includes a wider range of ideas and approaches than any one of the four theories considered above. While there are a number of common features in black feminist work, many (but by no means all) black feminists also identify with one of the other theories. We are therefore looking at black feminism not only as an important strand in its own right, but also as one which has had a profound effect upon other theories (although many black feminists would certainly suggest that the effect has not been profound enough).

Black feminism places race at the centre and does not assume that all women share common interests. It emphasises the importance of women and men fighting together against racism, and usually has an international approach. As well as being significant in its own right, black feminism has also had an enormous impact upon other types of feminist theory: all the theories discussed above now take far more account of race and of women's diverse experiences thanks to the vital work of black feminists.

Black feminism takes the experiences of black women as its starting point, but the way in which those experiences are analysed can vary enormously. In her introduction to *Black British Feminism: A Reader* (Routledge (1997)), Heidi Safia Mirza describes a theoretical shift during the 1980s from the coming together of ethnic minority women under the umbrella identity of 'black' to an emphasis upon cultural differences between 'black' women. She describes this as a shift 'away from confrontational struggle in the political and economic domain towards the struggle to be heard among ourselves in the social and cultural domain'. However, this shift caused its own problems: it focused upon personal behaviour rather than upon challenging oppressive structures, particularly the patriarchal discourse of whiteness. More recently, the emphasis has been upon how 'race' itself is constructed as a category.

A frequent theme in black feminist work is challenging the exclusion of black women's perspectives in mainstream feminism. The assumption that whiteness, white women's experiences and goals, were somehow universal was shown to be false. In the 1980s, socialist feminism was criticised for using the idea of 'ethnocentrism' to explain its exclusion of black women, rather than naming the problem as racism. In the 1990s, postmodernist feminism's emphasis on difference was challenged. First, a celebration of difference risks depoliticising feminism by removing any foundation for collective action; and second, the idea of difference assumes that one is different to something, ie whiteness, which is taken to be the norm.

Black feminism has had great impact upon all areas of feminist activism. One important example in the legal context is the work of Southall Black Sisters (SBS). This organisation has campaigned particularly upon domestic violence, and in consequence has a leading role in the campaign to reform the law in relation to battered women who kill. In particular, SBS supported and raised awareness of Kiranjit Ahluwalia, whose case helped transform the law on provocation (see Chapter 7). Their campaign used alliances with other groups, particularly radical feminists and Asian women. It was careful to balance, on the one hand, Kiranjit Ahluwalia's specific experience as an Asian woman and, on the other, the connections between her experience and that of other women in all sections of society (Pragna Patel, 'Third wave feminism and black women's activism' in Heidi Safia Mirza (ed), *Black British Feminism: A Reader*, Routledge (1997)).

3.7 Common themes

There are a number of themes which will run throughout this book. We will briefly consider some of them here.

Women and protection

As we saw in Chapter 2, apparently discriminatory rules are often presented as protecting women, rather than disadvantaging them. In the nineteenth century, judges argued that their decisions preventing women from going to university, entering certain professions or voting protected women from the burden of mental activity and responsibility. Women needed this protection, the judges suggested, because their biology meant that strenuous mental activity would cause physical and emotional problems.

Judges today would be unlikely to use such arguments. However, women are still seen as needing protection in some circumstances where men do not, particularly in relation to conception and pregnancy. A notorious example is *Page* v *Freight Hire (Tank Haulage) Ltd* [1981] ICR 299. Ms Page was an HGV driver, and among the loads carried by the firm's lorries was a substance called DMF. The manufacturers of DMF warned that the chemical was dangerous to foetuses, and so women of childbearing age should be protected from excessive exposure. On the basis of that warning, Freight Hire refused to allow Ms Page to drive loads containing DMF, so that she effectively lost her job.

Ms Page took her case to an employment tribunal on several grounds. First, she was not in the area when DMF was loaded and unloaded, so it was unclear that she would be exposed to it. Second, and crucially, she had informed her employers that she was not pregnant, did not want children, and was even prepared to grant them an indemnity. Nonetheless, the Employment Appeals Tribunal upheld the employers' actions on the basis that although Freight Hire had treated Ms Page unequally on the grounds of her sex, their action was taken to comply with the Health and Safety Act 1974. It thus fell within s51 of the Sex Discrimination Act 1975, which allowed discriminatory treatment which was in compliance with pre-existing legislation.

The judgment raises several important questions. First, what was Ms Page being protected from? There was no risk to her foetus, since she was not pregnant and had no intention of becoming pregnant. Second, why was this 'protection' extended only to a woman driver? DMF poses risks to both women's and men's health. Third, why was no consideration given to whether Ms Page could be protected from the risks in a non-discriminatory way? (In fact, her employer arguably already did so protect her since she was not exposed to the chemical during loading.)

The effect of the tribunal's judgment was to prevent Ms Page working in the already male-dominated field of lorry driving. This was done in the name of a protection which she neither wanted nor needed.

However, do women sometimes really need this protection? The issue is not always straightforward, as discussed in Chapter 2. It is also not purely historical: as the *Page* case illustrates, many of these questions are still pertinent today. There are special risks to pregnant women, from which they should be protected. Women often have little choice about taking risks if they are to keep their employment (especially as women often have more limited job options than men), so it is arguable that the law must step in to protect them. Protection for women might eventually lead to protection for all sections of society (this was the reason many people supported campaigns to shorten women's working hours in the nineteenth century: they thought that men's working hours would also have to change). However, feminists are very wary of such 'protection'.

It is often no more than an excuse for discrimination. As we saw in *Page*, men were at risk too: why should only women be protected? Women are currently protected mainly from risks to the foetus, but should women's whole working lives be defined by the relatively brief periods when they might be pregnant? Once the principle that men and women should be treated differently is accepted, why should improvements for men follow? In any event, some women are more protected than others: working class women in traditionally female occupations have rarely been given the same protection from occupational hazards as those in traditionally male occupations, or middle class women. Why can't women be trusted to decide what risks they will take?

Women and biology: hysteria and hormones

We will see again and again throughout this book that women are viewed by the law as governed by their biology. The fact that women menstruate, bear children and go through menopause is used to explain not just certain life events, but all aspects of our lives and behaviour. Women cannot do certain jobs because they may become pregnant; women are not trusted to make their own decisions during childbirth; premenstrual syndrome is used to explain 'unfeminine' violence.

The notion of a biological explanation for women's behaviour is certainly not new. The term 'hysteria' derives from the Greek word for 'womb', highlighting Victorian assumptions about the links between mental instability and female physiology. Neither is this use of biology neutral: it is not used to enhance women's rights and autonomy. Instead, hormones become a convenient excuse for controlling women's behaviour and explaining away conduct that might otherwise challenge stereotypes of 'natural' femininity. They are invoked to stop women from doing things viewed as 'male' (education in the nineteenth century, lorry driving in 1981), not to expand opportunities.

It is perhaps surprising then to realise that men have hormones too. Those hormones might make them behave in anti-social, irrational ways (consider testosterone). The levels of each hormone also change at different times, as do women's. However, when did you last see any suggestion that men should not make decisions, do particular jobs or be allowed full responsibility for their own actions because they are too 'hormonal'?

Irrational women, rational men

Women's biology is only part of the explanation for another myth: that women are innately irrational, while men are naturally rational beings. We have seen that this stereotype was used in the eighteenth century as a justification for withholding liberal rights from women. However, it is not just a historical curiosity: throughout this book we will see the stereotype of the irrational woman influencing her legal rights and responsibilities.

The idea that women are less rational and less able to make difficult moral decisions is a central theme of the law on abortion. The woman whose body contains the foetus and whose life will be deeply affected by it is not trusted to make a decision on abortion by herself. Instead, the final say is given to two doctors (legally envisioned as men). Likewise, the woman who is about to give birth is seen as irrational if she dares to disagree with the doctors and refuse a caesarean section. The court may respond by making an order which forces her to undergo the surgery.

As with most stereotypes, there is no concrete evidence to support this assumption. Indeed, Carole Gilligan has gone further and argued that women are actually better at making moral decisions than men (*In a Different Voice: Psychological Theory and Women's Development*, Harvard University Press (1982)). While not all feminists would accept her view, it is interesting to consider how different the law would be if it did recognise a superior decision-making ability among women. Can you imagine legal judgments allowing women to make similar decisions concerning men's bodies?

4

Women and Autonomy

4.1 Introduction

4.2 Forced caesareans

4.3 Female genital mutilation (FGM)

4.4 Forced marriages

4.1 Introduction

Autonomy is defined in the Oxford English Dictionary as 'personal freedom'. It is considered a fundamental element of being a fully functioning member of society and is what early feminists strove for in cases such as *Chorlton* v *Lings* (1868) LR 4 CP 374 (the recognition of women as persons with the right to make their own political decisions). Autonomy requires more than political or legal rights alone: to be autonomous is to have control over all areas of one's life. We will look at medical autonomy in instances such as forced caesareans, at autonomy over our sexual bodies in the area of female genital mutilation, and over our right to choose who we spend the rest of our life with under the topic of forced marriages.

However, it is important to note that the idea of autonomy is not unproblematic for feminists. Criticisms focus upon the problem that the idea of autonomy can be a liberal, individualistic one: personal autonomy rather than the liberation of all women. As we saw in Chapter 3, many feminists would dispute the idea that we should take such an individualistic view: we must look at the interests of women collectively.

The purely individualistic approach can lead to the endorsement of practices which are actively hostile to women's liberation. For example, prohibiting selective abortion of female foetuses in societies where boys are more desired has been seen as an infringement of personal autonomy by some libertarian feminists (discussed in F Moazam, 'Feminist Discourse on Sex Screening and Selective Abortion of Female Foetuses' (2004) 18(3) *Bioethics* 205).

The idea that everyone can have complete autonomy is also unrealistic: we all have some constraints upon our actions (the point is that they should be kept to a minimum rather than not exist at all). The difficulty, of course, is deciding where those constraints are permissible: should women be prevented from selecting the sex of their children? Should this vary according to cultural context, or to the sex chosen? Almost all our choices will impact upon other people: how much does our choice have to affect their autonomy before they have a right to interfere?

Autonomy can be a particularly problematic notion for pregnant women, since their body contains and maintains another body. How do we apply the notion of individual autonomy when the woman and foetus are not independent individuals? We will see that the law has not sought an answer to this dilemma: instead, it has claimed to uphold the woman's autonomy while simultaneously enforcing the view that her duty is to act in the best interests of the foetus, by denying her competence and rationality.

Nonetheless, despite these problems and reservations, we use the concept of autonomy here for convenience. We do not take a liberal view of the autonomous individual as separate from her wider social relationships; instead, we hope to show that each woman's autonomy is closely related to the legal and social position of all women. We are all constrained by the values and attitudes of the communities in which we live, and these affect (sometimes unjustifiably) the choices which we are allowed to make. If we do not change those wider factors, the greater autonomy of one woman is too often obtained at the expense of other women. In other words, if women as a group are to have autonomy, then individualistic solutions will not suffice.

4.2 Forced caesareans

Introduction

We have already seen that many women have had very little control or autonomy over their own lives, let alone their own bodies. Additionally, the social construction of motherhood demands that mothers should be self-sacrificing at all times, particularly during pregnancy. Forced caesareans occur when a pregnant woman is literally forced into having a caesarean section against her will. This is an extremely contentious area. In an age where more and more woman are now demanding caesareans, while others seek natural childbirth without medical intervention, women's choices about childbirth are sometimes viewed as problematic. The law and medical practice directly clash with the pregnant woman's assertion of autonomy. The pregnant women is not viewed by doctors as one patient, but rather two: the pregnant woman and her child (although of course the foetus has no legal personality: it has no rights of its own in law).

The current law

At first glance, the law in this area seems very straightforward. Every competent adult has the right to refuse medical treatment, as stated in *Re T* [1992] 4 All ER 649:

> 'Prima facie every adult has the right and capacity to decide whether or not he will accept medical treatment, even if a refusal may risk permanent injury to his health or even lead to premature death. Furthermore, it matters not whether the reasons for the refusal were rational or irrational, unknown or even non-existent. This is so, notwithstanding the very strong public interest in preserving the life and health of all citizens. However, the presumption of capacity to decide, which stems from the fact that the patient is an adult, is rebuttable.'

Re C (Adult: Refusal of Medical Treatment) [1994] 1 All ER 819 set out exactly when that capacity (competence) could be rebutted – only when the patient was unable to:

1. take in and retain the treatment information;
2. believe it; and
3. weigh that information, balancing risks and needs.

The facts of this case concern a male psychiatric patient (rather than a pregnant woman) and are worth noting. Whilst in Broadmoor Special Hospital, C developed a life-threatening gangrenous foot. C also suffered from schizophrenia and believed that he had an international career in medicine, during the course of which he had never lost a patient. He believed that although he couldn't guarantee it, if aided by God, the good doctors and nurses, he could survive without an amputation (and indeed he subsequently did). Justice Thorpe held in the High Court that although C's general capacity was impaired by the schizophrenia, he had satisfied the competence criterion and had arrived at a clear choice.

It is evident then that a psychiatric patient in Broadmoor, with delusions of a medical career, has been judged to be competent to refuse medical treatment. It would surely follow that a competent pregnant woman would have the same autonomous rights as the applicant in *Re C*? We should also remember at this point that the law only regards a foetus as having rights after it has been born alive (see Judge Helibron in *C v S* [1988] QB 135, agreeing with *Paton v British Pregnancy Advisory Service (BPAS) Trustees* [1978] 2 All ER 987).

We will see that in fact, this area of law has proved problematic. The courts have had difficulty in stating that the same principles apply to pregnant women as to others in apparent need of life-saving medical treatment. There has been significant progress, but it was by no means smooth.

Let us now turn to the most recent and authoritative case involving pregnant women: *St George's Healthcare NHS Trust v S; R v Collins and Others, ex parte S* [1998] 3 All ER 673. This case establishes that a pregnant woman has the right to refuse medical treatment, provided that she is legally competent. The forced caesarean in this case amounted to a trespass (a civil wrong, for which S was entitled to compensation).

The facts are both complicated and lengthy. S was a 30-year-old, pregnant veterinary nurse. When she sought to register herself as a new patient at her local GP's surgery, it was discovered that she was 36 weeks pregnant and suffering with pre-eclampsia. Prior to this she had not sought any kind of pre-natal care as she believed that pregnancy was a natural condition and wanted her child to be born naturally. At the request of the GP, S waited for two hours for a social worker to attend and another doctor was called. They all advised her that if they were untreated, both she and the foetus could die.

On application by the social worker and two doctors S was admitted to a safe place under the Mental Health Act 1983 for an assessment of her 'severe condition' (not a mental condition, rather her physical complaint of pre-eclampsia) and for monitoring. No reference was made in that Mental Health Act 1983 application to treatment for her mental disorder or depression. Once in hospital she continued her objection to treatment. Although S was assessed as being 'sad and distressed', she was recorded by the hospital as being legally competent. She was then moved to the maternity unit.

The following day the hospital sought an ex parte order from the High Court sanctioning a caesarean section. No evidence was laid before Justice Hogg (who dealt with the application during her lunch break), but she was informed that:

1. S had been in labour for 24 hours (in fact, labour had not started);
2. S had pre-eclampsia, and both she and the foetus would probably die without treatment;
3. this was a 'life and death' situation;
4. S had been admitted under the Mental Health Act 1983 for assessment, which was ongoing, although to date only moderate depression had been diagnosed.

Justice Hogg was not told that:

1. S was competent;
2. she had instructed solicitors; or
3. the truth about her stage of pregnancy (ie not yet in labour).

No one considered the issue of competence or suggested appointing the Official Solicitor on S's behalf. S was shown the order, spoke to her solicitors and decided that to physically struggle would be undignified. The caesarean was carried out at 10pm that evening, following which she rejected the baby, a girl. She received postnatal care for two days, and was then sent back to the psychiatric unit. There, she spoke to her solicitor, asking him to appeal her committal, and she was released the next day.

The Court of Appeal held that the caesarean carried out on S was a trespass. They held that a competent pregnant woman had the right to refuse medical treatment:

'In our judgment while pregnancy increases the personal responsibilities of a woman it does not diminish her entitlement to decide whether or not to undergo medical treatment.'

Further, they said (and indeed issued guidelines) that the Mental Health Act 1983 could not be used simply because the individual's reasoning was contrary to the majority of the community. Even when a woman was admitted for a mental disorder she could not be forced into a medical procedure unconnected with her mental condition (unless she was not competent according to *Re C*). The committal here was unlawful, as it was not for assessment of her mental condition, but for her pre-eclampsia. All such cases in the future should be heard inter partes, with the pregnant woman represented or assisted by the Official Solicitor.

History

The student would be forgiven for thinking that the law should have been perfectly clear even before *St George's Healthcare NHS Trust* v *S*. It had already been well established in law that the foetus is not legally a person before birth and has no rights (see *C* v *S* [1987] 1 All ER 1239; *Paton* v *BPAS Trustees* [1978] 2 All ER 987; *Attorney-General's Reference (No 3 of 1994)* [1998] AC 245; *Re F (In Utero)* [1988] FCR 529). Following *Re C* and *Sidaway* v *Governor of Bethlem Royal Hospital* [1985] AC 871 a pregnant woman should have full autonomy over her body provided she is:

1. an adult; and
2. competent.

Re C had confirmed that all adults had autonomy over their bodies, provided that they were competent. *Sidaway* (a tort case) established that all adults are free to refuse medical treatment, regardless of the consequences and despite the fact that such refusal may appear irrational, provided the adult is competent to make that decision (under the three-stage test in *Re C*).

The situation appeared to be remarkably clear: provided the adult pregnant woman was competent, she would be able to refuse medical treatment. However, difficulties arose concerning when a pregnant woman was competent (this may still arise today) and what constituted 'treatment' for a mental condition. These cases continue to have profound implications for women. We will analyse the cases chronologically.

In *Re S (Adult: Refusal of Medical Treatment)* [1992] 3 WLR 806, the hospital sought a declaration to enable it to carry out an emergency caesarean operation on S, a 30-year-old woman, six days past her due date, who was in spontaneous labour with her third pregnancy after her membranes had ruptured. Her condition was considered serious because the foetus was in a position of 'transverse lie', with an elbow projecting through the cervix. The doctors treating S feared that her uterus would rupture and that the situation was one of imminent life or death. They considered that the operation was essential to save S's life and that of her foetus; and that the foetus could not be born alive without the caesaerean. As a 'Born Again Christian', S (supported by her husband) refused to consent to the caesarean operation.

The Judge, Sir Stephen Brown, noted in his judgment that the couple were 'quite sincere in their beliefs'. Nonetheless, he ordered the declaration sought. His authority for granting the order was an obiter remark made by Lord Donaldson in *Re T (Adult: Refusal of Consent to Treatment)* [1992] 3 WLR 782. Lord Donaldson had suggested that a competent adult lost their right to refuse treatment where 'the choice may lead to the death of a viable foetus'. Sir Stephen Brown noted that the 'fundamental question appears to have been left open by Lord Donaldson in *Re T*'. He also noted that there was no English authority on the point, but that there was an American authority.

Quite how Sir Stephen Brown arrived at these conclusions is difficult to understand. Lord Donaldson's remarks were clearly obiter and it is well established in English law that a foetus has no legal rights. As for the American authority, he was wrongly relying on the US case *Re AC* (1990) 573 A 2d 1235. This truly tragic case concerned a woman with cancer (leukaemia) who refused a recommended caesarean because she knew that it would hasten her death. She had been clear of the cancer when she became pregnant. The caesarean was subsequently ordered by a court and carried out when she was 26 weeks pregnant, and both she and the foetus died. The Court of Appeal overturned the ruling of the lower court and said that the decision in virtually all cases resided with the woman. Only in exceptional cases should the woman's wishes be overridden.

Re S was a problematic decision. It led to women being forced to have unwanted caesareans: either following court orders or as a result of the medical profession using this judgment as a bargaining tool to elicit their co-operation. It was not until 1997, as a result of *Re MB* [1997] 2 FCR 541, that *Re S* was overturned. *MB* concerned a woman with a needle phobia. This was a genuine fear of needles, which were utterly terrifying to the woman. In their judgment the Court of Appeal doubted *Re S* and declared Lord Donaldson's obiter comment in *Re T* incorrect. Butler-Sloss LJ, giving judgment for the Court, commented obiter on a pregnant woman's autonomy:

> '[A] competent woman who has the capacity to decide may, for religious reasons, other reasons, or for no reasons at all, choose not to have medical intervention, even though … the consequences may be the death or serious handicap of the child she bears, or her own death. She may refuse to consent to an anaesthesia injection in the full knowledge that her decision may significantly reduce the chance of her unborn child being born alive. The foetus up to the moment of birth does not have any separate interests capable of being taken into account when a court has to consider an application in respect of a caesarean section operation. The court does not have the jurisdiction to declare that medical intervention is lawful to protect the interests of the unborn child even at the point of birth.'

This seems like an excellent principle. However, it was only stated obiter, because the woman in this instance was judged not to be competent. The High Court had already ordered the caesarean, which was then approved by the Court of Appeal. MB was not represented. The Court of Appeal said that her needle phobia had rendered her incompetent. Further, her panic, indecision and irrationality could be symptoms of incompetence. They felt that it was in her best interests to carry a full-term, healthy child, and therefore it had been correct to order a caesarean against her wishes.

Between *Re S* and *Re MB* was another disturbing case, *Thameside and Glossop Acute Services Trusts* v *CH* [1996] 1 FLR 762. Wall J developed a new and frightening approach to the problem of pregnant women refusing caesareans: rather than considering the pregnant woman's competence, he decided that a caesarean section operation could be used to treat a mental disorder.

CH was a schizophrenic, in the 38th week of her pregnancy. Her foetus failed to grow because the placenta was not working properly. Wall J ordered the caesarean as treatment for a mental disorder. CH was admitted to hospital under s63 Mental Health Act 1983, which states that 'the consent of a patient shall not be required for any medical treatment given to him for the mental disorder from which he is suffering'. Wall J considered that a caesarean (or alternatively, inducement of labour) was treatment for CH's schizophrenia because after delivery, her treatment for schizophrenia could resume. This is a very difficult decision to justify: if its reasoning is correct, then surely it could have been argued in *Re C* that the treatment for C's gangrene was treatment for his schizophrenia.

It would appear from these decisions that men with a mental disorder may be granted more autonomy than pregnant women. The courts have been prepared to follow dubious lines of reasoning in order to justify caesareans ordered by the court, in ways which were deemed unnecessary for the schizophrenic and gangrenous C.

Pain during labour is more probable than not, but has led to one woman not being allowed to refuse medical treatment on the ground that she was not competent to make such a refusal. In *Norfolk and Norwich Healthcare (NHS) Trust* v *W* [1997] 1 FCR 274, Johnson J found that a woman who had a history of psychiatric illness and who denied that she was pregnant, when she was in fact in labour, was not competent to refuse treatment because of the pain she was in during labour and the acute emotional distress that this caused. Such distress, they said, was aggravated by her medical history. She was judged not competent under the third limb of the test in *Re C*: incapable of weighing up the considerations that were involved. W clearly had an aggravating mental disorder, but the greatest difficulty with this case is that it opens the floodgates for courts to be able to judge women undergoing labour as not competent as a result of the pain and distress that they are experiencing.

Indeed, this happened whilst *Norfolk and Norwich Healthcare (NHS) Trust* v *W* was being heard. Johnson J considered (at the same time as the *Norfolk* case) an application from doctors in *Rochdale Healthcare (NHS) Trust* v *C* [1997] 1 FCR 274. The woman in this case was described as competent. Johnson J nonetheless said that she failed the *Re C* competence test because she was in the throes of labour: she was therefore suffering pain and emotional stress. C had undergone a caesarean in the past and said that she would rather die than go through another caesarean. Johnson J said that she saw death as inevitable and therefore was a patient who could not weigh up the considerations and make a valid decision. Compare this to *Re C*: he was delusional, he truly believed that he was an internationally acclaimed doctor and he, too, was fully prepared to die.

Despite *St George's Healthcare NHS Trust* v *S*, there are still problems faced by women during labour with regard to their personal autonomy. Needle phobia, pain during labour or an unwillingness to repeat the ordeal suffered following a past caesarean may all lead to a woman being judged incompetent and subjected to treatment that she does not want to have.

A caesarean is not a minor operation, it is major surgery. Most women do their very best to act in the best interests of the child they are carrying. We should take care not to allow the law to assume that a refusal of recommended medical treatment is made on a whim: it may be made on a very real and honestly-felt conviction. If a paranoid schizophrenic in *Re C* is allowed total autonomy, why not a pregnant woman?

Why is this a feminist issue?

The fundamental issue concerning forced caesareans is one of bodily autonomy. The law has stipulated that all competent adults have the right to refuse medical treatment. Feminists have argued that pregnant women should not lose this basic degree of bodily autonomy. As soon as bodily autonomy is removed, women lose a basic human right. Bridgeman and Millns argue that 'to override the refusal of consent of a pregnant woman denies her the respect for autonomy enjoyed by other competent adults and facilitates invasion of her bodily integrity' (*Feminist Perspectives on Law*, Sweet and Maxwell (1998)).

However, this issue does not exclusively concern autonomy. The legal approaches thus far also represent a furtherance of the myth that women are hormonal, hysterical and 'mad'. The women making these difficult decisions tend to be portrayed as unthinking, irrational and unable to reason. For example, Lieve Gies argues that in *St George's Healthcare NHS Trust* v *S* the Court of Appeal, despite its decision that the caesarean should not have been ordered, accepted the view that the actions of the doctors and social worker were 'necessary, spontaneous and commonsensical' while S was 'difficult', 'unreasonable' and 'eccentric'. Refusal of medical treatment – the failure of the mother to sacrifice herself in the foetus' interest – is portrayed as morally repugnant. Thus, although its decision supported the autonomy of the mother, the Court's reasoning reinforced the stereotype of self-sacrificing motherhood as normal and natural ('Contesting the Rule of Emotions? The Press and Enforced Caesareans' (2000) 9(4) *Social and Legal Studies* 515).

In *Re MB, Thameside and Glossop Acute Services Trusts* v *CH* and *Norfolk and*

Norwich Healthcare (NHS) Trust v *W*, all the women were considered irrational. MB had a fear of needles, CH denied that she was in labour and W was suffering the pain of labour and said that she would rather die than have a caesarean. Compare their treatment to that of the patient in *Re C* who was judged to be competent, despite his mental condition.

The courts' application of the test of competence appears to be inconsistent. If we assume that women have their reasoning clouded by the pain of labour, and we assume that this 'clouded reasoning' removes their ability to be competent, how many women in labour could be said to be competent? Probably none. Yet it is not until labour is in progress that the need for many emergency caesarean sections becomes apparent.

Another concern with these cases is the frightening frequency with which these women were not legally represented. Since the guidelines in the *St George's* case, this should not happen in the future. However, it remains troubling that many women will be advised of the outcomes in these cases whilst in hospital and will reluctantly consent without their challenge reaching a court of law.

Further, the level of force that may be used to carry out medical procedures is worrying. In *Re MB*, Butler-Sloss LJ condoned physical force being used to make the woman submit to treatment and also said that 'the extent of the force or compulsion which may be necessary can only be judged in each individual case and by the health professionals'. Aileen McColgan commented in *Women Under the Law* (Longman (2000)) that health professionals 'appear to pay scant regard to the physical autonomy of women in labour'.

The barrister Barbara Hewson wrote in the *Independent* (5 March 1997) that the decision in *Re MB* meant:

> '... women who reject their doctors' advice could be ... convicted of "incompetency", and subjected to house arrest, torture or inhuman and degrading treatment in state hospitals. Forced epidurals, forced episiotomies, forced pubic shaving, forced forceps deliveries, forced general anaesthetic, forced caesareans, forced medication, forced in utero foetal surgery, forced detention, forced vaginal examinations, forced AIDS testing, forced foetal screening, forced abortions.'

Finally, all of these cases raise the question of the nature of foetal rights. We have rehearsed these arguments above and return to them in considering abortion law (see Chapter 6). The law is quite clear that the foetus is not a legal person until born alive, yet all these cases appear to show some consideration for either the life of the foetus, or (as in *Re MB*) the mother's need for the foetus to be born alive. Yet, at law, the foetus has no rights: it is the mother's rights that should be considered. The mother, surely, does not need to be told of the importance of her own desire to see her child born alive! The courts should follow established legal principle, rather than bending the law to avoid what may be a morally unpalatable outcome.

Opposing views

There is a lack of legal literature which supports the use of forced caesareans. However, it is clear from the judgments that both judges and doctors treat these cases as though they concern two patients: the foetus and the pregnant woman. It must be very difficult for the medical profession not to envisage that they have two patients, and it will generally be appropriate medical practice to proceed on that basis (since usually the pregnant woman will want her child's medical interests to be protected as well as her own). Health professionals' concern is with providing quality care for the safe delivery of babies.

However, difficulties arise where the mother wishes to act in a way which may conflict with the foetus' interests. Health carers in these cases seem to view the healthy, innocent baby as being trapped inside an unwilling mother's body.

The difficulty has been twofold. First, there is professional frustration that a patient who has presented herself for care then refuses to take medical advice (although we know from the number of litigation cases involving hospitals that the medical profession does not always know best). Of course, such frustration cannot be a justification for overriding a woman's personal autonomy.

Second, the legal rights of the foetus are unclear. We have seen that the case law now states that a competent woman's decision takes precedence in this situation. In other circumstances, though, the foetus does seem to have rights: with regard to abortion, to some injuries caused to it in the womb, etc.

Given the law's lack of a clear set of principles, it is perhaps not surprising that doctors also have difficulty in putting women's aut;omony first. Faced with a child dying, their instinct is to act rather than stand back. It is therefore for the courts to provide a principled approach which respects women's personal autonomy. However, the vague status of the foetus and troubling attitudes to assessing competence mean that such an approach has proved difficult to achieve.

4.3 Female genital mutilation (FGM)

Introduction

FGM is also known as female circumcision. However, unlike male circumcision, female circumcision is designed to prevent the woman from experiencing sexual pleasure. It is defined by the World Health Organisation as 'all procedures involving partial or total removal of the external female genitalia or other injury to the female genital organs whether for cultural or other non-therapeutic reason'.

The procedure performed depends on the custom of the particular area that the woman is from (most commonly east or west Africa and parts of the Arabian Peninsula, although it is now carried out in other countries where there has been immigration from these areas, including Britain). It can range from removing part of the clitoris to the total removal of the labia. Sometimes the whole of the woman's external genitalia are removed and she is sewn up (infibulated) with only a small opening left in the vagina to allow menstruation and urination. The procedure is carried out (normally on a pre-pubescent girl, and often in unhygienic conditions by medically untrained people, with no anaesthetic) in order to make her marriageable. In cultures where FGM is common, many men prefer circumcised wives as the procedure is supposed to ensure that a woman's lack of interest in sex will prevent her from having affairs, therefore ensuring her 'purity' and the paternity of her children.

The current law

FGM is a criminal offence under English law. Section 1 Prohibition of Female Circumcision Act 1985 makes it an offence for any person to:

1. excise, infibulate or otherwise mutilate the whole or any part of the labia majora or labia minora or clitoris of another person; or
2. to aid, abet, counsel or procure the performance by another person of any of those acts on that person's own body.

Section 2 makes it lawful where it is carried out by a doctor for the physical or mental health of the person. This does not include a belief in a custom or ritual (s2(2)).

In practice, the principal problem arises when girls are taken out of this country in order to have the operation performed in a country where it is legal. In these situations the authorities, if alerted in time, may apply for a care order under s32(2) Children Act 1989 (see *Re H and R (Minors) (Sexual Abuse)* [1996] AC 563).

Why is this a feminist issue?

Feminists believe that women should have autonomy over their bodies. FGM prevents this in three different ways.

1. The procedure is usually carried out on girls before they reach puberty. They are therefore not in a position to give informed consent, and generally have no choice about whether to undergo the procedure.
2. Women can suffer serious complications (and even death) as a result of the procedure. Such complications can occur not only when the FGM is carried out, but also on first sexual intercourse and during childbirth. Infections can also occur at other times.
3. FGM can deny women the ability to function fully as sexual beings. Its very purpose is the control of female sexuality. Indeed it was carried out in nineteenth century Britain and America for that reason (as a 'medical treatment' for socially unacceptable female sexual conduct, such as nymphomania or masturbation).

Alternative arguments

It has been argued that the law is racist, as it prevents an ethnic tradition from being carried out. It has been asserted that this is a western idea that is being imposed on other cultures. This is a rather complicated issue. On the one hand, women from outside cultures where FGM is common are certainly criticising another culture. However, it would be wrong for feminists to fail to do so, and thereby accept that it is somehow alright for women in other cultures to have less rights than, say, white British feminists themselves have or seek. On the other hand, the assumption that feminist criticisms amount to one culture attacking another is itself simplistic. In the words of Katha Pollitt:

> '[F]eminism sets itself in opposition to virtually every culture on Earth ... feminism interrogates and challenges all cultural traditions.' (Cited in Jennifer Mather Saul, *Feminism: Issues and Arguments*, Oxford University Press, 2003.)

It also renders invisible the feminists within those communities who are campaigning on this issue. It is insulting to those women to assume that they are somehow ignorant dupes of white feminism (particularly given the enormous efforts many ethnic minority feminists have made to challenge racist assumptions in white feminism as well as sexism within their own communities).

Nonetheless, there are problems with Western feminists addressing issues such as FGM. The first is the risk of misunderstanding the issue (for example, assuming that all FGM is in the most serious form, involving infibulation; this is simply not true). Second, the practices which seem most shocking to Western feminists may not be the most urgent for women in those communities. The answer is for feminists to listen carefully to each other. White feminists, in particular, must be very careful not to assume that they know best, and to acknowledge the expertise of feminists within ethnic minority communities both in understanding the issues in their own communities and in determining priorities.

Many women who are brought up in cultures where FGM is the norm find uncircumcised genitalia aesthetically displeasing. Is FGM (particularly in its less drastic versions) necessarily any more mutilating than other procedures women undergo for aesthetic reasons, such as cosmetic surgery? After all, rhinoplasty can result in the loss of the sense of smell, which also removes a key sensual element from one's life. The difficulty from a feminist perspective with this argument is that we oppose the pressure on women to undergo any oppressive practice in order to conform to an aesthetic ideal. FGM is no more justifiable on this ground than cosmetic surgery (see Chapter 10).

Nonetheless, there is an important issue here: we should not condemn practices from other cultures yet ignore similar practices in our own (which seem normal, because we are so used to them). We must be critical of all practices which harm women, not just those which are unfamiliar to us.

Finally, it should be remembered that marriage is the central reason for this surgery. Without FGM, many of these women would not be able to marry men within the same culture. The inability to marry may seem more damaging than the procedure itself. Once again, then, a practice harmful to women is the result of a sexual double standard which demands purity from women but not from men: the same double standard which pervades many aspects of the English law (see, in particular, the discussion of rape myths in Chapter 8).

4.4 Forced marriages

Introduction

Forced marriage affects not only women, but also men. However, it is women who tend to suffer most because they are the ones who are in a weaker position: in the gender hierarchy women are still subordinate. Women are normally the ones who stay at home, raise children and are thus in less of a position to make demands. It is often the man in this kind of arrangement who has the choice of whom to marry because of the perception that men are more important – they are the ones who receive the dowry.

It is a problem that has affected almost every culture at some point. In Britain, you only have to look as far as the royal family in the 1980s: we have to ask what choice did Prince Charles really have in choosing a bride? His future wife had to be a virgin and of a certain class.

In 1999 the government established a Working Group to look into the problem of forced marriages. Their paper is published at: www.homeoffice.gov.uk, and is called 'A Choice by Right'. The Working Party for the government defined a forced marriage as:

> 'A marriage conducted without the consent of both parties, where duress is a factor.'

Forced marriages are repugnant to our society because they prevent a person from being autonomous. Married people vow to live with the other person for the rest of their life. It is a serious commitment. In the cultures where forced marriages are most common, divorce also carries stigma and the parties to a marriage may be put under enormous pressure not to end the marriage.

The current law

Relevant provisions
There is not a specific law on forced marriages, but the following provisions of English and international law are relevant and important.

1. Section 12(c) Matrimonial Causes Act 1973 states that a marriage is voidable if either party to the marriage did not validly consent to it, whether in consequence of duress, mistake, unsoundness of mind or otherwise.

2. Art 16(2) Universal Declaration of Human Rights 1948 states that:

> 'Marriage shall be entered into only with the free and full consent of the intending spouses.'

3. Art 16(1)(b) Convention to Eliminate All Forms of Discrimination Against Women 1979 (CEDAW):

> 'State parties shall ensure on a basis of equality of men and women ... the same right freely to choose a spouse and to enter into marriage only with their full and free consent.'

4. General Recommendation No 21 (1994) UN Committee on the Elimination of All Forms of Discrimination Against Women:

> 'A woman's right to choose a spouse and enter freely into marriage is central to her life and her dignity as a human being.'

5. Art 12 European Convention on Human Rights 1950 provides for a person's right to marry.

The legal validity of forced marriages

There is no statutory definition of marriage. The Matrimonial Causes Act (MCA) 1973 instead defines marriages that are void or voidable and what formalities are required.

Section 11 MCA 1973 makes marriages void where they do not meet the formal legal requirements (ie the parties are not legally able to wed because of their age, sex, family relationship or an existing marriage). Thus forced marriages are not usually void. However, they are voidable: in other words, the courts can declare them invalid if an application is made. If no application is made then the marriage is as legally valid as one freely entered into. Section 12 provides:

> 'A marriage shall be voidable if ...
> (c) either party to the marriage did not validly consent to it, whether in the consequence of duress, mistake, unsoundness of mind or otherwise.'

Other reasons that render a marriage voidable include non-consummation, mental disorder and either venereal disease or pregnancy caused by some person other than the spouse at the time of the marriage.

The judicial definition of marriage can be found in *Hyde* v *Hyde and Woodmansee* [1866] LR 1 P & D 130:

> '... [marriage] is the voluntary union for life of one man and one woman to the exclusion of all others.'

This definition clearly has its basis in Christianity. Its emphasis upon monogamy and heterosexuality reinforce patriarchal definitions of the family.

Married women are no longer considered legally invisible as regards contracts, torts, property or domestic violence. But the underlying attitudes to married women arguably still persist. We will consider in Chapter 5 how the law has struggled (and still struggles) to accept that violence in a marriage is as serious as other types of violence. Think also of married women taking the title 'Mrs' to show that they are married: why does this matter, since men are 'Mr' whether married or not? For a woman, marriage may still be considered a status which bestows some social worth, or proves some kind of moral good character.

How easy is it for women to invoke the law?

For a marriage to be voidable the applicant must prove that there was no valid consent to the marriage. The courts have attempted to identify the boundaries between valid and invalid consent.

In *Singh* v *Singh* [1971] 2 All ER 828 a Sikh couple who had never met each other before were married at a registry office. She was 17 years old and he was 21 years old. She said in evidence that when she saw him she was repulsed. She refused to go ahead with the religious ceremony. She petitioned for a decree of nullity on the grounds of duress and her incapacity to consummate the marriage. Karminski LJ held that she had no sexual aversion and therefore refused to annul her marriage.

However, a year later another case came before the court: *Kaur* v *Singh* [1972] 1 WLR 105. Here the couple again went through with the civil ceremony, but he refused to go ahead with the religious ceremony. She was entitled to void the marriage for his non-consummation. This is a very difficult case to explain in relation to *Singh* v *Singh*: presumably the change reflects a developing awareness of the social issues rather than the consistent application of any legal principle.

Later, in 1981, the Court of Appeal held in *Kaur* v *Kaur* (1981) 11 Fam Law 152 that immense family pressure was not enough to render the marriage voidable. Again, however, a year later the courts changed their approach. In *Hirani* v *Hirani* [1982] 4 FLR 232 the Court of Appeal adopted the law of contract to determine whether valid consent had been given:

> 'The crucial question ... in these cases is whether the threats, pressure or whatever it is is such as to destroy the reality of consent and overbear the will of the individual. It seems to me that ... this is a classic case of a young girl, wholly dependent on her parents being forced into a marriage with a man she has never seen in order to prevent her (reasonably from her parents' point of view) continuing in an association with a Muslim which they would regard as an abhorrence. But it is as clear a case as one would want of the overbearing of the will of the petitioner and thus invalidating or vitiating her consent.'

Because of these inconsistent approaches, it can be difficult to explain exactly what is sufficient to render a marriage void. However, it is to be hoped that the later of each pair of cases now reflects the law, indicating a greater recognition of the pressures which can be brought to bear upon young people to enter marriages against their will.

Other legal remedies

For cases involving children under 18, the court has a wide range of powers at its disposal. These are particularly important where a girl is to be taken out of the country in order to enter into a forced marriage abroad.

1. Section 31 Children Act 1989 allows a child to be made a ward of court. This power was used in *Re KR* [1999] 2 FLR 542 where the court made a girl a ward of court to ensure her safe return to England.
2. Under s44 Children Act 1989 the courts have the power to make an Emergency Protection Order.
3. Section 46 Children Act 1989 allows the police to remove a child to suitable accommodation if they believe that she will otherwise suffer significant harm.
4. Section 17 Children Act 1989 places a duty on each Local Authority to safeguard and promote the welfare of any child within their area who is in need.
5. Section 8(4) Children Act 1989 provides that children aged between five and 16 must receive suitable education.

For adults over 18 there are no such powers, although a woman in her late teens can still be put under enormous pressure by her family. In these instances the only legal remedies available form part of the criminal law. A forced marriage may involve offences of assault, battery, kidnap, rape and so on. However, prosecution for these offences happens only after they have taken place, too late to prevent the forced marriage. Additionally, the victim of the offences may not want a prosecution: she will gain little practical benefit from it, and despite the circumstances of her marriage, she may still love and feel loyalty to her family, and may not wish to see them convicted and imprisoned.

Why is this a feminist issue?

Feminists believe that all women should be able to live as fully autonomous individuals. The right to choose whether to enter a marriage is fundamental to this. Forced marriages therefore provide another example of women's subordination within society and demonstrate the hierarchy of gender.

Alternative arguments

Forced marriages occur in order to maintain language and cultural traditions. Western cultural practices may be seen as harmful and undesirable in upsetting traditional relations between men and women, and in giving personal and sexual autonomy to women which is inconsistent with their expected roles. Many families who force their children into marriage say that it is part of their religion. (In fact, no religion requires this.) It maintains family wealth, and brings together families of similar wealth and beliefs. Families usually act in this way in the belief that they are ensuring the best future for their children.

In other words, forced marriage often happens because families want to do the best for their children. They want to ensure that they are married into a similar family, with similar beliefs and standards. Parents (of all cultures) often think that they know better than their children – they have a wealth of experience which their child lacks.

Conclusion

The unjustified coercion of women is wrong. All people ought to be able to choose their life partner. That is their autonomous right. Any form of duress, whether economic, violent or otherwise, is unacceptable. Once violence is used or threatened, or expulsion from the family and ostracism occurs, the pressure is inappropriate, regardless of any good intentions which may also be involved.

Many feminists believe that we need a specific law on forced marriages (despite the Home Office Working Party's view to the contrary), as it is impossible to reach many affected women and men under the current law. Even if the people involved are educated about the issues and the law, it is often impossible to encourage them to use the law. The principal reason for this is that, if the affected person is over 18, then the law offers only criminal prosecution. The problem is similar to that of battered women: the victims of forced marriages are often in a relationship of love and dependence with their families (and often economically dependent). Further, our legal system is a terrifying system for most non-lawyers because of its adversarial nature. The people involved are designated as opponents by the courts, which may make it difficult to combine the prevention or ending of the unwanted marriage with the maintenance of good family relations.

5

Choosing (Not) to Mother

5.1 Introduction

5.2 Contraception

5.3 Surrogacy

5.4 Assisted fertility

5.1 Introduction

One of the most significant developments for British women in the twentieth century was the increasing availability of technology allowing them to choose whether or not to bear children. However, as we shall see, the apparently greater choices have not invariably been beneficial. The growth of these technologies has created its own problems, dilemmas and pressures.

One of the central questions raised by reproductive technologies such as in vitro fertilisation, and options such as surrogacy, is what it means to be a mother. The link between genetic or biological motherhood and social motherhood (ie the actual rearing of the child) have never been complete – think of adoption, for example. However, there are more complicated permutations now than previously: the biological mother of a child (the woman who was actually pregnant) need not be the genetic mother (since the egg could have come from another woman). Either or neither of these women may then become the social mother.

While the law grapples with these questions, it also continues to define motherhood in a different way. The myth of the 'ideal mother' is a powerful one, which we examine in more detail in Chapter 6. Its significance here is the way in which women who choose not to have children, or who do choose to have them but use new technologies to do so, can be characterised as selfish. A selfish woman is the opposite of the ideal mother.

To counter this negative stereotype, some of those promoting the availability of new technologies have portrayed their users as desperate victims of childlessness. However, such a stereotype poses its own problems for women: are we really only complete when we have children? Always sad and unfulfilled when we do not? Feminists would generally dispute such a claim.

5.2 Contraception

Introduction

We will consider abortion as an issue of women's personal autonomy. In the same way, contraception enables women to take control over their fertility, which consequently increases their autonomy. However, access to contraception has not always been straightforward. We will consider both the current law and the history of women's access to contraceptive methods.

Existing forms of contraception are not perfect. Some are less reliable; others are more reliable but pose health risks. Some, but not all, contraceptives also offer protection against sexually transmitted diseases. We will not go into detail about these health issues here, but it is important to bear them in mind. In particular, the inadequacies of contraceptive methods are part of the reason why access to contraception does not eliminate the need for abortion to be legally available.

The issues which we will concentrate upon here are, first of all, who has legal access to contraception? Second, who has practical access to contraception? In other words, it is not enough for someone to legally be allowed to use contraceptives if they cannot find somebody to prescribe them or supply them, or if they cannot afford them.

Current law

Women's access to contraception is ensured by s5 National Health Service Act 1977:

> '(1) It is the Secretary of State's duty ...
> (b) to arrange, to such extent as he considers necessary to meet all reasonable requirements in England and Wales, for the giving of advice on contraception, the medical examination of persons seeking advice on contraception, the treatment of such persons and the supply of contraceptive substances and appliances.'

Thus the NHS is obliged to provide access to contraceptives, along with appropriate medical advice.

Girls under 16 years old

The age at which women can legally consent to sexual intercourse (or any other sexual activity) is 16. Arguably, the giving of contraceptive advice to a girl below that age amounts to aiding and abetting the criminal offence that would be committed by a male sexual partner (it is not illegal for the girl herself to have sexual intercourse below that age). However, the House of Lords rejected this approach in the leading case of *Gillick* v *West Norfolk and Wisbech Area Health Authority* [1986] 1 AC 112.

Victoria Gillick, who had five daughters under the age of 16, brought this case against her local health authority. A Memorandum of Guidance had been issued to area health authorities by the Department of Health and Social Security in May

1974. It stated that the decision to prescribe contraception without a parent's consent was a matter for 'the clinical judgment of the doctor', although it emphasised that this was to be done only exceptionally. The local area health authority refused to undertake not to prescribe contraception for Mrs Gillick's daughters without her consent, as 'treatment prescribed by a doctor is a matter for that doctor's clinical judgment taking into account all the factors of the case'. Mrs Gillick sought a court declaration that contraceptive advice and treatment could not be given to a child under 16 without at least one parent's consent.

The House of Lords held by a majority that doctors were entitled to prescribe contraception for some girls under 16 without parental consent. By so doing, they would not be aiding and abetting a criminal offence. According to Lord Scarman, 'parental right yields to the child's right to make his ... own decisions when he reaches a sufficient understanding and intelligence to be capable of making up his own mind on the matter requiring decision'.

A doctor can therefore give contraceptive advice and treatment to a child under 16 without their parents' knowledge or consent if satisfied that:

1. the child will understand the advice;
2. the doctor cannot persuade her to inform her parents or allow the doctor to inform her parents;
3. she is very likely to have sexual intercourse with or without contraceptive treatment;
4. unless she receives contraceptive advice and/or treatment, her physical and/or mental health are likely to suffer; and
5. her best interests require the doctor to give her contraceptive advice and/or treatment without parental consent.

History

By the 1920s, access to birth control had become a feminist issue. Marie Stopes had published her book *Married Love*, AC Firfield, 1918; the Co-operative Guilds had debated the issue; and campaigners such as Eleanor Rathbone (later an MP and leading campaigner for the family allowance) saw it as an important welfare measure to improve women's lives. However, most of these campaigns did not seek access to birth control for all women. Instead, the emphasis was upon contraception for married women. Although many feminists did oppose the ideology of the nuclear family and favoured greater sexual autonomy for women, others did not. There was also a perception that advocating contraception for all women, including those who were not married, would undermine public support. The public arguments which prevailed were those which portrayed women's control over fertility as a means of improving married life by both permitting married women to limit their pregnancies, and allowing the couple to have an active sex life. Thus the patriarchal institution of the nuclear family was supported by these arguments even as women's autonomy was identified as a goal.

We can also see the connections here to the parliamentary debates on abortion (some 40 years later) which we will consider in Chapter 6. Conduct which seems on its face to amount to a rejection of motherhood is reinterpreted as a way of embracing it. The woman using contraceptives, like the mother-of-six seeking an abortion, is doing so because she wants to be a better mother to the children she does bear. In the context of contraception, married women's duty to please their husbands (particularly sexually) was also invoked. Thus the release of women from unwanted pregnancy was portrayed as a way of fitting them more firmly into their traditional roles of wife and mother.

Some campaigners went further. Janet Chance, one of the founders of the Abortion Law Reform Association, argued that women who had not enjoyed heterosexual sex were unsuitable for public office. She dismissed them as 'non-orgasmic' and 'spinster-minded' (Barbara Caine, *English Feminism 1780–1980*, Oxford University Press (1997)). Such views did little to forward women's sexual autonomy, since they identified the only acceptable form of sexuality as heterosexuality (by implication, within marriage). The view that a woman is incomplete without a man bears more resemblance to reactionary, sexist views than to any recognisable feminist principle.

Equally troubling is the attachment some groups campaigning for birth control had to eugenic principles. Eugenics was a pseudo-scientific theory popular in the early twentieth century, which supported the idea that the race or nation would be stronger and better if the quality of its children was improved. Thus birth control techniques (or more drastic methods of preventing births such as sterilisation) were to be targeted at the lower classes, the insane and the disabled. Eugenics could also have strong racist overtones, often incorporating attitudes about the superiority of one race over another. Its most infamous expression was in the Nazi policies of the 1930s and 1940s, which included not only sterilisation but also the killing of disabled and mentally ill people, and ultimately genocide. However, in the 1920s eugenicist views were still respectable, and indeed held by some socialists and feminists.

The provision of birth control was never illegal in Britain (although information about it was sometimes prosecuted as obscene material: for example, in 1877 Annie Besant and Charles Bradlaugh were prosecuted for publishing a booklet on contraception, although they were acquitted on a technicality). However, in the early part of the twentieth century the clinics which did provide such services were all private. A 1930 Department of Health Memorandum gave local authorities the power (but not the duty) to provide contraceptive advice to married women. Thirty-six authorities did so (V Walsh, 'Contraception: The Growth of a Technology' in Jo Bridgeman and Susan Millns, *Feminist Perspectives on Law: Law's Engagement with the Female Body*, Sweet & Maxwell (1998)).

In 1949, the Royal Commission on Population recommended that the NHS should be under a duty to provide advice on contraception to all married persons who wanted it. However, it would be almost 25 years before any such duty was placed on the NHS. Change came in the 1960s, when Scarlett Pollock argued that contraception came to be seen as 'the lesser of two evils':

> 'In the attempt to maintain the patriarchal family structure as the stable unit of society, fears of condoning women's "promiscuity" have had to be weighed against the evidence of pregnancy and childbirth outside of marriage.' ('Sex and the Contraceptive Act', in Jo Bridgeman and Susan Millns, *Feminist Perspectives on Law: Law's Engagement with the Female Body*, Sweet & Maxwell (1998).)

The next important step was the National Health Service (Family Planning) Act 1967 (note that this was passed in the same year as the Abortion Act 1967). Local health authorities were empowered to give advice, to medically examine those seeking such advice and to supply contraceptives. The Act recognised social as well as medical criteria for providing contraceptives, and rejected restrictions on the grounds of age or marital status.

Under s4 National Health Service Reorganisation Act 1973 the power to provide these services became a duty. Health authorities were not simply allowed to provide these services: they now had to provide them. The provisions in the 1973 Act have since been replaced by the National Health Service Act 1977. Critically, shortly after the 1973 Act was passed, the provision of free contraceptives was ensured for the first time by a circular issued in May 1974 (Circular HSC (IS) 32).

Feminist perspectives

As we will discuss further in relation to abortion (Chapter 6), to have control over one's reproductive capacity is crucial to a woman's autonomy. Its effects go beyond the avoidance of unwanted pregnancy and childcare: the ability to control one's own fertility makes long-term plans, including education and career progression, possible. It can allow greater sexual autonomy, as one's sexual behaviour is no longer governed principally by the risk of pregnancy. The idea that the availability of contraception is liberatory for women was enthusiastically endorsed by Lord Scarman in *Gillick*: he asserted that the contraceptive pill granted women 'a degree of independence and of opportunity undreamed of until this generation and greater ... than any law of equal opportunity could by itself effect'.

However, the picture is not completely rosy. The idea that contraception is unequivocally good for women ignores a number of difficulties, one being the health risks involved in using many contraceptive methods. Some such risks are unknown or uncertain. In England and Wales, there is no duty for a doctor to give full information: *Blyth* v *Bloomsbury Area Health Authority* (1989) 5 *Professional Negligence* 167 held that 'there was no obligation on the hospital to give the patient all the information available to the hospital'. If a doctor acts in accordance with accepted professional practice, they have fulfilled their legal obligations. In *Blyth*, a woman was given a contraceptive injection (Depo-Provera) without being informed of all the potential health risks, such as depression, severe headaches, menstrual disturbance and possibly osteoporosis.

If she cannot make a fully-informed decision about something which profoundly affects her own health, but is forced to rely upon what a doctor chooses to tell her, a woman clearly does not have bodily autonomy. This issue particularly affects ethnic minority women: Jill Rakusen describes the administration of Depo-Provera injections without adequate information, and sometimes with deliberate misinformation or without consent at all, to predominantly ethnic minority women in Britain. Women with mental health problems have also received Depo-Provera injections without their knowledge or consent ('Depo-Provera: The Extent of the Problem. A Case Study in the Politics of Birth Control' in Jo Bridgeman and Susan Millns, *Feminist Perspectives on Law: Law's Engagement with the Female Body*, Sweet & Maxwell (1998)).

The construction of contraception as a medical issue does have some advantages (notably the provision of contraceptive services through the NHS), but as with abortion (Chapter 6), authority is given to (rational) doctors rather than (irrational) women. This issue is most clearly highlighted in the *Gillick* judgment. Little attention was given to the autonomy of teenage girls who had the maturity to make medical decisions. Instead, the debate was constructed as one of clinical judgment against parental rights. For example, in his dissenting judgment, Lord Templeman argued that Parliament ought to decide whether 'the doctor prevailed over the parent … [or] the parent prevailed over the doctor'. The legal effect of this approach was the *Gillick* test, which goes far beyond the ordinary competence test used for adults.

Lewis and Cannell argue that the rejection of bodily autonomy for teenage girls was more fundamental than this. They suggest that although the debate was 'in terms of parental rights versus those of the medical profession … the subject of the debate was in fact the control of female sexuality and the role of mothers'. The beliefs underlying the judicial approaches to this issue are that 'sex and reproduction belong inside marriage [and] "the good mother" would stop teenage sex' ('The Politics of Motherhood in the 1980s: Warnock, *Gillick* and Feminists' (1986) 13 *Journal of Law and Society* 321). Again the belief that contraception has a role to play in the preservation of the patriarchal family is crucial to understanding the development of the law in this area. The social good thus promoted is generally the limiting of 'bad mothers' (eg teenagers) rather than the extension of female autonomy.

Health risks are not the only disadvantages of contraception for women. Some feminists would not dispute the popular notion that the contraceptive pill was an important factor in the 'sexual revolution' of the 1960s, but would dispute that that 'revolution' benefited women. On the contrary, it can be seen to have had some very unrevolutionary effects, most ironically by undermining women's sexual autonomy. This was achieved in two ways.

1. It reinforced compulsory heterosexuality by emphasising this as 'real sex' and as somehow liberating and vitally important for women.
2. It limited women's ability to refuse sexual intercourse. Not wanting to engage in sexual intercourse was not accepted as a valid choice for women: instead, it was characterised as problematic repression or uptightness.

For further discussion of the sexual revolution as disadvantageous for women, see Sheila Jeffreys, *Anticlimax: A Feminist Perspective on the Sexual Revolution*, The Women's Press (1990).

Almost all existing contraceptive methods place the full responsibility and burden upon women (the exception being the condom). Thus women have to spend the time and money and take the health risks involved in contraception. While sexual health education in relation to Aids did place more of an onus on men to take responsibility through using condoms, not all men are prepared to do so. Where sexual intercourse within a particular relationship apparently does not pose a risk of disease, the burden is likely to return to the woman. However, this is to some extent inevitable since it is the female partner who will have to bear the main consequences of any contraceptive failure. As a result, many women suggest they would not trust a man to take contraceptive measures, such as the often-suggested 'male pill'.

Conclusion

Access to safe, reliable contraception can make a real difference to women's lives. The law has certainly facilitated such access, but at a cost. Birth control is seen as a medical issue, with women's autonomy being secondary to doctors' professional standing. Further, legal approaches to the use of contraception are influenced by ideas of supporting patriarchal family structure and discouraging the birth of babies to 'bad mothers'. In the process, the autonomy of all women, but in particular women from ethnic minorities, women with mental health problems and women with learning disabilities, is undermined.

5.3 Surrogacy

Introduction

Surrogacy refers to the practice whereby a woman (the surrogate mother) goes through pregnancy and childbirth in order to bear a baby for somebody else (the commissioning party). When the baby is born, it is given to that other person.

Current law

The Surrogacy Arrangements Act 1985, at s1, defines a surrogate mother:

'(2) "Surrogate mother" means a woman who carries a child in pursuance of an arrangement –
(a) made before she began to carry the child, and
(b) made with a view to any child carried in pursuance of it being handed over to, and parental responsibility being met (so far as practicable) by, another person or other persons.'

Surrogacy is legal in England and Wales, provided that there is no commercial element. Payments to the mother (beyond 'reasonable expenses') are not permitted. Section 2 Surrogacy Arrangements Act 1985 prohibits third parties from becoming commercially involved in surrogacy arrangements, while s3 prohibits advertisements (including by the parties themselves) either offering a surrogacy arrangement or seeking a surrogate mother. The commissioning parent(s) and the surrogate mother will usually draw up an agreement, but this is not legally enforceable by either party (s1A Surrogacy Arrangements Act 1985, inserted by s36 Human Fertilisation and Embryology Act 1990).

Six weeks after the baby is born, the intended parents can apply to the court for a parental order under s30 Human Fertilisation and Embryology Act 1990 which extinguishes the surrogate mother's rights over the baby and vests them in the commissioning parents. Thus the baby legally belongs to the commissioning parents, and the surrogate mother has no further rights in respect of the baby. The order will only be made where:

1. the applicants are married;
2. the applicants are domiciled in Great Britain;
3. they are over 18 years old;
4. at least one of the parents is a biological parent of the baby;
5. the baby is between six weeks and six months old;
6. the baby's home is with the husband and wife seeking the order;
7. both the father of the child (where he is not the husband) and the woman who carried the child must have freely and unconditionally agreed to the order;
8. the court must be satisfied that no money or benefit (other than for expenses) has been given or received by the husband and wife.

Where these conditions are not met, the commissioning couple can seek to adopt the child or to have it made a ward of court. The relevant test will then be the best interests of the child (*Re P (Minors) (Wardship: Surrogacy)* [1987] 2 FLR 421). In *Re P*, the children's bonding with the surrogate mother (they had lived with her for five months by the date of hearing) meant that she was awarded residence: '[t]he fact that she is their mother' was seen as a weighty factor, indicating that motherhood is viewed by the courts as a natural and biological role.

History

While it has probably existed for far longer, surrogacy became an issue in the mid-

1980s. The Cotton case (*Re C* [1985] FLR 846), where surrogate mother Kim Cotton bore a baby for another couple, brought the issue into the newspapers and the law courts. She was portrayed as Britain's first surrogate mother (see: www.news.bbc.co.uk). Although the parties wished to carry out the agreement after the child was born, the local authority obtained a place of safety order which meant that the baby remained in the hospital's care. The commissioning (and biological) father then issued wardship proceedings which were successful (*Re C* [1985] FLR 846). At around the same time, the Warnock Report (*Report of the Committee of Inquiry into Human Fertilisation and Embryology*, Cmnd 9314, 1984) made recommendations on a number of reproductive issues including surrogacy.

The Warnock Report opposed surrogacy arrangements, and in particular recommended the prohibition of commercial surrogacy. The Report's arguments rested on three broad grounds.

1. Procreation should take place within a marital relationship (a view the Report argued was supported by public opinion).
2. Surrogacy is contrary to human dignity, both for the surrogate mother and for the child who is 'bought for money'.
3. The relationship between mother and child is distorted when a woman becomes pregnant in order to carry a child she will give away.

One result of the Warnock Report was the Surrogacy Arrangements Act 1985. However, the issue has remained controversial. In 1997, the Brazier Report was published. The focus of this report was not the desirability of surrogacy per se, but rather the payment of expenses to surrogate mothers and the regulation of surrogacy arrangements. It made the following recommendations.

1. Payments to surrogate mothers should be limited to genuine, verifiable expenses.
2. Non-commercial agencies involved in surrogacy should be registered with the Department of Health (commercial agencies are already illegal).
3. The Department of Health should draw up a Code of Practice for agencies.
4. The Department of Health should collect statistics from agencies.
5. Parental orders should only be available from the High Court, in cases where the Code of Practice has been complied with.
6. These recommendations should be incorporated into a new Surrogacy Act.

However, no Surrogacy Bill has yet been placed by the government before Parliament.

Feminist perspectives

Against regulation of surrogacy
Both the Warnock and Brazier Reports have emphasised that surrogacy should not be permitted on a commercial basis. In particular, the surrogate mother should receive no payment beyond her actual financial expenses. However, why should

surrogacy only be permitted on a non-commercial basis? If it is damaging and undignified for a woman to bear a child for a third party, why is it less so if she is unpaid? The Warnock Report addressed this as an issue of non-interference in (albeit undesirable) private arrangements. However, given that same Report's emphasis upon supporting the nuclear family, it may be that other considerations are also at work in the opposition to commercial surrogacy.

First, while other technologies sometimes involve third parties as gamete donors (and of course involve a number of third parties in the form of medical personnel), there is generally no risk of extending the definition of the family since such donors are usually anonymous. By contrast, surrogate mothers often continue to have a relationship with the commissioning parents and the child (MacCallum, Lycett, Murray, Jadya and Golombok, 'Surrogacy: The Experience of Commissioning Couples' (2003) 18(6) *Human Reproduction* 1334). Thus the boundaries of the family are expanded, and the patriarchal model is threatened:

> 'At the core of the dilemma relating to surrogacy is that whilst the aim of an arrangement is the creation of a child (possibly for a heterosexual couple and possibly genetically related to one of the commissioning parties), it represents a distortion of the "normal" family relationship and challenges dominant constructions of motherhood.' (Jo Bridgeman and Susan Millns, *Feminist Perspectives on Law: Law's Engagement with the Female Body*, Sweet & Maxwell (1998).)

Second, if childbirth is commercialised, this upsets the idea of childbearing and childrearing as something women should (by nature) do gratuitously for love. The idea that women's reproductive role has a significant economic and social value threatens its devaluation within patriarchal society. At the same time, the idea of mothers having a special natural relationship with their children is one of the justifications for the unequal burden of childcare which they bear, and ultimately for the idea that women's place is in the home (the private sphere).

Third, the Warnock Report's opposition to surrogate motherhood can be seen to be based upon supporting the patriarchal family and the myths of motherhood, notably that of the self-sacrificing mother. A surrogate mother does not sacrifice all in the interests of her child: instead, she quite deliberately conceives, bears and gives birth to a child with the intention of giving it away. That she could choose such a course contradicts some of the strongest myths of maternal devotion.

While a surrogate mother (particularly in a non-commercial arrangement) is arguably sacrificing herself, she is doing so for third parties rather than for her own child/nuclear family unit. The development of such bonds between women and beyond patriarchal families can be threatening to the status quo. Additionally, surrogacy gives the status of 'mother' to a woman who not only has not borne the child herself, but who has chosen motherhood in her own interests rather than those of, for example, an otherwise unparented child (as in adoption or fostering). This 'mother' again fails to fit the stereotype of self-sacrifice since she has gained her maternal status as a means, rather, of self-gratification. Feminists take a critical approach to such discourses which divide women into the selfless (good mother) and selfish (bad mother).

Surrogacy can be conceptualised as an issue of female autonomy. If women have full control over their bodies, that must include the right to use them in this way. The Warnock Committee's approach is then viewed as 'paternalistic', rejecting female autonomy to argue that '[a] woman should not be allowed to use her uterus for financial profit' (Michael Freeman, 'After Warnock – Whither the Law?' [1986] *Current Legal Problems* 33). One should note that Freeman's formula of 'us[ing] her uterus' is misleading: pregnancy and childbirth have effects upon the whole of a woman's body, not simply her womb. However, the general argument remains unaffected: why should women be forbidden to use their bodies for profit in this context? After all, what does other paid employment do but use our bodies?

Popular perceptions of surrogacy have concentrated upon the idea that such arrangements are likely to go wrong. However, it appears that this view is mistaken: some arrangements break down, and some surrogate mothers want to keep the babies they bear, but these cases are very much the exception. Around 98 per cent of surrogacy arrangements involving members of the voluntary surrogacy organisation Childlessness Overcome Through Surrogacy (COTS) reach a successful conclusion (COTS statistics 2004: www.surrogacy.org.uk). A study of 34 surrogate mothers approximately a year after giving birth concluded that they did not generally experience major difficulties in handing over the baby or in their relationship with the commissioning couple (Jadya, Murray, Lycett, MacCallum and Golombok, 'Surrogacy: the Experiences of Surrogate Mothers' (2003) 18(10) *Human Reproduction* 2196).

Against surrogacy

Feminists who oppose surrogacy would largely agree with the criticisms of the nuclear family and ideals of motherhood already mentioned. However, they would differ on the question of whether surrogacy is therefore a positive choice for women.

Andrea Dworkin takes issue with the idea that surrogacy does in fact break away from patriarchal models of reproduction. She argues that motherhood has been based upon a 'farming model' whereby women are 'tended' and valued for their reproductive capacity (in the same way as a farmer tends and values his livestock and land). However, surrogacy moves away from this not towards greater female liberation but rather towards the 'brothel model' (previously related only to prostitution) whereby a woman sells her body parts and acts to a series of men. She is not acting autonomously because it is the patriarchal state itself which creates the conditions for such a sale (*Right-wing Women*, A Dworkin, The Women's Press (1983)).

V E Munro makes the crucial point that surrogacy involves a two-person model of the maternal-foetal relationship. Acceptance of such a model in this context could affect perceptions of the relationship between mother and foetus in all pregnancies. ('Surrogacy and the Construction of the Maternal-Foetal Relationship: The Feminist

Dilemma Explained' (2001) 7(1) Res Publica 13). We have already seen in relation to forced caesareans (see Chapter 4) that to view the woman and the foetus as separate individuals poses a real threat to women's autonomy. In particular, the more the foetus is perceived as having its own separate personhood, and thus rights, the less account is taken of the mother's rights so that she becomes an 'invisible' carrier whose liberty may be restricted in the presumed interests of the foetus.

Further, rejecting patriarchal mythology about motherhood does not necessitate accepting that childbearing is physical labour like any other. In Chapter 6 we will discuss the conception that the relationship between a woman and the foetus she carries as one of intimacy. Few other occupations (with the exception of prostitution) demand a relationship of such bodily intimacy. Shelley Roberts rejects the idea that a comparison with other employment is valid:

> 'The surrogate is "on duty" 24 hours a day, every day. There is no possibility of terminating the employment (without incurring criminal, or at least moral sanctions by having an abortion). The commissioning couple seeks to assert control not over work, but over aspects of personal life such as diet, medical care, sexual relations, the ingestion of alcohol and tobacco and even psychological attitude ... Thus, such an agreement does not seem to be employment, as we know it, but rather something akin to slavery.' ('Warnock and Surrogate Motherhood: Sentiment or Argument?' in Jo Bridgeman and Susan Millns, *Feminist Perspectives on Law: Law's Engagement with the Female Body*, Sweet & Maxwell (1998).)

Nonetheless, this level of control over the surrogate mother is rarely openly acknowledged; nor is the physical reality of pregnancy and labour. Far from 'renting her womb', a surrogate mother will be affected throughout her body (common effects of pregnancy can include back pain, severe heartburn, nausea, haemorrhoids, the need for stitches after labour, to name a few). She will also be affected socially, since pregnancy is rarely secret and for all its relegation to the private realm, is often a focus for moral judgments about the mother (think about press reporting of, and legal attitudes towards, women who smoke or take harmful substances during pregnancy, women who become pregnant outside a stable, heterosexual relationship, etc). However, popular conceptions of surrogacy take little account of these wider effects. The law also fails to give them any value, limiting financial compensation to the loss of earnings and other clearly defined expenses, such as maternity clothes. Thus ultimately, surrogacy may serve to further devalue pregnancy.

Conclusion

Surrogacy has proven both legally and theoretically problematic. On the one hand, it involves issues such as childbearing which are seen as private and thus largely outside the scope of the law. The women involved can be seen as fulfilling the typically feminine roles of nurture, care for others and maternity.

However, on the other hand, surrogacy challenges these notions. It extends and alters the patriarchal family unit, and contradicts the myth of the altruistic woman putting her child before all else (on the contrary, she gives it to another couple for their benefit). It suggests that childbearing is not a purely private matter, and that it has significant economic value.

How should feminists respond to these issues? There is no straightforward answer. One could argue that the challenge to patriarchal notions of privacy, the family and the domestic sphere are to be welcomed. Conversely, the emphasis of women's reproductive role, the devaluing of childbearing as 'renting a womb' and the idea of the foetus as somehow separate from the mother all pose problems. Thus, while many feminists have serious concerns about the growing use of surrogacy, there is not a single feminist position on surrogacy law reform. Nonetheless, most feminists would criticise the current emphasis of the law upon recognising only heterosexual couples as valid surrogate parents.

5.4 Assisted fertility

Introduction

In recent years, reproductive medicine has progressed enormously with the development of a number of new procedures to help women bear children. In-vitro fertilisation (test-tube babies) had its first successful birth in 1978. Currently, there are regular announcements of plans to produce human babies using genetic cloning techniques. Given how quickly the technology is developing, we will not look at specific methods here. Instead, we will focus upon the wider legal issues raised by, and the implications for women of, these new technologies.

As reproductive technologies developed, they raised an increasing number of legal and ethical questions. These were considered by the *Report of the Committee of Inquiry into Human Fertilisation and Embryology*, Cmnd 9314, 1984 (the Warnock Report), which formed the starting point for the Human Fertilisation and Embryology Act 1990.

We will concentrate upon two particular issues. First, is there a right to treatment? Second, where donor gametes are used, who are the legal parents?

Current law

Access to treatment
The availability of treatment is governed by two factors: first, NHS resources (or the financial means of those seeking treatment where it is not available through the NHS). Second, the Human Fertilisation and Embryology Act 1990 contains a number of restrictions upon treatment.

We will not consider the first factor in any depth here. However, by way of example, in February 2004 the National Institute for Clinical Excellence recommended that three cycles of IVF should be offered to couples in which the woman is aged between 23 and 39 years old (see: www.nice.org.uk). However, the Department of Health responded by advising the NHS to offer at least one cycle of treatment to these women, from April 2005, with the aim of progressing towards full implementation in the long term. Thus growing demand from the infertile cannot be met fully, and political decisions are made upon the use of limited resources.

Other limitations upon both what treatment is available, and who has access to it, are contained in the Human Fertilisation and Embryology Act 1990. The main such provisions are considered below.

1. Section 5 establishes the Human Fertilisation and Embryology Authority (HFEA). This body has various powers, particularly in relation to licensing.
2. There are several absolute prohibitions. Section 3 prohibits, inter alia, the implantation of non-human gametes or embryos in a woman. Section 3A (inserted by the Criminal Justice and Public Order Act 1994) additionally prohibits use of female germ cells (eggs) taken from a foetus or an embryo.
3. Certain activities are prohibited without a licence. Section 3 prohibits the creation, keeping or use of an embryo without a licence. Section 4 states that a licence is required for gamete storage, treatment using donor eggs or sperm and the placing of sperm and eggs in a woman.

Beyond the restrictions mentioned above, there are also provisions in the Act aimed at restricting the access of single and lesbian women to reproductive technologies. Under s13, it is a condition of each clinic's licence that:

> '(5) A woman shall not be provided with treatment services unless account has been taken of the welfare of any child who may be born as a result of the treatment (including the need of that child for a father), and of any other child who may be affected by the birth.'

Who are the parents?

When the gametes (egg or sperm) do not come from the woman or couple involved, difficult questions arise. Traditionally, parentage has been defined genetically: the people who provided the eggs and sperm were generally the parents. Exceptions did exist, such as adoption where parentage passed from the genetic parents to the adoptive parents. However, those exceptions did not have to deal with situations as complex as where the genetic and biological mothers are different people, as a result of egg donation. New definitions of parenthood are therefore required where fertility treatments have taken place, and these are provided by the Human Fertilisation and Embryology Act 1990.

Defining 'mother' has proved relatively straightforward. Under s27:

> '(1) The woman who is carrying or has carried a child as a result of the placing in her of an embryo or of sperm and eggs, and no other woman, is to be treated as the mother of the child.'

In other words, motherhood is identified firmly with pregnancy. By contrast, defining fatherhood has proved considerably more problematic. Above all, the legal desire to preserve fatherhood as important is in conflict with the concern to ensure that social rather than genetic fathers are acknowledged. Since the technology permits motherhood without social fatherhood, and allows anonymous genetic fatherhood or even posthumous fatherhood, a short definition does not suffice to deal with the situations which arise. Instead, there are a series of definitions of 'father' where the sperm was not provided by the mother's partner. They are contained in s28, which defines 'father' in the following ways:

1. if the woman was married and her husband consented to the artificial insemination or embryo implantation, he is the father;
2. if the services were provided to an unmarried woman together with a man, he is the father;
3. if the genetic father was dead at the time of the embryo's creation, then he will be the father provided that either:
   a) the couple were married and the man had consented in writing to such use of the sperm and to being the father; or
   b) the couple were unmarried but receiving treatment together, and the man had consented in writing to such use of the sperm and to being the father.

Bridgeman and Millns point out that the definition of 'mother' and 'father' 'shores up the traditional nuclear family, seeking to ensure that, for the most part, children born via reproductive technologies are not fatherless' (*Feminist Perspectives on Law: Law's Engagement with the Female Body*, Sweet & Maxwell (1998)). Thus the law's response to new reproductive technologies has centred upon ensuring that the ideology of the patriarchal family is preserved.

The third part of the definition of 'father' (where the man's gametes are used after his death) was inserted by the Human Fertilisation and Embryology (Deceased Fathers) Act 2003. This Act resulted from the case concerning Diane Blood. She was a widowed woman, whose husband died suddenly and unexpectedly of meningitis. Shortly before his death, while he was in a coma, sperm was taken from him. Diane Blood later sought to use that sperm to become pregnant, arguing that she and her husband had planned to start a family together and that he would have wanted her to proceed with that plan despite his death.

The HFEA informed her that the sperm could not be stored legally in Britain, or exported for use abroad, since her husband had not given his permission. She sought judicial review of the Authority's decision, and her case eventually reached the Court of Appeal (*R* v *Human Fertilisation and Embryology Authority, ex parte Blood* [1997] 2 All ER 687). They ruled that while use of the sperm would be unlawful in Britain, European Community law on the freedom to obtain medical services required that she be allowed to export it for use in treatment abroad.

Following this case, Diane Blood received treatment in Belgium and had two sons. However, the litigation did not end there. When she registered the birth, she was not allowed to name her late husband as the father: instead, the relevant section of the birth certificates was left blank. She again took her case to court on the ground that her and her sons' rights under art 8 European Convention on Human Rights (the right to private and family life) had been breached. The government conceded this, and as a result the Human Fertilisation and Embryology (Deceased Fathers) Act 2003 was passed, amending the definition to include the third situation above. When the Act came into force, Diane Blood re-registered her children with her late husband named as father.

Feminist perspectives

The growing range of methods available to enable apparently infertile women to bear children might appear to empower women. After all, American feminist Shulamith Firestone famously argued that reproductive technology could free women from 'the tyranny of biology' by enabling artificial reproduction (*The Dialectic of Sex*, Morrow (1970)). However, while some women gain new options, the position of women overall is not necessarily improved. Reproduction is being placed under male (medical and legal) control. Just as childbirth has become increasingly medicalised, so conception is increasingly a medical procedure too. Thus doctors and judges have growing power to articulate and enforce their own views of who should and should not become a mother.

The form in which this power is given encourages its use to limit access to those who live within a traditional, patriarchal family. The provision of services to single women and lesbians is discouraged by the explicit statement in s13 that the 'welfare of the child' includes 'the need ... for a father'. Thus heterosexuality is enshrined as an ideal in a way which has more to do with patriarchal ideology than any disinterested analysis of child welfare. Indeed, there is a growing body of research which confirms that the children of lesbian mothers are not disadvantaged (see for example Lynne Harne and Rights of Women, *Valued Families: The Lesbian Mothers' Legal Handbook*, The Women's Press (1997)).

As a result of such research, the family courts have increasingly accepted that a mother's lesbianism does not pose a risk to the welfare of the child and is not a ground for refusing residence or contact. Implicitly, the HFEA Code of Practice (2004) allows licensed clinics to take a similar view:

> '3.3 Treatment centres are expected to ensure that they have clear written criteria for assessing the welfare of any child ... Those criteria are expected to include the importance of a stable and supportive environment for any and all children who are part of an existing or prospective family group.'

However, the presumption in favour of heterosexual couples does mean that both women not in heterosexual relationships and women in unmarried heterosexual relationships will face greater scrutiny:

> '3.14 Where the child will have no legal father the treatment centre is expected to assess the prospective mother's ability to meet the child's/children's needs and the ability of other persons within the family or social circle willing to share responsibility for those needs.

3.15 Where the couple are not married couples are expected to be advised that their legal position as parents, whether or not donated gametes are used, may require legal advice in order for full parental responsibility to be achieved.'

This area of legal and medical discourse also reinforces motherhood as women's presumed goal. As contraception and legal abortion have enabled many women to choose not to have children (either at a particular time or, increasingly, ever), so reproductive technologies have created new pressures upon women to bear children. Significantly, they also affect perceptions of women's choice not to have children: since the discourse in the media and elsewhere is medicalised, there is frequently an assumption that women are childless because of infertility (viewed as a medical problem) rather than through choice (the exercise of autonomy).

The medical view of conception is not one which is ultimately empowering to women. Orly Shachar, in a survey of the medical literature and of feminist criticisms, concludes that women are absent, reduced to a few body parts, referred to by such terms as the 'uterine milieu' and 'embryo transfer sites'. This represents a devaluation of the role of women, and an emphasis instead upon the role of (and shift of power to) the doctor ('The Invisible Female Patient: The New Reproductive Technologies Discourse in the Medical Literature', www.pantaneto.co.uk, 2001). As the subject becomes more technical and specialised, so the courts increasingly defer to doctors (as Parliament has done in relation to abortion): thus medical discourse impacts upon legal discourse too.

Conclusion

Assisted fertility poses many difficulties, both for feminists and for the law. First, there is the issue of how parenthood is defined and understood. The reality of different genetic, biological and social parents for one child would appear to pose a significant threat to patriarchal understandings of the family. However, as we have seen, the Human Fertilisation and Embryology Act 1990 does its utmost to defuse this threat by defining parenthood in a way consistent with 'traditional' understandings and giving importance to the marital status of the social parents.

Second, assisted fertility allows people to bear children when this would not have been possible before. The obvious situation is where one or both heterosexual partners are infertile, and the technology enables them to have a child. However, it can also be used in other ways: for example, to enable single women, lesbian couples and post-menopausal women to have children. The law's concern has been with regulating access to such treatment. However, feminists might ask different questions. For example, does this technology improve women's lives by increasing their choices? Does it damage women's interests by further emphasising motherhood as women's highest achievement and source of fulfilment? Do we want women's lives to be further medicalised? Does the technology encourage negative attitudes towards women's bodies within the medical profession (for example, defining women as 'embryo transfer sites')?

There are no easy answers, and the progression of these technologies will raise more and more difficult questions. As we write, human cloning has not yet been achieved but is being debated. If it becomes a reality, or if other technologies emerge, more of these complex questions will continue to be generated.

6

Bad or Mad Mothers?

6.1 Introduction

6.2 Infanticide

6.3 Abortion

6.1 Introduction

One of the strongest patriarchal ideologies is that which identifies womanhood with motherhood. There is an assumption that women achieve their greatest fulfilment through bearing and raising children. However, motherhood on its own is not enough: instead, women are measured against a mythical figure, the 'ideal mother'. Her characteristics are defined both socially and legally and include the following.

1. Age: consider how the media define teenage motherhood as a social problem, women who wait until their forties to have children as career-obsessed and those seeking post-menopausal fertility treatment as both selfish and unnatural. Thus the ideal mother must be in her twenties or thirties.
2. Marital status: since single parents and lesbian mothers are viewed as proof of society's decline, the ideal mother must be heterosexual and married.
3. Self-sacrificing: 'good' mothers are those who put their children before themselves. Women who seek their own fulfilment as well are frequently condemned as 'selfish'.
4. Solvent without full-time employment: while women dependent upon benefits appear in the tabloids as 'dole scroungers', and in political discourse as a problem to be solved by 'helping mothers back to work', those with demanding careers are portrayed as neglecting their children and lacking commitment to motherhood. The ideal mother, then, only works while her children are at school (if at all) but doesn't need state support, so is likely to be middle class and married.
5. Endlessly patient: the ideal mother doesn't shout at her children in the supermarket, get frustrated or complain about putting her child first all the time.

This mythical figure is culturally specific. She would be different in other societies, and she has changed over time. She also sets a near-impossible standard which all women with children are nevertheless criticised for not meeting.

The mythology depends upon the idea that this is how 'real' mothers, 'good' mothers are: that this is the natural way for women to be. Thus when a woman rejects motherhood (on one occasion or for life), or uses fatal violence against her child, the myth is challenged. If women can behave like that, is 'ideal motherhood' really the only natural way for women to be? In this chapter, we consider the legal discourses used to reconcile abortion and infanticide with the mythology of self-sacrificing motherhood. In particular, we will see how women whose behaviour contradicts the stereotype are portrayed as hapless victims of their biology and circumstances, rather than as autonomous adults.

6.2 Infanticide

Introduction

Infanticide is defined in law as the killing of a child under 12 months by its mother. The legal definition explains her behaviour by blaming her actions on her body: she has not recovered from childbirth. Recent cases, such as Sally Clarke's and Trupti Patel's, have brought some of the issues surrounding infanticide into the public arena. It is a crime that society finds shocking, because this is not the behaviour of a 'mother'. Mothers are supposed to be loving, caring, self-sacrificing and devoted. They are the one person that we believe a child should be safe with, because it contradicts all our stereotypes of motherhood for a mother to kill her child.

What happens when a mother kills her baby? There is a huge reluctance to accept that the myth of the perfect mother is just that: a myth. Instead, the courts look for explanations consistent with the mythology: that she did not really want to kill her child, but did so because she was unwell. In particular, her treacherous female body betrayed her. Thus, the law has developed almost to excuse the mother's behaviour, because any alternative view would be unconscionable. However, by blaming the woman's body, the law stigmatises and stereotypes women as being 'slaves' to their hormones. The law fails to address the social and economic reasons of why some women commit infanticide.

Not all women can be excused in that way, however. Some women will be seen as having gone too far. For example, both Sally Clarke and Trupti Patel were charged with murder, not infanticide. They were alleged to have killed several children, thus putting them in the category of 'evil' rather than irrational. Ania Wilczynski suggests that 'good mothers' will be convicted of infanticide, 'bad mothers' of murder (in Jo Bridgeman and Susan Millns, *Feminist Perspectives on Law: Law's Engagement with the Female Body*, Sweet & Maxwell (1998)).

Current law

Infanticide Act 1938

Section 1 Infanticide Act 1938 creates both an offence of infanticide and a defence to murder. In other words, a woman who kills her baby can either:

1. be charged with infanticide; or
2. be charged with murder, but argue that she should be convicted of infanticide instead.

It states:

> 'Where a woman by any unlawful act or omission causes the death of her child being a child under the age of 12 months, but at the time of the act or omission the balance of her mind was disturbed by reason of her not having fully recovered from the effect of giving birth to the child or by reason of lactation consequent upon the birth of the child, then, notwithstanding that the circumstances were such that but for this Act the offence would have amounted to murder she shall be guilty of felony, to wit of infanticide, and may for such offence be dealt with and punished as if she had been guilty of the offence of manslaughter of the child.'

To be guilty of infanticide a person must therefore be:

1. a woman – the offence/defence is gender specific;
2. suffering from a condition that has been caused by a change in her hormones;
3. that change in her hormones must have been caused by:
   a) giving birth in the past 12 months; or
   b) breast-feeding after giving birth;
4. the Act does not provide a defence if she has also killed an older child or adult.

History

The first legislation involving infanticide was very different to the 1938 Act. The Stuart Act 1623 (21 Jac I, c27) 'to prevent the destroying of bastard children' reversed the presumption of innocence (the mother of the dead baby was presumed guilty of its murder unless she could prove her innocence). The Act provided that: if a woman had given birth to an illegitimate child; and had concealed the birth of the child; and the child was found to be dead, the woman 'shall suffer death as in the case of murther' – unless she could provide a witness to state that the child had been stillborn.

This Act was gender specific and was confined to unmarried mothers only. Married mothers were tried for murder. Think about unmarried woman at that time: stigmatised, alone, maybe in employment where they were open to abuse (such as domestic servants). They may have had little choice except infanticide (as difficult and repugnant as this may be). Additionally, the reality for babies who survived was very different prior to the twentieth century, which also had an effect upon attitudes to infanticide.

One such example of these different attitudes can be seen in the practice of 'baby farming'. Working class women who had to work often had no alternative but to leave their babies with paid foster carers. However, these carers often took in large numbers of young children, or combined the childcare with other work requiring their attention, and relied upon dangerous methods such as gin or opium to keep the children quiet and docile. Too much of these substances could kill a child. Some of the most unscrupulous baby farmers deliberately killed the babies to minimise costs and effort while maximising profit.

However, even the best cared for baby was at great risk from a range of diseases. There was therefore a cultural acceptance of high infant mortality, which inevitably affected at least some people's attitudes to infanticide as well. The Stuart Act 1623 was therefore unpopular, as juries were unwilling to convict women of an offence carrying the death penalty when they were faced with these desperate choices.

The 1623 Act was repealed in 1803 with Lord Ellenborough's Act. This was called the Offences Against the Person Act 1803. It reinstated the presumption of innocence, so a woman charged with killing her baby was innocent until proven guilty. The baby was presumed to have been born dead. Therefore the burden was on the prosecution to prove that the child had been born alive and was later killed. There were many acquittals as a result of the lack of proof that the baby had been born alive: it was extremely difficult for the prosecution to prove this beyond reasonable doubt.

However, the 1803 Act contained another offence of concealing a death, which carried a maximum sentence of two years' imprisonment. This was used where there was no evidence to prove that the child had been born alive. Juries were more willing to convict women of this offence: it better reflected contemporary attitudes concerning such women's blameworthiness than one which carried the death penalty.

In 1922 a new piece of legislation was passed to deal with infanticide. The Infanticide Act 1922 had the effect of reducing the offence from murder (and thus the death penalty) to manslaughter. Legislators hoped that this would raise the number of convictions, as juries had proved unwilling to convict when the death penalty would be involved. The Act provided that infanticide occurred where a woman killed her new born child by a willful act or omission as at that time she had not recovered from the effect of giving birth, because the balance of her mind was disturbed. This was the bedrock for the legislation that we have today.

The 1922 Act provided a medical excuse for the woman's behaviour. Compare the 1938 Act with the 1922 Act and you will see two differences:

1. the 1938 Act changed the definition of 'new born' to 'under 12 months'; and
2. the 1938 included lactation as a reason for the mother's behaviour.

Because the medical theory that the 1938 Act is based on is now recognised as incorrect, there have been many calls for reform. The 1960 Criminal Law Revision Committee (CLRC) looked at infanticide. They argued that some women killed because of the emotional and social pressures on them, and didn't believe that the defence of diminished responsibility could adequately replace infanticide, as under its very different definition some women would be convicted of murder. They accepted that the medical reasons the Infanticide Act 1938 puts forward are not accepted today. For example, there is no such thing as lactational insanity as there was thought to be in 1938. They recommended that the reference to lactation be removed.

Fifteen years later, the 1975 Butler Committee requested that the section be amended to include the wider causes of wife battering. Unlike the 1960 CLRC report, Butler considered that manslaughter by diminished responsibility would adequately cover the situation. They agreed that the medical principles on which the 1938 Act is based are not relevant today, accepting evidence that the causes of infanticide were:

1. the stress of caring for the infant; or
2. an unwanted or a difficult child; or
3. personality disorders.

Why is this a feminist issue?

1. The 1938 Act perpetuates the stereotype that women are 'hormonal' and 'mad'. It excuses child killing on that basis. Women are considered not responsible for their actions; but that leniency comes at the price of medicalisation and stereotyping. This myth of being at the mercy of one's hormones is a stereotype that applies to all women: they are supposedly ruled by their hormones, while men are not. Female hormones are assumed to be bad, while men's are good.
2. The 1938 Act works on the presumption that 'normal' and 'sane' women are natural mothers. That is a woman's primary and ideal role. It is this stereotype that has been used as a tool for subordinating women and for keeping women out of the workplace.
3. The 1938 Act reflects the notion of an ideal mother, a very difficult role for any woman to fit in to.
4. A woman who kills her child departs from the expected norm of womanhood. She also departs from what we expect of a mother. Mothers are supposed to be loving, self-sacrificing and completely fulfilled by caring for their child. Infanticide offers an explanation of why a woman would act in this way – because her hormones made her do it. This explanation works to preserve these cultural norms.
5. The 1938 Act uses the woman's body as an excuse/explanation of her crime rather than looking at the social, cultural and historical circumstances of the crime. It fails to look at external factors such as poverty, poor housing, an unwanted pregnancy and lack of support.
6. The 1938 Act is now outdated. The medical theory that the law is based on is not good medicine. Judges are left to fit women's social and economic

circumstances into the Act, reinterpreting them as hormonal disturbance. The law is therefore in need of reform.

7. It makes no sense to reduce the crime from murder to manslaughter where the child is under 12 months but not do the same if the child is only a few days older. It is also a nonsense to have the situation where, if the woman kills a baby and an older child at the same time, one is classed as infanticide while the other is considered to be murder.

8. Stereotypes of women which are put before the court have a huge effect on defendants are treated. Women will only benefit from the Act if the court sees them as 'good' mothers.

Alternative arguments

A somewhat different attitude can be seen in one particular American court case. The case involved an English woman, Caroline Beale. It is discussed in detail in *Infanticide and the Nation: the Case of Caroline Beale* (1997) 32 New Formations. Caroline was discovered at JFK Airport, New York with the body of a new born baby under her clothes.

She had spent a two-week holiday in New York City with her boyfriend and his two brothers. On the eve of her return to Britain she gave birth secretly. Believing the baby to be dead she put it in a bag. The next day she put the bag containing the baby into the waistband of her trousers and went to the airport. She was reluctant to go through the security check: this aroused the suspicions of the staff and they searched her. The baby was found, and Caroline Beale was charged with murder.

Her defence claimed that her best friend had been diagnosed with breast cancer and had had to have her ovaries removed to try and stop the disease. Caroline realised that she was pregnant and was too embarrassed, distressed and guilty to tell anyone. Over the course of her pregnancy she became convinced that the baby had died. Throughout her trial she maintained that the baby was born dead. British medical specialists confirmed this but there were contradictory opinions from American specialists. The prosecution said that her motivation in killing her baby had been to keep her relationship with her boyfriend.

After plea bargaining she admitted manslaughter. Her lawyer considered that the medical evidence in her defence would not be considered conclusive and recommended that she accept the manslaughter plea bargain and return to London. Her mitigation was constructed around her own mental health: she had medical evidence to show that she was depressed as a result of the death of her friend and that this was made worse by the traumatic birth. Caroline Beale was sentenced to eight months' imprisonment (which she had already served) plus five years' probation and at least one year's psychiatric treatment.

If the baby had been born a day later, when she was back in England, then she would have received different treatment. She would almost certainly have been tried under the Infanticide Act 1938 and the emphasis would have been upon medical treatment rather than custodial sentence. The English law considers mothers to be mentally unstable rather than criminally culpable. In New York, there is no such legislation: the law on homicide makes no distinction on the basis of the victim's age.

Caroline's father spoke to the press and said that British law shows humanity for mothers who kill their children. The English courts were thus portrayed as being kinder, more humane and more civilised. However, the American judge (New York Supreme Court Judge Hanophy) responded with a very different argument based upon child protection:

> 'Granting parents a law to kill their children when their children are under the age of one is a law which is primitive and uncivilised. Granting parents a law to kill their children harkens to uncivilised times. I say to our friends in Britain, God bless America.'

While the judge misstates the effect of the Infanticide Act 1938, he makes a valid point. Why is the age of the child a relevant factor in assessing the mother's blameworthiness? English law, in seeking to preserve the myth of the ideal mother, ignores the real reasons why women kill. Instead, it appears to suggest that a baby's life is somehow of less value than that of an older child or adult.

6.3 Abortion

Introduction

The medical termination of pregnancy is a controversial area, and one which is directly regulated by the law. It is also an area which directly affects the lives of very many women: about one in three women will have an abortion at some time in their life (Royal College of Obstetricians and Gynaecologists, *The Management of Infertility in Tertiary Care*, 2000). Government statistics show that in 2001, 176,364 abortions were carried out on women living in England and Wales, almost 90 per cent of them in the first 12 weeks of pregnancy.

Nonetheless, most women know very little about their rights under the law: in a recent survey of British women, only 24 per cent knew that the written consent of two doctors was required, while just 13 per cent of women knew the time limit for abortion (*Women's Perceptions of Abortion Law and Practice in Britain*, Marie Stopes International, 2002).

'Abortion' actually means the ending of pregnancy in any circumstances – thus 'spontaneous abortion' is a medical term for miscarriage. However, the word 'abortion' has become the common term for the medical or voluntary termination of pregnancy. Throughout this chapter, we will use the word in this narrower sense.

Current law

Legally, a foetus only becomes a person at birth. Thus killing a foetus – however old – while it is in the womb is not murder, and abortion has therefore had to exist as a separate offence, because the injury is not being caused to somebody who is a legal person. It is important to remember this so that the law on abortion makes sense.

The starting point for the current law is the Offences Against the Person Act 1861, which makes having or performing an abortion illegal. Section 58 states that:

> 'Every woman, being with child, who, with intent to procure her own miscarriage, shall unlawfully administer to herself any poison or other noxious thing, or shall unlawfully use any instrument or other means whatsoever with the like intent and whosoever, with intent to procure the miscarriage of any woman, whether she be or not with child, shall unlawfully administer to her or cause to be taken by her any poison or other noxious thing, or shall unlawfully use any instrument or any other means whatsoever with the like intent, shall be guilty of an offence, and being convicted thereof shall be liable to imprisonment.'

In other words, both a pregnant woman obtaining an (unlawful) abortion and a person carrying out an (unlawful) abortion on a woman they think may be pregnant – whether she really is or not – commit an offence for which the maximum sentence is life imprisonment.

The Infant Life (Preservation) Act 1929 is also relevant, which created the offence of child destruction where a person causes a child to die before birth when it was capable of being born alive. Evidence that the woman has been pregnant for 28 weeks or more creates a rebuttable presumption that the child was capable of being born alive. The 1929 Act was actually concerned with children killed during birth – ie too late for the killing to count as procuring a miscarriage, but before the child was born and thus became a legal person who could, at law, be murdered. However, the 1929 Act later became relevant to the law on abortion for two reasons. First, it contained a defence which was extended to offences under s58 Offences Against the Person Act 1861 (see *R* v *Bourne* [1939] 1 KB 687, below). Second, it created an offence of child destruction committed wherever a foetus is capable of being 'born alive': it is not limited to the situation where labour has begun.

The meaning of 'born alive' has proved difficult. Advances in medicine mean that it is now possible, in some cases, to keep a baby alive when it is born earlier than 28 weeks into the pregnancy. The case of *C* v *S* [1987] 1 All ER 1239, where a man tried to prevent his girlfriend having an abortion, turned upon this issue. The man argued that since the foetus was between 18 and 21 weeks, it could be born alive (defined as showing some evidence of life, such as beating of the heart), although after birth it would inevitably die very quickly. The opposing argument was that a foetus was only capable of being born alive if it was viable, in other words 'capable of independent human existence separate from the mother'. Before approximately 24 weeks, the foetus does not have sufficient lung development for that to be possible.

Heilbron J held that the term 'born alive' is ambiguous and capable of different definitions. She rejected the definition put forward by the man, and instead favoured the concept of viability although she did not attempt to formulate a precise definition. The Court of Appeal upheld her decision, holding that a foetus which could never breathe either naturally or with mechanical assistance (such as a ventilator) could not be capable of being born alive.

Both abortion and child destruction are serious criminal offences. However, there is a defence to both offences, created by s1 Abortion Act 1967 (as amended by the Human Fertilisation and Embryology Act 1990). It applies where the abortion is carried out for specified reasons, following a specific procedure:

> '(1) subject to the provisions of this section, a person shall not be guilty of an offence under the law relating to abortion when a pregnancy is terminated by a registered medical practitioner if two registered medical practitioners are of the opinion, formed in good faith,
> (a) that the pregnancy has not exceeded its twenty-fourth week and that the continuance of the pregnancy would involve risk, greater than if the pregnancy were terminated, of injury to the physical or mental health of the pregnant woman or any existing children of her family; or
> (b) that the termination is necessary to prevent grave permanent injury to the physical or mental health of the pregnant woman; or
> (c) that the continuance of the pregnancy would involve risk to the life of the pregnant woman, greater than if the pregnancy were terminated; or
> (d) that there is a substantial risk that if the child were born it would suffer from such physical or mental abnormalities as to be seriously handicapped.
> (2) In determining whether the continuation of a pregnancy would involve such risk of injury to health as is mentioned in paragraph (a) or (b) of subs(1) of this section, account may be taken of the pregnant woman's actual or reasonably foreseeable environment.'

In other words, an abortion can be carried out if two doctors agree that the woman is less than 24 weeks pregnant, and:

1. that continuing with the pregnancy would involve risk to her physical or mental health greater than if the pregnancy was terminated; or
2. that continuing with the pregnancy would involve risk to the physical or mental health of any existing children in her family.

The 24-week limit does not apply if:

1. the woman's life would be at risk if the pregnancy continued; or
2. if there is a risk of grave permanent injury to the physical or mental health of the pregnant woman if the pregnancy continues; or
3. if there is substantial risk that the child would be born with a serious disability.

Since the Abortion Act 1967 was passed, there have been a number of attempts to repeal it or attempt to further restrict the law. None of those has been successful. However, there has been one important change to the 1967 Act. Originally, under s5, the upper time limit for abortion was explicitly governed by the Infant Life (Preservation) Act 1929 which prohibited the killing of a foetus capable of being born alive and created a presumption that at 28 weeks' gestation, a foetus was so capable. Because it is now considered possible to keep alive a child born after about 24 weeks of pregnancy, the Abortion Act 1967 was amended to introduce a time limit in line with current medical practice. Section 37 Human Fertilisation and Embryology Act 1990 therefore introduced the upper time limit of 24 weeks for most abortions. However, there is no time limit at all for the narrower grounds, which allow an abortion to be carried out after that time.

History

Abortion was first made illegal in the early nineteenth century, by the Offences Against the Person Act 1803, which made it a capital offence to procure an abortion after what was described as the 'quickening stage' (when movement could be felt by the pregnant woman, at about 16–18 weeks). This was thought to be the time when the soul of the foetus entered the body. Abortion was also more dangerous than childbirth at that time, and often caused death to the woman concerned.

Later legislation removed the distinction between the quickening and non-quickening stages, making abortion an offence at any stage of the pregnancy. By 1861, ss58 and 59 Offences Against the Person Act 1861 defined the offence in terms which still apply today. The 1861 Act made it illegal to procure a miscarriage at any stage of pregnancy. The maximum penalty for such an offence was life imprisonment. Anyone who supplied or used a 'poison or other noxious instrument or other means' to induce abortion was also guilty of a criminal offence under s59 of the 1861 Act. Thus abortion in any circumstances was a serious criminal offence, and all abortions were illegal – which meant that they were often carried out in unsuitable conditions and by dubious (or even dangerous) methods.

Early in the twentieth century, there were campaigns by women such as Stella Browne to make abortion available to women legally and safely, but legislative reform was slow to arrive. The law did ease a little in 1938, with a reading of the child destruction defence into abortion law in the case of *R v Bourne* [1939] 1 KB 687. Dr Bourne carried out an abortion on a 14-year-old girl who had been raped by a gang of soldiers, and then invited the police to prosecute him. The police did indeed prosecute him for abortion contrary to s58 of the 1861 Act, but he was acquitted. The court said that he could use the defence in the Infant Life (Preservation) Act 1929, that being that he had acted in good faith to preserve the life of the girl, who might otherwise have become a 'physical and mental wreck'. Lord McNaughten, directing the jury, effectively widened the law in two important ways.

1. He stated that the defence in the 1929 Act reflected the common law. The word 'unlawfully' in s58 Offences Against the Person Act 1861 indicated that there

were situations where abortion was not illegal. Those situations were the same as for the 1929 Act (where the doctor acted in good faith to preserve the mother's life). *Bourne* effectively stated for the first time that abortion was legal in certain, very narrow circumstances.

2. The defence applied where 'the act which caused the death of the child was ... done in good faith for the purpose only of preserving the life of the mother'. By holding that this included a situation where the mother would become a 'wreck', *Bourne* broadened the defence.

Bourne, then, changed the law a little, allowing doctors – but not others – to carry out an abortion where there was a serious risk to the woman's life. However, it carefully restricted the exception to very serious cases where the abortion was carried out by a doctor: there was no defence for other people who carried out abortions, or where the reason was anything but the preservation of the mother's life. The very limited terms of this exception effectively meant that doctors would have to be very cautious in relying upon it. However, the case also highlighted the issue, and in 1939, a government committee chaired by Norman Birkett recommended that the law on abortion be amended: unfortunately, the outbreak of the Second World War prevented any reform from taking place.

Throughout this time, very little birth control was available to women. What was available was very expensive and even among those who could afford it, was often available only to married women. Thus unwanted pregnancies were much harder for most women to avoid. The result was that abortions took place illegally, and were often attempted by doctors who had been struck off, by non-medically qualified people or by the pregnant women themselves.

Such illegal, 'backstreet' abortions often used dangerous methods, such as the taking of poisonous substances where miscarriage was one of the side effects, the injecting of various liquids into the uterus or the use of non-surgical implements like knitting needles. London hospitals would clear beds on Friday nights and Saturdays in preparation for women whose illegal abortions had gone wrong; in the worst cases, women permanently injured their health or even died as a result of these backstreet abortions. While some qualified doctors would carry out abortions, relying on the *Bourne* judgment, they charged a great deal of money and most women could not afford their services: campaigner Diane Munday describes paying a Harley Street doctor £90 for an abortion in 1961, equivalent to about £1,200 today (British Pregnancy Advice Service, *Abortion Law Reformers: Pioneers of Change* (1997), see: www.bpas.org).

However, campaigners for abortion law reform were not motivated only by the dangers of illegal abortions. They also pointed out that without control over their fertility, women could not fully control their lives. The legalisation of abortion would free women from the fear that they would have to have an unplanned, unwanted child. This meant that they could have the confidence to pursue education, careers and other long-term goals. There was particular concern for working class women, since they simply could not afford the high fees charged by medical practitioners, and so were disadvantaged by the law in a way which better off women were not.

Despite such campaigning, and a series of private members' bills brought before Parliament during the 1950s and 1960s, there were no further changes to the law until it was reformed by the Abortion Act 1967. This, for the first time, clearly allowed abortion in certain circumstances. Although the law has been criticised from various perspectives, as outlined below, it has not changed substantially since that Act was passed.

Why is this a feminist issue?

The fundamental issue concerning abortion is whose rights take precedence: those of the mother, or those of the foetus? Anti-abortion campaigners take the view that the rights of the foetus must be fully protected. Those who favour a woman's right to choose take an opposite position on the fundamental principle: they argue that a woman's right to bodily autonomy takes precedence over the rights of the foetus. (But note that some feminists go further and argue that we should move beyond using the concept of rights, since that will always risk placing the rights of the woman in conflict with those of the foetus.)

Pro-choice critics of the law point out that the foetus does not exist independently, floating in space. Instead, it is inside a woman's body, taking its nourishment from her, changing her body as it grows and profoundly affecting her. Margaret Little discusses this relationship as one of intimacy, and argues that this is a 'particularly intimate physical relationship' which women should not be forced into, any more than we would support the enforced physical intimacy of rape ('Abortion, Intimacy, and the Duty to Gestate', 2 Ethical Theory and Moral Practice 296). For feminists, given this extraordinarily close relationship between mother and foetus, it makes no sense to talk about the foetus having rights separate from, or even superior to, the mother's. It is also unjustifiable to suggest that anyone else could make the decision for the woman. Her own judgment should be respected, and so the current legislation is opposed on the basis that it imposes significant and unjustified restrictions on that right.

In particular, the requirement that she obtain the approval of two doctors effectively gives precedence to the judgment of medical practitioners over that of the woman herself. Women do not have the right to choose: instead the final choice is left to doctors. (They cannot force a woman to have an abortion she does not want, but they can refuse permission for her to have one she does want). Thus the law encourages and endorses medical paternalism – the idea that doctor knows best – allowing doctors to substitute their own views for those of the woman herself.

One issue that needs to be raised concerns the fact that there are, of course, a number of doctors who are opposed to abortion. Doctors may not declare their own moral objections to abortion, making it difficult or impossible for a woman to obtain the consent she needs; delay at this stage causes additional distress and anxiety to the woman, and may mean that a more invasive procedure with higher risks is required. Marie Stopes International's report, *General Practitioners: Attitudes to Abortion* (1999) found that a quarter of GPs who considered themselves 'broadly anti-abortion' did not believe that doctors should reveal such views. Even if the doctors concerned do not have personal objections, the mere fact that the consent of two doctors is required can result in delay at a time when speed is often of the essence. Trying to justify a very personal and difficult decision to a stranger can also be both patronising and distressing to many women, and it is a situation for which most doctors do not receive any special training.

The terms of the law also leave doctors a great deal of discretion in deciding if a woman falls within the terms of the 1967 Act. This discretion again allows doctors to impose their own views, and inevitably some doctors will interpret the law more strictly or more liberally than others. This means that there is real inconsistency between doctors' decisions, which is wholly unsatisfactory.

Sally Sheldon ('Who is the Mother to Make the Judgment? The Constructions of Women in English Abortion Law' (1993) 1 *Feminist Legal Studies* 3) argues that doctors are given a particular construction under the law: they are seen in parliamentary debate as male, and more specifically as professional medical men. Such men are portrayed as skilled, dedicated and altruistic, and therefore best able to make the decision – despite frequently hardly knowing the woman and not being aware of all the complex social and emotional issues involved for her. This is in contrast to the woman seeking the abortion, who is constructed as being immature, irresponsible and irrational, reflecting debates which portrayed such women either as unstable victims of their circumstances (according to those supporting the 1967 Act), or as selfish and morally childlike (according to its opponents).

She also argues ('The Law of Abortion and the Politics of Medicalisation', in Jo Bridgeman and Susan Millns, *Law and Body Politics: Regulation the Female Body*, Dartmouth (1995)) that the Human Fertilisation and Embryology Act 1990 has reinforced doctors' control over women's access to abortion, by relying solely upon medical definitions of viability for the terms of the amended 1967 Act. The debate took place in a medical framework without acknowledging the other considerations involved. Sheldon points out that women make decisions about abortion in the context of much more complex considerations than simply the viability of the foetus, including the social sustainability of bringing up the child for 18 years. The type of medical discourse involved in discussing viability as an abstract issue fails to recognise that the foetus does not exist in this abstract way: it is in reality very much attached to and dependent upon the woman who carries it. Rosalind Petchesky makes this point very strongly:

> '[N]o foetus is actually viable. Foetuses are biologically dependent on a pregnant woman and will be physically and socially dependent on her after birth. This dependence provides the basis for both her moral obligation to regard the foetus with care and her moral right to decide whether to keep it.'

In other words, when considering abortion we should look at the competing rights in a broader context: that of the social obligations of motherhood as well as the physical facts of foetal development and of pregnancy. It is because women do take the bearing of children seriously, and view it as entailing a continuing obligation to the child rather than just the short-term physical sustenance of the foetus, that they seek abortions.

A number of pro-choice organisations are therefore continuing to campaign for the law to be changed, so that abortion on request is available during the first three months of pregnancy. For example, the Abortion Law Reform Association wants the law to be changed so that the woman sees a doctor for counselling but the decision is her own in the first three months of pregnancy. Thereafter, up until 24 weeks, the consent of one doctor only should be required. Throughout, doctors with a conscientious objection to abortion should declare it and advise the woman of her right to see a different doctor.

On a purely practical level, there are several other problems with the current law. First, the procedure required can result in delay, yet it is desirable that abortions are carried out as quickly as possible. Second, there is no right to a free NHS abortion. In practice, NHS provision varies drastically between areas so that the availability of a free abortion depends upon where the woman lives. Private abortions are available through private clinics and several national charities, but cost from around £450.

Opposing views

Although most feminists support the right of the woman to choose – in other words, they accept that her personal autonomy takes precedence over the foetus – not all feminists take this position. Some opponents of abortion argue from a feminist perspective that abortion undermines women's rights for a number of reasons. Underlying many of these reasons is the idea that the ready availability of abortion actually undermines women's choices.

First, it is argued that abortion is in the interests of men because they can engage in sexual activity with even less fear of being held responsible for an unwanted pregnancy. Indeed, men can put women under pressure to have abortions. When a woman has an abortion under pressure from others, rather than because she really does not want to continue with the pregnancy and have a child, then her autonomy is being seriously undermined rather than respected.

Pro-choice critics also condemn male irresponsibility and, above all, anyone's actions aimed at reducing a woman's bodily autonomy. However, they would challenge the conclusion that making abortion unavailable could increase that autonomy. The responsibility men are forced to take for pregnancy is usually financial only, so it is unlikely that the possibility of abortion alone makes a great deal of difference to their behaviour. By contrast, the enormous responsibility of childbearing and childrearing would be forced upon women were abortion prohibited.

Second, many women come under social pressure to abort as a result of housing and financial issues, and the answer is improved social provision rather than the availability of abortion. Indeed, the fact that abortion is an option makes it easier for these pressing social issues to be disregarded, to the detriment of all women. Women can only have real control over their fertility if they can make choices secure in the knowledge that society will support them in the valuable work of childrearing. If women are forced to abort for economic reasons, then they do not make a free choice but rather are being forced into the path which is cheapest and least disruptive for society as a whole. Unfortunately, however, it is far from certain that in reality, the absence of legal abortion would see any real increase in support for mothers: many politicians opposed to abortion have also favoured limits upon social security and other welfare provision for women.

Third, it is argued that abortion can itself be damaging to the woman, particularly psychologically. In fact, most evidence suggests that this is not the case, particularly when compared with women who go ahead with unwanted pregnancies.

Fourth, abortion on demand risks allowing the abortion of female foetuses where male babies are more prized. Thus in China in 2000, 117 boys were born for every 100 girls, largely as a result of abortions carried out for reasons of sex selection. However, is restricting women's access to abortion the answer? Restrictions on tests identifying the sex of the foetus and, more fundamentally, changing social norms so that women are valued, would better address this problem than the prohibition of abortion (which to some extent has replaced older practices such as infanticide or the abandonment of female babies). The Chinese figures are particularly distorted because of the pressures placed upon families to have only one child: in India, there is still a problem but the figures are much less skewed, at 107.9 boys to 100 girls in 1994 (the usual figure is 105 to 100). In the context of English law, there is little evidence of such abortions and couples who wish to choose the sex of their babies seem as likely to want a girl as a boy.

Fifth, some abortions are carried out because the foetus is disabled, and respect for all women including those with disabilities raises the question of how we can justify abortion on the grounds of (sometimes relatively less serious) disabilities. The answer is that bringing up a child with serious disabilities is very difficult and demanding, and can have a great impact upon the whole of the family. The choice being made by a woman who aborts in that situation is not to do so because she does not respect the rights of disabled people and the value of their lives, but because she does not feel able to bring up such a child herself. It is important to remember that such abortions are almost always of hitherto wanted pregnancies, and the decision is one which will have been very difficult for all the parties involved.

However, opposition to abortion is not primarily based upon feminist arguments. It often focuses upon the notion of conception as the moment when life begins, and presumes that from that moment the foetus has the right to life. If the right to life begins at the moment of conception, then the argument is that that right is greater than the woman's right to bodily autonomy, and so the foetus must be protected by the prohibition of abortion. In other words, no difference is recognised between an existence which is entirely dependent upon the mother's body and life after birth.

Exactly when a foetus becomes a member of the moral community, entitled to rights, is a philosophically difficult question. There are various possible answers, discussed by Jennifer Mather Saul (*Feminism: Issues and Arguments*, Oxford University Press (2003)).

1. A foetus is human and alive, and therefore a person. However, is simply being biologically human enough? If so, it would also be murder to switch off a life support machine in instances where the individual being kept alive is brain-dead. What of cancer cells, which are biologically human and alive too?
2. Arguably we only become members of the moral human community (and therefore entitled to a right to life) when we become a person. However, it is not necessarily easy to define when this happens. Definitions based upon self-consciousness would often exclude newborn babies as well as foetuses, which most of us would not accept. For example, Michael Tooley says that a person 'possesses a concept of itself as a continuing subject of experiences and other mental states, and believes that it itself is such an entity'. Newborn babies would not meet that test.
3. Mary Anne Warren suggests that we can accept that a person must be self-conscious yet still give newborns a right to life: it may be appropriate to treat them as if they were such persons because (unlike foetuses in utero) they can be treated in this way without treating women as if they were less than persons.
4. Don Marquis says that the important issue is not whether the foetus is a person, but whether it has a future significantly like ours. By aborting a foetus, we are preventing it from having a life like the one we ourselves have and value. However, surely this makes contraception wrong too, since the birth control pill violates a zygote's right to life?

The argument that the foetus has a right to life is not necessarily seen as dependent upon its being a person. This is particularly true of those who oppose abortion on religious grounds. For example, the Roman Catholic Church has accepted that there is no clear theological authority pronouncing when a foetus becomes a person with a soul:

> 'This declaration expressly leaves aside the question of the moment when the spiritual soul is infused. There is not a unanimous tradition on this point and authors are as yet in disagreement.' (Sacred Congregation for the Doctrine of the Faith (Vatican), Declaration on Procured Abortion, 1974.)

Nonetheless, there is support for the view of Pope Pius VI, who declared in 1869 that the soul is present from the moment of conception. In the Catechism of the Roman Catholic Church, the foetus is given the rights of a person:

> 'Human life must be respected and protected absolutely from the moment of conception.

> From the first moment of his existence, a human being must be recognised as having the rights of a person – among which is the inviolable right of every innocent being to life.'

If the foetus does have a right to life, how far does that right extend? To most anti-abortionists, the right is absolute and always takes precedence over the woman's right to bodily autonomy. On this basis, the main anti-abortion organisations, such as the Pro-Life Alliance and the Society for the Protection of the Unborn Child, oppose abortion under any circumstances. David Alton MP, an active campaigner against abortion who sought to introduce legislation restricting or removing the right to abortion, argued in the House of Commons that abortion is always the greater of two evils: it amounts to choosing to take another's life. The Pro-Life Alliance state that '[a]bsolute respect for innocent human life from the one-cell embryo stage until natural death is the keystone of justice'. They rely upon anti-feminist arguments to rebut any suggestion that abortion should be available in extreme circumstances, such as where the pregnancy is a result of rape: 'violent rape is extremely unlikely to end in pregnancy ... It is also extremely difficult to prove the truth or falsehood of an allegation of rape'. Thus the stereotypes of 'violent rape' as the only significant form of rape, and of women as deceitful, are invoked in an attempt to deny women personal autonomy.

However, why should any right of the foetus be absolute and take precedence over the mother's rights (including her right to life, where continuing the pregnancy puts her at a real risk of death)? After birth, we have no such unconditional right to life: think of the law on self-defence, for example. In addition, we are not morally obliged to keep other born persons alive (for example, even the relatively unintrusive, quick and straightforward act of blood donation is not compulsory even though it saves others' lives), so why should a woman be placed under a moral obligation to keep her foetus alive, with her own blood and inside her own body, for nine months?

For most (but not all) opponents of abortion, the issue is a religious one. We are each created by God: we are not expendable. Only God, and not any one of us, has the right to take a life, and that life begins at the moment of conception:

> 'All human life, including life developing in the womb, is created by God in his own image and is, therefore, to be nurtured, supported and protected.' (Church of England, General Synod Resolution, 1983.)

Nonetheless, most religions such as Anglican Christianity, Judaism, Hinduism and Islam allow abortion in certain circumstances, such as where the life of the mother is in danger.

Fathers' rights

The mother and the foetus are of course those most intimately and directly affected by abortion. However, there is a third party who has sometimes sought the legal right to be involved in the decision: the father. The courts have ruled on several occasions upon the claims of men that they have a right to prevent women from having an abortion.

The issue was first considered in detail in *Paton v British Pregnancy Advisory Service (BPAS) Trustees* [1978] 2 All ER 987. Mr Paton applied to the court for an injunction restraining his estranged wife from having an abortion without his consent. He sought to make the application on his own and the foetus' behalf. His case was dismissed.

The first point made by the court was that the foetus does not have any legal existence independent of its mother. Mr Paton therefore could not seek to bring an action on behalf of the foetus. Any right he might have to prevent his wife from having an abortion would therefore have to depend upon his own rights as the father.

Did the father of the foetus have such rights? An unmarried father would clearly have had no rights under the law as it then stood, because an unmarried father had to apply to the court for parental rights after the child's birth. However, Mr Paton was married to the mother of the foetus. Did he have rights as a husband? The court concluded that he did not. Historically, husbands had the right to force their wives to live with them – a right which no longer existed but in any event did not compel a wife to conceive and bear her husband's children. The court would not seek to enforce matrimonial obligations by injunction if they included matters such as sexual intercourse or contraception. They would not grant an injunction to stop sterilisation or vasectomy. While spouses could apply for non-molestation orders, they were to protect the spouse or living children. By analogy to all these instances, the court would therefore not grant an injunction to a husband to prevent his wife from having an abortion.

Having lost his case in the English courts, Mr Paton took it to the European Commission of Human Rights in *Paton v UK* (1981) 3 EHRR 408. The Commission considered whether English abortion law contravened either art 2 of the European Convention on Human Rights, which guarantees the right to life, or art 8, which guarantees the right to family life. The Commission decided that art 2 did not give an absolute right to life to the foetus, given the connection between it and the woman sustaining it: 'The "life" of the foetus is intimately connected with, and cannot be regarded in isolation from, the life of the pregnant woman'. To give it an absolute right to life would mean to regard its life as of higher value than that of the woman carrying it. There was no conflict with art 8 since the interference with Mr Paton's family life was justified as necessary to protect Mrs Paton's rights.

In *C v S* [1987] 1 All ER 1239 the court also considered whether the woman's boyfriend had locus standi – in other words, whether as the father of the foetus he had any legal standing to bring the case at all. The court concluded that he did not.

The law is therefore clear: the father of the foetus has no right to a say in the decision to abort. However, this does not mean that men are generally excluded from such decisions: in one study, 84 per cent of men felt that the decision to abort was a joint resolution of the matter between themselves and the woman (Shostak and

McLouth, cited in David Nolan, 'Abortion: a Man's Right to Choose?', *Spiked Online*, www.spiked–online.com). These cases do, however, raise one question: if the courts are clear that the decision is one for the woman alone to take, why does the Abortion Act 1967 still require her to obtain the approval of two doctors?

7

Domestic Violence

7.1 Introduction

In this chapter, we consider the issue of domestic violence. We begin by analysing what remedies the law makes available to those who are experiencing domestic violence, and the limitations of those remedies. We then go on to consider what happens in a particular situation where the legal system has failed: that of the abused woman who kills her abuser. We will see the ways in which the criminal law poses real difficulties for women, but also the ways that it has responded to feminist criticisms.

7.2 What do we mean by domestic violence?

As the name implies, domestic violence is violence within the home. However, it is used more specifically to refer to violence between adult members of the same family, and in particular violence by one spouse or partner against another. Although it is not limited to violence by men against women, that is by far the most common form of it, and we will limit our discussion to that particular form.

There is no definition of domestic violence in English statute. Many organisations (for example, Women's Aid and the Women's National Commission) favour the definition in New Zealand's Domestic Violence Act 1996:

'(1) In this Act, "domestic violence", in relation to any person, means violence against that person by any other person with whom that person is, or has been, in a domestic relationship.

(2) In this section, "violence" means:

(a) physical abuse;

(b) sexual abuse;

(c) psychological or emotional abuse, including, but not limited to,
(i) intimidation;
(ii) harassment;
(iii) damage to property;
(iv) threats of physical abuse, sexual abuse or psychological abuse;
(v) in relation to a child, abuse of the kind set out in subs(3) of this section [allowing them to see or hear abuse of someone else].'

Domestic violence is very under-reported, and as we shall see is not always taken seriously when it is reported to the police and courts. However, various studies have arrived at a common figure: around one in four women experience domestic violence (for example, see Catriona Mirrlees-Black, *Domestic Violence*: *Findings from a New British Crime Survey Self-Completion Questionnaire*, Home Office Research Study 191, 1999; Stanko, Crisp, Hale and Lucraft, *Counting the Costs: Estimating the Impact of Domestic Violence in the London Borough of Hackney*, Crime Concern, 1998; British Medical Association, 1998). In other words, about a quarter of women will suffer domestic violence at some point in their lives. Nonetheless, it remains largely invisible since it happens in the private sphere: the home, which in patriarchal ideology is represented as a place of safety and refuge.

The term 'domestic violence' covers a whole range of assaults, but at its most serious can be life-threatening or even fatal. The majority of female murder victims are killed by family members. Of total homicides (during 1982–1986), nearly a fifth (18 per cent) were the result of husbands killing wives, while only 2 per cent were the result of wives killing husbands. In this country, two women are killed by domestic violence every week (see the Home Office statistics at: www.homeoffice.gov.uk).

7.3 What role do the courts and police play in protecting women?

Criminal law

There is no difference in criminal law between domestic violence and any other kind of violence. Such assaults are offences under the Offences Against the Persons Act 1861, and depending on the severity of the injury may amount to either common assault, assault occasioning actual bodily harm or grievous bodily harm. Other offences such as rape or attempted murder can also be committed: the relationship between perpetrator and victim has no effect upon any part of the definition of these offences.

The Protection from Harassment Act 1997 has also created two offences which can be particularly relevant to situations involving domestic violence. Section 1 defines harassment as:

'... a course of conduct –
(a) which amounts to harassment of another, and
(b) which he knows or ought to know amounts to harassment of the other.'

Note that the mens rea of the offence is tested objectively: what matters is whether the defendant ought to know the conduct was harassment (whether a reasonable person would have known). Thus the fact that a defendant has mental health problems, or wrongly and unreasonably believes that the victim welcomed the attention, is not a defence.

A course of conduct need not be over a long period of time: thus three telephone messages left within five minutes of each other and later listened to by the victim all at once amounted to a course of conduct, since each call was separate and distinct (*Kelly* v *DPP* [2003] Crim LR 45). Conversely, *Pratt* v *DPP* (2001) 165 JP 800 was concerned with two incidents three months apart. The magistrates had regard to the context of the incidents (attacks on the defendant's estranged wife during the breakdown of the marriage) and the fact that the second incident breached the defendant's undertaking not to harass his wife, and held that they amounted to a course of conduct. The High Court upheld the conviction.

However, a similar time gap was an important factor in finding that there was no course of conduct in *Lau* v *DPP* [2000] 1 FLR 799. The High Court noted that the fewer the number of incidents and the greater the time between them, the less likely that they amounted to a course of conduct.

Section 2 of the 1997 Act makes such conduct a criminal offence punishable by up to six months' imprisonment. Where the conduct causes the person to fear violence will be used against them, that is a more serious offence punishable by up to five years' imprisonment (s4).

If an offender is convicted of an offence under the 1997 Act, the court has the power to impose a restraining order in addition to any term of imprisonment or other punishment. Section 5 provides:

> '(2) The order may, for the purpose of protecting the victim of the offence, or any other person mentioned in the order, from further conduct which –
> (a) amounts to harassment, or
> (b) will cause a fear of violence,
> prohibit the defendant from doing anything described in the order.
> (3) The order may have effect for a specified period or until further order.'

Breach of the order is a criminal offence. However, we will see some of the problems with such orders when we consider the civil remedies below.

Despite the availability of criminal offences, the criminal law has real drawbacks. First, domestic violence is not always taken as seriously by either the police or the courts as other crimes of violence. Second, it is not always in the best interests of the victim to prosecute, and she may not wish to do so. Even if she does, many of the benefits are short term: bail conditions which may keep the abuser away last only until the end of the case, and the sentence may provoke rather than prevent further violence. Only where the charge is one of harassment can the court make a restraining order.

However, it is not only because of the limited effects of such prosecutions that women do not proceed with such cases. Actually calling the police, giving a statement and ultimately giving evidence in court can be difficult for many reasons. First, the police tend to be called only as a last resort. The violence, after all, is coming from somebody the woman may still love, and who may be the father of her children. Even when she finally takes this step, the police officers themselves may be unsympathetic and fail to arrest or charge the offender. This is a problem for all women, and ethnic minority women in particular: studies by Amina Mama (cited at www.womensaid.org.uk) found that black women are particularly reluctant to call the police because of their fears concerning police racism. Some black women have themselves been threatened with arrest when the police have responded to their calls.

The Crown Prosecution Service can also decide not to proceed with the case, or to accept a plea to a lesser charge (common assault instead of assault occasioning actual bodily harm, for example). If the case does go to trial, the woman may be very reluctant to give evidence. The courtroom can be intimidating and the abuser, perhaps together with his family and friends, will be present. Discussing the intimate details of the relationship in public can be very difficult, particularly where there is pressure to protect the family's reputation or honour.

Should a case go to court and be successfully prosecuted, matters may not be improved for the woman. Sentences tend to be low, often consisting of a fine or a suspended sentence. Even imprisonment provides only a temporary respite. Meanwhile, the proceedings themselves can trigger further and greater violence, thus leaving the woman in a worse, rather than better, position.

Nonetheless, the criminal courts could have an important role to play in addressing domestic violence. Ruth Lewis argues, based on her study of a number of male perpetrators and their female partners ('Making Justice Work: Effective Legal Interventions for Domestic Violence' (2004) 44 *Brit J Criminal* 204), that criminal prosecutions can help prevent future violence where:

1. there is a focus upon rehabilitation (such as a probation order with a condition of attendance at an abuser programme);
2. there is both coercion and control (such as the threat of a jail sentence if further violence is committed or the perpetrator does not attend the programme);
3. women's agency is recognised and supported: taking the issue out of the private sphere into the courts gives women more confidence and more access to support.

In spite of its failings, the criminal law could prove valuable provided that suitable programmes for offenders are available, and the courts take full advantage of them as a sentencing option.

Civil law

There are a number of measures in civil law aimed at protecting victims of domestic violence. These are now governed by Part IV Family Law Act 1996, which brings together a variety of remedies previously contained in various Acts which applied to different courts, including the Domestic Proceedings and Magistrates' Courts Act 1978, the Domestic Violence and Matrimonial Proceedings Act 1976 and the Matrimonial Homes Act 1983. The main remedies available to victims of domestic violence from their spouses or partners are discussed below.

Non-molestation orders

Section 42 Family Law Act 1996 sets out the court's power to make non-molestation orders. Section 45 allows such orders to be made ex parte 'where it considers that it is just and convenient to do so'. A full hearing (one for which both parties are given notice) must then be held 'as soon as just and convenient'.

Non-molestation orders provide emergency protection. They prohibit the abuser from molesting the applicant (s42). They can include a power of arrest, which enables the police to arrest the abuser for a breach of the order. Section 47 states that where the abuser has used or threatened violence, a power of arrest should be attached unless the court is satisfied that the applicant will be adequately protected without it.

If an order without power of arrest is breached, then the applicant must apply to the court through committal proceedings for the respondent to be imprisoned for breach of the injunction. Imprisonment may be suspended if he 'purges his contempt' by apologising to the court.

Occupation orders

These orders are made under ss33 and 35–38 Family Law Act 1996. They can:

1. exclude the violent partner from the home (or part of it);
2. exclude the violent partner from a defined area in which the home is included;
3. if he has already left, prevent him from returning to it;
4. if the other partner has left, order him to readmit her.

They are available both where a couple are married (ss33, 35 and 37) and to heterosexual cohabitees who are living or have lived with each other in the same household as husband and wife (ss33, 36 and 38). The different sections contain provisions for married couples or cohabitees with different types of rights to occupy their home. The orders are temporary interferences with the man's right of occupation, made either for a specified period, until the occurrence of a specified event or until further order.

In deciding whether to make an order, s33 directs the court to consider:

'(6)(a) the housing needs and housing resources of each of the parties and of any relevant child;
(b) the financial resources of each of the parties;
(c) the likely effect of any order, or of any decision by the court not to exercise its powers

under subs(3), on the health, safety or wellbeing of the parties and of any relevant child; and

(d) the conduct of the parties in relation to each other and otherwise.'

The court must also consider the 'balance of harm' (s33(6)): it must make an order where the applicant would otherwise suffer significant harm, unless the harm suffered by the other party is likely to be as great or greater. Note that similar considerations are set out for occupation orders under the other sections.

Section 41 adds another consideration where the partners are unmarried cohabitees:

'(2) Where the court is required to consider the nature of the parties' relationship, it is to have regard to the fact that they have not given each other the commitment involved in marriage.'

Just as we discuss elsewhere in other contexts (see, for example, assisted fertility in Chapter 6), the legislation here aims to reinforce the primacy of heterosexual marriage, thereby reinforcing patriarchal norms and values.

Other powers of the civil courts

The court has further powers in relation to divorce proceedings and the protection of children. It also has an inherent jurisdiction to grant injunctions in proceedings in tort for assault and trespass, nuisance and intimidation: thus such proceedings are necessary to obtain an injunction against a partner with whom the woman has not lived. The court does not, however, have the power to attach a power of arrest to injunctions granted in such proceedings.

The Protection from Harassment Act 1997 also creates civil remedies. For further details, see Chapter 11.

Feminist perspectives

The remedies available in instances involving domestic violence have been criticised. The most obvious point to note is that they do not save large numbers of women from experiencing domestic violence, or a smaller number from being killed by abusive partners. Women's experiences of such orders can vary widely: in one study, 36 per cent of women who had used protection orders said that the abuse stopped; a further 39 per cent said that the orders were of some help, although they were breached. However, 25 per cent of the women found the orders to be of no help (Cathy Humphreys and Ravi K Thiara, 'Neither Justice Nor Protection: Women's Experiences of Post-Separation Violence' (2003) 25(3) *Journal of Social Welfare and Family Law* 195).

Criticisms of the orders concern all aspects of the procedure, from the first steps in making an application, through to dealing with breaches of injunctions. First, can women access the orders at all? To do so, the woman being abused must know that the orders exist. However, not all women are aware of them. In particular, women who do not speak English will have difficulty in accessing information and support.

Once somebody has overcome this first hurdle, realising that a legal remedy may be available, she must obtain appropriate legal advice: again, this may be far from straightforward. Women may be reluctant to approach solicitors, particularly male solicitors. There is much silence and shame surrounding abusive relationships, and discussing those circumstances can therefore be a difficult step to take. It may be particularly difficult where a woman has not decided to end the relationship.

There can be social stigma in acknowledging living in a violent relationship or in taking a husband to court. This can combine with social pressures, including a feeling of obligation to preserve family honour, to make the reality of court action very difficult.

Financial issues can also deter or prevent women from obtaining legal advice and pursuing a case. Solicitors' services are costly, and may not be affordable for women who are not eligible for public funding. The financial limits on eligibility mean that many people are not eligible for free legal advice, but cannot afford to pay privately either. In the context of domestic violence, there may be particular problems as many abusers take control of the couple's finances, so that the woman cannot accumulate savings to pay for legal representation.

If the woman proceeds through these steps to court, her problems are by no means over. First, the experience of going to court is itself intimidating and often unpleasant. Most courts have limited facilities and no childcare provision. There can be long waiting times before hearings and court staff, including the judge, may be prejudiced or unsympathetic.

Once inside the courtroom, the woman may be left feeling that it is her behaviour which is under scrutiny. She has to show the judge that she is a deserving victim rather than someone who has provoked or deserves the violence. In particular, the courts can have regard to the 'conduct of the parties' when deciding whether to grant an occupation order, so the abuser can use the victim's behaviour (such as her parenting, housework, and so on) to justify the violence.

Many types of abuse may not fall clearly within the law. The civil law is rather vaguely worded, giving a margin of judicial discretion. There can be particular difficulties where the violence is psychological in nature. The law focuses on a comparatively small range of violent behaviour, which in reality forms only one type of domestic violence. Abusive behaviour may consist principally of humiliating, undermining and psychologically abusing a woman rather than rely upon the use of physical force.

Where the woman has not lived with her abuser, she will have no remedy unless she can show either that there has been a formal promise of marriage, or that there are children for whom both she and the abuser have parental responsibility. Thus many women are excluded from the 1996 Act's protection altogether.

Even where an order is made, it does not always solve the problems the woman is experiencing. Serving an order upon the abuser can itself trigger further violence against the woman. Some men have no respect for the court order, and will continue their behaviour. Any enforcement of the order by necessity will always come too late: after the violence has happened (although such enforcement may prevent further violence).

Enforcement can prove difficult, particularly if there is no power of arrest attached to the order. The woman herself must then bring proceedings to enforce the order by applying to have the abuser committed to prison for breaching it. Committal proceedings are very technical, and any error is likely to result in the man not being imprisoned. Even if the procedure is correctly followed and the breach proven, the man may be allowed to 'purge his contempt' by apologising to the court. The imprisonment will then be suspended.

Where a power of arrest is attached, that empowers the police to arrest the abuser following a breach. It does not force them to arrest him. Thus police attitudes and failure to respond can render the power of arrest worthless. Part of the difficulty here is that the police have tended to view domestic violence as less serious than other types of crime. Attitudes are now changing: all police forces have policies on domestic violence, and many police stations have domestic violence units. However, police attitudes outside these specialist units may remain dismissive of domestic violence; and the availability of such units is variable.

Finally, there is also a theoretical problem with this system of civil court orders. They reinforce the public/private divide, first because they are only usually available to those who live or have lived together, and second, because they deal with what are in fact serious criminal offences in the civil courts. Arguably they reinforce the idea that marital violence is different to, and less serious than, other violent crime.

The consequences of these failings are that it can be very difficult for women to escape abusive relationships. However, women stay in violent relationships for many reasons, only a few of which can be addressed by court orders. Just a few of these reasons are listed below.

1. The act of leaving can provoke further and more serious violence. This is the most dangerous time of all for women in violent relationships.
2. Leaving does not necessarily end the violence. One recent study found that 76 per cent of women suffered further harassment and abuse after ending the relationship; for more than a third, the abuse was continuing (Cathy Humphreys and Ravi K Thiara, 'Neither Justice Nor Protection: Women's Experiences of Post-Separation Violence' (2003) 25(3) *Journal of Social Welfare and Family Law* 195).
3. Economic issues may make leaving very difficult. The woman may have been encouraged to give up work by her abusive partner; have had to account for all money spent and so had no opportunity to save money; or may have had children and therefore not been in full-time employment. Without money, it can be very difficult to leave home and set up a new household elsewhere. Further barriers, such as racism and lack of childcare, can make it difficult for women to find employment after leaving an abusive relationship.

4. Women subject to immigration control are often subject to a condition that they do not have recourse to public funds: ie they are not allowed to claim benefits. This can have devastating effects if they need to leave a violent relationship and have no other means of financial support. One study found that of 251 abused women with no recourse to public funds, only nine could be accommodated in refuges (Imkaan, *A Place to Stay?*, 2003).

5. The effects of the relationship itself can make leaving difficult. The abuse can lead to the woman losing ties with family and friends, and losing confidence in herself. Isolating the woman from friends and family is a very common form of control in these relationships.

6. There can be enormous social and cultural pressure on people to stay in a marriage. Pressure from an abuser's (and even from the woman's own) friends and family is often used to try to persuade a woman to return to a relationship.

7. It is difficult to stay away from the abusive partner, as many will go to enormous lengths to find their victims. This is particularly true where there are children involved, as the courts will enforce access except in the most exceptional circumstances. Even if the parties do not meet during these access arrangements, the children themselves can be asked for information on where they now live, told to give messages to their mother, etc.

8. The violence comes out of a relationship which was probably once loving. It may be difficult for the woman to accept that her partner's promises to change won't be kept, and that the best thing for her to do is leave.

The Domestic Violence, Crime and Victims Bill 2003

In June 2003 the government published the *Safety and Justice* consultation paper on domestic violence. That consultation paper and the responses to it led to the Domestic Violence, Crime and Victims Bill 2003. At the time of writing (September 2004) the Bill had reached its second reading. If passed in that form, the following provisions will be included.

1. Breach of a non-molestation order will become a criminal offence, removing the need for difficult civil committal proceedings.

2. The definition of 'cohabitants' in the Family Law Act 1996 will be extended to include same-sex cohabitants.

3. Protection will be extended to those who have never cohabited provided 'they have or have had an intimate personal relationship with each other which is or was of significant duration'.

4. Domestic violence homicide reviews may be held where a person over 16 is killed by a member of their household or someone with whom they had been in an intimate relationship, with a view to identifying the lessons to be learned from the death.

5. Members of the House of Lords tabled an amendment (based on Southall Black

Sisters' proposals) to entitle victims of domestic violence subject to immigration controls to welfare benefits. However, the government opposed this amendment.

It can be seen that these proposals address some of the difficulties with the current law. However, there are many more issues left unaddressed, in particular those which require social as well as legal change. As with most issues discussed, the law is only part – albeit an important part – of the problem (or solution). Women's position in society can be fundamentally changed only by legal and social change together, not by the law alone.

7.4 Women who kill

Introduction

The law on homicide provides a range of defences for people who have killed others. These defences form one of the most criticised areas in the criminal law's treatment of women (another is sexual offences: see Chapter 8). On first appearances, the defences appear to be gender neutral: the same rules apply to women or men. However, the impact of those rules is very different for women.

The defences of provocation, self-defence and diminished responsibility have been criticised for their failure to properly take account of women's experiences. The particular context in which they have been analysed and developed is that of battered women who kill their abusers. This is not the only situation in which women kill, but it highlights the problems raised by the law with particular clarity. Not only the legal requirements of the defences, but also the role of expert psychiatric evidence of 'battered woman syndrome' (BWS) have come under scrutiny. We will therefore consider both the use of BWS, and the defences to murder, in the context of battered women who kill.

There is also a gender specific defence to murder: that of infanticide, which has been dealt with earlier in this chapter.

Battered women who kill

We have already discussed the enormous difficulties facing women who suffer domestic violence. Sometimes, women respond to the threat to their own lives by killing their abuser. They then face criminal charges for the killing, and if convicted of murder must be sentenced to life imprisonment. The availability of a defence is therefore very important, as it will reduce a conviction to manslaughter and enable a lesser sentence to be given; or in the case of self-defence, result in a 'not guilty' verdict.

Historically, the criminal courts have not taken adequate account of the circumstances surrounding these killings. Many women who killed their abusers were convicted of murder and sentenced to life imprisonment. By contrast, men were more often able to use the defence of provocation when killing their partners and thus receive drastically different sentences. One notorious case was that of Joseph McGrail, who in 1991 was convicted of manslaughter. His wife had been an alcoholic, and swore at him. His defence was that he had been provoked into killing her by kicking her repeatedly in the stomach. The judge said that 'this lady would have tried the patience of a saint' and gave him a two-year suspended prison sentence.

The law has made a number of changes in recent years, which have had positive effects. It is now relatively unusual for a battered woman who kills her abuser to be convicted of murder and serve a life sentence. Most women in this situation are more likely to be convicted of manslaughter: Nicholson and Sanghvi 'More Justice for Battered Women' (1995) *New Law Journal* 1122 comment upon this:

> 'The approach now seems to be to allow battered defendants great latitude in putting forward circumstances and characteristics relevant to their provocation defences. At trial level it has become common for murder charges to fail or not even be attempted in the case of battered defendants.'

However, less positively, injustice continues to exist. Women from ethnic minorities can be particularly ill-served by the law in this area. For example, the courts have sometimes shown a willingness to accept 'honour killings' of women as provoked. Southall Black Sisters have highlighted the case of Shabir Hussain, who killed his sister-in-law by driving a car over her several times. He did so because she was having an affair, although at his original trial his defence was that he was not the driver. He was convicted of murder in 1996, but subsequently won an appeal and was retried in 1998. In this second trial, he admitted the killing but claimed he was provoked, on the basis of the shame and distress his sister-in-law's behaviour brought upon him and his family, and was convicted of manslaughter. He was sentenced to three years' imprisonment. Hannana Siddiqui, of the Southall Black Sisters, said in an article taken from *The Guardian* (3 October 2003): 'Cultural defences which use notions of honour to justify murder or other offences of domestic violence have been accepted by the courts, which has led to differential treatment of black and minority women and a system colluding with that justification'.

By contrast, the cultural pressures on Zoora Shah have not been recognised by the courts. After being abandoned by her husband, she lived with a man called Mohammed Azam, who took her in in return for sex. He abused her physically and sexually for a period of 12 years. He then turned his attention to her daughter, and seeing no other way out of the situation, Zoora poisoned him. Depression, feelings of shame and fear of dishonour meant that she did not tell the police or the court about the abuse she had suffered. She also feared the effect upon her daughters if she spoke out about what had happened to her. She was convicted of murder in 1993 and sentenced to life imprisonment with a tariff (the minimum time she has to spend in prison) of 20 years. Her appeal on the basis of diminished responsibility was unsuccessful, as the Court of Appeal failed to understand why she had not spoken out earlier. In 1997 the Home Secretary reduced her tariff to a still substantial 12 years.

Where women are found guilty of manslaughter rather than murder, most convictions are on the basis of diminished responsibility. Thus a woman who does something which may be a rational response to circumstances will nonetheless be categorised by the courts as irrational. We consider elsewhere how that stereotype denies women's agency and ability to make their own decisions in situations such as childbirth and abortion. In this chapter, we will see the courts using the myth of women's irrationality to rule that they are not fully responsible for their own actions even when committing the most serious offence in criminal law, murder.

Provocation

What is provocation?

The defence originated at common law as a concession to human frailty. Lord Hoffmann set out its history in his judgment in *R* v *Smith* [2000] 4 All ER 289:

> 'It comes from a world of Restoration gallantry in which gentlemen habitually carried lethal weapons, acted in accordance with a code of honour which required insult to be personally avenged by instant angry retaliation and in which the mandatory penalty for premeditated murder was death. To show anger "in hot blood" for a proper reason by an appropriate response was not merely permissible but the badge of a man of honour. The human frailty to which the defence of provocation made allowance was the possibility that the man of honour might overreact and kill when a lesser retaliation would have been appropriate. Provided that he did not grossly overreact in the extent or manner of his retaliation, the offence would be manslaughter and execution avoided.
>
> The situations which were considered to be proper occasions for anger reflected the code of honour of the time ... [In] *R* v *Mawgridge* (1706) ... the court listed four categories of case which were "by general consent" allowed to be sufficient provocations. The first was the quarrel which escalated from words to physical assault ("by pulling him by the nose, or filliping upon the forehead"). If the assaulted party drew his sword and immediately slew the other, it would be "but manslaughter". The second was a quarrel in which a friend of the person assaulted joined in and gave the deadly blow. The third was where someone took the part of a fellow-citizen who was being "injuriously treated" and the fourth was killing a man in the act of adultery with one's wife ("for jealousy is the rage of man and adultery is the highest invasion of property").
>
> The nineteenth century judges had to adapt this law to a society of Victorian middle class propriety. They changed it in two ways. First, they generalised the specific situations which the old law had regarded as sufficient provocation into a rule that whatever the alleged provocation, the response had to be "reasonable" ... The second change was to shift the emphasis of the law from the question of whether the angry retaliation by the accused, though excessive, was in principle justified, to a consideration of whether the accused had lost his self-control.'

This history contains no mention of women, except in a purely passive role, as the object of adultery. The person losing their reason due to strong provocation and instantly reacting with fatal force is seen as male. This is because the law has taken (white, middle and upper class) men as the norm and based its requirements around their behaviour, with women left to fit themselves in as best they can.

These problems are not purely historical, as we shall see below. However, before considering criticisms of the current law, we must first understand what it says. Provocation is a common law defence. Its classic definition was set out by Lord Devlin in *R v Duffy* [1949] 1 All ER 932:

> 'Provocation is some act, or series of acts done by the dead man to the accused, which would cause in any reasonable person and actually causes in the accused, a sudden and temporary loss of self-control, rendering the accused so subject to passion as to make him (or her) for the moment not the master of his mind.'

Certain aspects of the common law were amended by s3 Homicide Act 1957, which states:

> 'Where on a charge of murder there is evidence on which the jury can find that the person charged was provoked (whether by things done or by things said or by both together) to lose his self-control, the question whether the provocation was enough to make a reasonable man do as he did shall be left to be determined by the jury; and in determining that question the jury shall take into account everything done and said according to the effect, which, in their opinion, it would have on a reasonable man.'

This section makes two particularly important changes to the *Duffy* test. First, the issue of provocation is placed very firmly in the hands of the jury. Second, the provoking incident can take the form of words as well as acts.

Further changes have also been made by the case law. For example, the provocation no longer needs to come from the victim or be directed at the defendant (an interpretation consistent with the wording of s3). We will not consider the law in detail here, but rather concentrate upon those aspects of the test for provocation which have proved particularly problematic from a feminist perspective. That test was summarised in the form of two questions in the case of *R v Brown* [1972] 2 All ER 1328, which says that the judge should ask two questions.

1. Did the defendant, as a result of provocation, lose self-control?
2. Was the provocation sufficient to make the reasonable man behave as the defendant did?

The first question is subjective: did this particular defendant lose self-control as a result of some provoking words or acts? That loss of control must be 'sudden and temporary': any gap between the provocation and the killing may be treated as 'time for cooling' in which reason can reassert itself (*Duffy*).

The second question is objective; it requires the jury to consider what a 'reasonable man' would think or do in that situation. It asks, would a reasonable person in the defendant's position be as provoked by the words or acts? How would a reasonable person who was so provoked react?

There are two aspects of provocation which have been particularly criticised.

First, it is clear from the case law (beginning with the leading case of *Duffy*) that the loss of self-control must be angry, 'sudden and temporary'. This requirement has caused particular problems for women who have killed their abusers, since in many cases there has been a delay between the provoking words or acts and the killing.

Second, the objective test is based upon the reasonable man. Since the case of *R v Camplin* [1978] 2 All ER 168, the courts have been clear that the age and sex of the accused are characteristics which can be given to the reasonable man, so he can become a teenage boy or a woman, for example. However, it has been less clear whether that reasonable man could share other characteristics of the accused. Since suffering domestic violence has had such a profound effect upon the defendants we are concerned with, it would seem sensible for that to be a possible characteristic of their 'reasonable woman'. Unfortunately, the law has not always been clear that this is the case.

Loss of self-control

A loss of self-control could include all sorts of mental states. Imagine being so despairing and desperate that you cannot think clearly about what to do any more. Or so upset and frightened that you're hardly in control of how you strike out. Unfortunately, the law has not used its imagination in that way: the only loss of control recognised in relation to provocation is one caused by anger.

Not only must the loss of self-control be an angry one; it must also be sudden and temporary (*Duffy*). This requirement makes sense when we consider the history of provocation. It was established to help men who, faced with a terrible insult from a physical and social equal, reacted immediately with fatal force. However, women do not necessarily respond in the same way, and in particular, women who suffer domestic violence are unlikely to respond with that kind of instant violence. The classic view of provocation, then, is based upon a specifically male typology of anger.

There are two important differences in the way that women who have suffered domestic violence might react to a provoking incident. First, that incident will be one of a whole series in the relationship (including previous insults, abuse and violence). The effect which the provoking incident has upon the woman may only make sense in the context of the full history of the abusive relationship. It is not a single event, but the latest in a long series, the final straw: it may be trivial in itself, but on top of the past incidents, becomes too much for the woman to bear. This is what is known as 'cumulative provocation'.

Second, most women tend to face strong cultural pressures throughout their lives not to react with immediate violence to something which upsets them. As a result, a requirement that they instantly 'snap' is unrealistic. What often happens is that the woman will not react instantly, but will think about the incident, and the more she considers it, the more upset she becomes. Finally, a little while after the original event, she will lose self-control. This is known to the courts as 'slow burn provocation'.

Ironically, the case which emphasised that a loss of self-control must be 'sudden and temporary', with delay liable to interpretation as 'time for cooling ... for reason to regain dominion over the mind' (*Duffy*) itself concerned a battered woman who killed her violent husband. After he made threats one evening, Mrs Duffy waited until he was asleep to kill him. This delay was construed as a cooling-off period, and she was convicted of murder.

After more than 40 years, two cases returned to this issue and redefined the term 'sudden and temporary'. First, *R v Ahluwalia* [1992] 4 All ER 889 looked again at the issue of delay. The accused, Kiranjit Ahluwalia, had been subjected to repeated violence and sexual abuse from her husband throughout their marriage. She was also prevented by him from seeing family and friends. She had obtained court injunctions and attempted to leave, but without success. One evening he made further threats. She didn't react immediately. She went to bed, but was unable to sleep and continued thinking about his behaviour. Instead, she went downstairs, poured petrol into a bucket, lit a candle, then returned and set fire to her husband's bed. He died from his injuries.

Ahluwalia appealed against her conviction for murder. The Court of Appeal said that the requirement in *Duffy* of a sudden and temporary loss of self-control was still good law. However, the defence of provocation could be available in cases where there was a delayed reaction: the loss of self-control had to be sudden, but need not be immediate. Thus the court recognised 'slow burn' provocation, but emphasised that the longer the delay, the stronger the evidence of deliberation, and thus the more likely it will be that the prosecution will be able to negate the defence of provocation. This reflects the court's concern to differentiate between genuine provocation (where the defendant is not master of their own mind) and premeditated revenge.

Because the judge's direction in *Ahluwalia* on the need for a sudden and temporary loss of self-control was correct, her appeal on that point did not succeed. The court did, though, accept medical evidence of endogenous depression and reduced her conviction to manslaughter on the basis of diminished responsibility.

Ahluwalia's interpretation of the loss of self-control as sudden and temporary, but not necessarily immediate, was confirmed by *R v Thornton (No 2)* [1996] 2 All ER 1023. Sara Thornton had also killed her husband following a history of violence. He was an alcoholic ex-policeman, and was jealous and possessive. After several days of arguments, she went out one evening to the pub. When she returned, another argument developed and she went to the kitchen to look for something to defend herself with, should he attack her. She took and sharpened a knife, then returned to the sitting room. She asked him to come to bed, but he refused and threatened to kill her in her sleep. She then stabbed him with the knife.

It was again confirmed that the words 'sudden and temporary' are still appropriate. However, the defence of provocation was not ruled out as a matter of law either because the provocation extended over a long period (cumulative provocation) or because there was a delayed reaction. Lord Taylor explained the effect of cumulative provocation:

'A jury may more readily find there was a sudden loss of control triggered by even a minor incident, if the defendant has endured abuse over a period, on the "last straw" basis.'

The vital issue to ascertain is that the act was not premeditated. On this basis, Thornton's appeal was successful and she was convicted of manslaughter at her retrial (although it is not known whether this was on the basis of provocation or diminished responsibility, both of which were argued).

Feminists' concerns over this specific aspect of the law of provocation therefore seem to have been addressed by the courts. However, it is notable that despite the more favourable interpretation of the 'sudden and temporary' requirement, Kiranjit Ahluwalia still did not fall within the defence. Instead, her appeal succeeded on the basis of diminished responsibility.

The 'reasonable man'

Provocation also contains an objective test based upon the reasonable man. He can be given limited characteristics of the defendant, including their age and sex (*R* v *Camplin* [1978] 2 All ER 168). Critics have pointed out that this means in law, there is not a 'reasonable woman' but rather a 'reasonable man who happens to be a woman'. The man is very much the norm, with being female something to be appended. This emphasises the extent to which the law has been based on and developed around men, with women being required to adapt to the standards set for men.

A particular difficulty for battered women was the limited range of characteristics which could be given to the 'reasonable man' in the provocation test. *Camplin* effectively divided the second, objective question into two stages.

1. How provoked would a reasonable man of the defendant's age and sex, and 'sharing such of the accused's characteristics as … would affect the gravity of the provocation' be? This is sometimes referred to as the gravity of the provocation.
2. How would a reasonable man of the defendant's age and sex, 'having the power of self-control of an ordinary person' (ie not sharing other characteristics relevant to their ability to control themselves) react to that degree of provocation?

Thus relevant characteristics of the defendant could be used to assess the gravity of the provocation but not the reasonable person's reaction to it.

The problem has been particularly serious for women who have killed their abusers. The abstract reasonable woman has not suffered the things which they have undergone. The identification of Battered Woman Syndrome (BWS), a psychiatric disorder which showed how battered women would not react like the abstract reasonable woman, added to concerns over the court's refusal to take such characteristics into account.

The court looked at this point in *R* v *Humphreys* [1995] 4 All ER 1008. Emma Humphreys was a young woman in a relationship with a partner who had a history of violence towards her. One evening, she took knives from the kitchen and cut her wrists. Her partner taunted her, saying that she had not made a good job of it. He also indicated that he wanted sex with her. She stabbed him with one of the knives. Psychiatric evidence indicated that she had 'immature, explosive and attention-seeking traits'.

Emma Humphreys was convicted of murder. On appeal, the Court of Appeal considered whether her 'immature, explosive and attention-seeking traits' were relevant characteristics of the reasonable woman. They concluded that her immaturity and attention-seeking were relevant for the purpose of assessing the gravity of the provocation. However, her explosiveness was not a relevant characteristic to be given to the reasonable person in deciding whether they would have reacted in the way she did. In other words, to judge how upset the reasonable person would have been, the jury could consider a reasonable person with the defendant's relevant characteristics. However, when deciding how a reasonable person who was that upset would react, that reasonable person could not have the accused's characteristic of explosiveness.

The confirmation that her psychiatric condition was relevant to the gravity of the provocation was valuable. However, the refusal to allow it to be relevant to the reasonable person's reaction to the provocation meant that the defence of provocation was still difficult to apply to many battered women.

The House of Lords recently looked at the characteristics of the reasonable man again in the leading case of *R* v *Smith (Morgan)* [2000] Crim LR 1004. The defendant, Morgan Smith, suffered from depression. One of its effects was to limit his capacity for self-control. He and his friend, the victim, were alcoholics and drinking partners. He argued with his friend, accusing him of stealing some tools with which Morgan Smith earned his living. The friend refused to admit this and the defendant lost control, stabbing him to death with a knife.

The House of Lords held that for both parts of the objective test – deciding on the gravity of the provocation and deciding how the reasonable man would respond to provocation of that gravity – the reasonable man should be given the characteristic of the defendant's depression. In other words, characteristics which meant that the defendant would not have an ordinary level of self-control could now be given to the reasonable man. This represents a very important change in the law: it means that the reasonable person can have the relevant characteristics of the defendant throughout the objective test.

Indeed, Lords Hoffmann and Clyde suggested that juries do not need to be directed in terms of the 'reasonable man' at all. Instead, they should simply be told that an acceptable standard of self-control should be expected from everyone (taking into account certain characteristics such as depression – but not bad temper or excessive jealousy – which affect the defendant's self-control). The House of Lords therefore substituted the defendant's conviction for murder with a conviction for manslaughter.

This case concerned two men having a single argument, but arguably represents a positive outcome for battered women who kill, too. The impact of feminist campaigns on the judgments was clear. For example, they emphasised that there are still certain characteristics which cannot be taken into account, such as an unusually jealous nature or violent disposition. Lord Hoffmann said:

> 'Male possessiveness and jealousy should not today be an acceptable reason for loss of self-control leading to homicide, whether inflicted upon the woman herself or her new lover.'

However, even with these changes provocation is a much more difficult defence to establish for battered women than diminished responsibility, and with the risk of a life sentence it is a gamble many women cannot afford to take. Instead, they have to accept the false stereotype of the irrational woman which the use of diminished responsibility in these circumstances helps to create.

Morgan Smith isn't unproblematic for women, either. It may help some women successfully plead provocation when they kill their abuser, but it may also help men who kill their wives, perhaps on much more trivial provocation. The further the defence is widened, the greater the risk of opening it to people who take calculated revenge, who overreact to trivial incidents and who carefully premeditate killing. The problem is arguably a more fundamental one: not how do we fit women into provocation, but how do we ensure that the law deals appropriately with women who kill?

Self-defence

What is self-defence?
Self-defence is complete defence. This means that somebody who is found to have acted in self-defence will be found 'not guilty'. It applies to all offences including murder.

Self-defence is a common law defence. It also appears in statutory form in s3 Criminal Law Act 1967:

> '(1) A person may use such force as is reasonable in the circumstances in the prevention of crime, or in effecting or assisting in the lawful arrest of offenders or suspected offenders or of persons unlawfully at large.'

The defence is defined largely subjectively (ie according to the defendant's understanding of events): 'if the defendant may have been labouring under a mistake as to the facts, he must be judged according to his mistaken view of the facts ... whether the mistake was ... a reasonable mistake or not' (*R* v *Gladstone Williams* (1984) 78 Cr App R 276). However, there is an objective element: the 1967 Act requires that the degree of force used must be reasonable in the circumstances as the defendant believed them to be.

1. Whether self-defence was necessary is judged subjectively (on the facts as the defendant believed them to be).

2. The degree of force necessary to defend oneself is judged objectively (on those facts, what would the reasonable person think was required?).

Self-defence has proved very difficult for women to plead successfully. The emphasis on a proportionate response and upon the imminence of the threat mean that women face difficulties in showing first, that it was reasonable to use a weapon against an unarmed man and second, that it was reasonable to use deadly violence against a drunk or sleeping man rather than to run away. Thus the defence is very rarely available to battered women who kill. By contrast, most such women themselves describe their actions in terms of defending themselves and saving their own lives and perhaps those of their children.

Imminent threat

The facts are judged subjectively, so it must be shown that the defendant believed she was in imminent danger of violence. However, it can be very difficult to convince a jury that she had such a belief where she killed her abuser while he was drunk or sleeping (as in *Ahluwalia*, for example).

The law does allow pre-emptive strikes: it is permissible to use violence to prevent a violent attack, before it actually happens. *Beckford* v *R* [1988] AC 130 states that 'a man about to be attacked does not have to wait for his assailant to strike the first blow or fire the first shot; circumstances may justify a pre-emptive strike'. However, the requirement of imminence still applies. The defendant must believe that the danger is imminent: that the attack is just about to happen. *Palmer* v *R* [1971] AC 814 suggested that if a person was in 'immediate peril' or 'imminent danger', then immediate defensive action might be necessary, but if the attack were over then the force 'may be by way of revenge or punishment or by way of paying off an old score or may be pure aggression'.

However, Aileen McColgan argues that the case law has been misinterpreted, and that in fact imminence is not an absolute requirement, just evidence that the force was used in self-defence rather than from some other motive ('In Defence of Battered Women Who Kill' (1993) 13 OJLS 508). Nonetheless, there are no reported cases of women who have killed their abusers successfully using this approach in practice.

If the attack could be prevented in some way other than by the use of force, then self-defence will not be available. The most relevant issue here is whether the defendant could have retreated and thus avoided the need for violence. The fact that the victim was sleeping or otherwise temporarily incapacitated can be interpreted as creating an opportunity to retreat (ie leave the house) rather than use force.

The law has softened a little so that there is no 'duty to retreat' (Michael Allen points out that if there were, pre-emptive force could never be justified: *Textbook on Criminal Law*, 7th Ed, Oxford University Press (2003)). Instead, the failure to leave is a factor in deciding whether the use of force was necessary (*R* v *Bird* [1985] 1 WLR 816). Unfortunately, though, misapprehensions concerning the ability of battered women to escape their abusers are critical here. The courts have tended to believe that women could simply walk out of the house, while in fact such a course of action is liable to increase rather than remove the danger they face.

Proportionate force

Someone is entitled to the defence of self-defence if, on the facts as they believed them to be, the amount of force used was proportionate to the violence threatened.

1. The facts are judged subjectively – what did the defendant herself believe the situation to be?
2. The degree of force is judged objectively – what force would a reasonable person use in that situation?

When an unarmed man is killed by a woman armed with a knife or other weapon, the violence she used may seem disproportionate. However, is this really true? Many men are stronger than women, and (particularly in the case of violent abusers) more used to using violent force. In those circumstances, a woman can only effectively defend herself with a weapon. Nonetheless, the apparent mismatch between bare hands and a murderous implement may appear disproportionate to the jury. Again, the problem is that the law assumes a male defendant, who has defended himself against an attack from an equally-matched male adversary. That approach cannot work fairly for a female defendant who has had to protect herself from an ongoing (perhaps escalating) series of attacks by a larger, more violent adversary.

Diminished responsibility

What is diminished responsibility?

Diminished responsibility is a partial defence to murder, reducing it to manslaughter. The defence was created by s2 Homicide Act 1957:

> '(1) Where a person kills or is a party to the killing of another, he shall not be convicted of murder if he was suffering from such abnormality of mind (whether arising from a condition of arrested or retarded development of mind or any inherent causes or induced by disease or injury) as substantially impaired his mental responsibility for his acts and omissions in doing or being a party to the killing.'

To plead the defence successfully:

1. the accused must suffer from an abnormality of mind;
2. that abnormality must have been caused by arrested or retarded development, and any inherent cause or disease or injury; and
3. its effect must have been to impair the accused's mental responsibility for the killing.

What are the criticisms of the law and how have the courts responded?
The principal feminist criticism of diminished responsibility is that it has been used to provide a medical explanation for women's behaviour. In other words, it fits them into the stereotype of the irrational or 'mad' woman. On the contrary, a woman who kills a violent abuser may be acting very rationally to save her own life. However, diminished responsibility shifts the focus from the danger her abuser created for her to her own mental state.

Some of the cases we have already discussed provide examples of this tendency to medicalise women's responses to life-threatening violence. For example, Kiranjit Ahluwalia's appeal succeeded on the basis of diminished responsibility but failed on provocation. Thus criticisms of this defence centre not on its terms, but on the way that it is used when other defences might more accurately reflect the circumstances in which women have killed.

One way in which the abuse a woman suffers can be translated into diminished responsibility is through a diagnosis of Battered Woman Syndrome. The syndrome can also be used to support the defence of provocation (as one of the relevant characteristics of the reasonable person). It has therefore been useful in reducing individual convictions from murder to manslaughter, but as we see below, feminists are very wary of this syndrome.

Battered Woman Syndrome

What is Battered Woman Syndrome?
Psychologist Lenore Walker developed Battered Woman Syndrome (BWS) to explain the effect of domestic violence. There are two elements to the syndrome. First, a cycle of violence is identified – the violent incident, followed by a period of loving contrition when the abuser is apologetic and pleasant, followed by building tension until the cycle begins again with another violent incident. Second, the effect of undergoing this cycle is described as 'learned helplessness': the woman comes to believe that she cannot fight back or escape.

What are the benefits of BWS?
BWS has benefitted individual defendants and has helped support useful changes in the law.

1. As a recognised psychiatric condition, BWS can form the basis of a defence of diminished repsonsibility.
2. The syndrome allows expert evidence to be admitted explaining the background to the killing and the effect of the victim's violence upon the defendant.
3. It can help the jury understand how a battered woman might experience 'slow burn' provocation so that her loss of self-control, although sudden and temporary, does not immediately follow the provocation.
4. BWS can also be one of the characteristics of the 'reasonable man' in

provocation. The objective test thus becomes more responsive to the particular situations of battered women.

5. It helps counter criticisms of the woman's behaviour, for example that she could have left her abuser.

What is wrong with BWS?

Many feminists have reservations about using BWS. These relate to the validity of the research; the impact of BWS upon legal proceedings; and ways in which BWS has been used against victims of domestic violence.

1. The admissibility of BWS evidence depends upon the status of the syndrome as a recognised psychiatric condition. However, Walker's methodology has been severely and quite convincingly criticised. Much of the research her theory is based upon used not human subjects, but dogs. Her own data shows that some battered women react other than with 'learned helplessness', and that many abusers do not go through the 'loving-contrite' stage of the cycle (see Donald Nicholson, 'What the Law Giveth, It Also Taketh Away: Female-Specific Defences to Criminal Liability' in Donald Nicholson and Lois Bibbings (eds), *Feminist Perspectives on Criminal Law*, Cavendish (2000)). If the syndrome is discredited, the evidence will cease to be admissible.

2. The emphasis on 'learned helplessness' may explain why a woman did not leave her abuser, but also makes it difficult to understand how she came to use fatal violence. It is hard for juries to imagine how a state of passivity and fear could be consistent with a decisive murderous act.

3. 'Learned helplessness' also enables the courts to ignore the wide range of other factors preventing a woman from leaving a relationship. It is easier to blame individual psychology (and stereotypes of women as passive) than to face up to the wider failure of our society to provide adequate protection for abused women.

4. Domestic violence is made to seem unusual, so much so that it needs to be explained by a psychiatrist. In fact, it is shockingly common, affecting about one in four women.

5. The psychiatrist interprets and explains the defendant's experience, speaking on her behalf. Sheehy, Stubbs and Tolmie point out that this means that her explanations are taken over by the expectations of other people.

6. Once a woman is shown to suffer from a psychiatric condition such as BWS, diminished responsibility will appear a more appropriate defence. Thus BWS helps to confirm the legal perception of women who kill as 'irrational'.

7. It also supports the stereotype of women as passive victims, and is thus likely to be most successful where the defendant can demonstrate her conformity to the law's stereotypes of femininity (Donald Nicholson and Rohit Sanghvi, 'Battered Women and Provocation: The Implications of *R* v *Ahluwalia*' [1993] Crim LR 728).

Although BWS was developed by a feminist and intended to help women in court, we can see from these criticisms that in practice, the syndrome has not proved an unmixed blessing. Instead, it can worsen some of the problems faced by battered women in the criminal courts. Nicholson and Sanghvi summarise many of its limitations in the above article:

> '[E]ven if BWS is developed to address the pertinent issues, it will always actively shift the emphasis from the reasonableness of the defendant's actions to her personality in a way which confirms existing gender stereotypes, silences battered women and conceals society's complicity in domestic violence.'

A final area of difficulty is that BWS can actually be used against women who have suffered prolonged abuse. It becomes misused as a definition of the 'real' battered woman, so that the abuse suffered by women who do not fall within the syndrome is dismissed or disbelieved. This has already happened in the United States. BWS then functions not to help battered women but to provide another obstacle in their search for justice.

Conclusion

The overall criticism from feminists is that the law relating to homicide is modelled on male behaviour and designed by and for men. It has proved difficult to adapt it to women's needs. More fundamentally, none of the existing defences is ideally suited to instances where battered women kill their abusers.

Recent cases – particularly those concerning battered women which were the focus of a lot of campaigning and press attention, such as *Humphreys* and *Ahluwahlia* – have gone some way to improving the law for battered women. They have changed the law on provocation first, by accepting cumulative provocation and slow burn provocation; and second, by extending the characteristics of the reasonable person. More generally, the courts are now more aware of, and at least somewhat more sensitive to, the position of women who have killed their abusers.

However, the situation remains far from perfect. We have considered the ways in which the existing defences simply fail to meet women's needs. The question is, what should be done? Can the defences be further reformed; should a new defence be created; should the law on murder itself be reformed so that the life sentence is no longer mandatory?

These questions are now being asked by the government. In 2004, it was announced that there would be a review of this area of the law, and in particular of whether the defence of provocation should be abolished. The Law Commission expected to produce its final report in the late summer of 2004.

Can we keep and reform the existing defences?
The response of the courts to these cases has been to alter the parameters of existing defences. This approach has brought some real gains. However, it is not without its problems, and for provocation, has probably gone as far as realistically possible.

One difficulty is that the defences apply to everyone accused of murder, in any circumstances. Although reforms may have been made in the context of battered women killing their abusers, not only those women will benefit. We have already seen how men's behaviour tends to fit more readily within these defences, sometimes when they have killed for quite trivial reasons. The more the defences are widened, the greater the risk that they will benefit abusers who kill their victims as much as victims who kill their abusers. Thus, while the aim may be to benefit women, the result of further reform could be to undermine their legal protection against the most extreme form of domestic violence.

Another problem is that the defences can only be changed to a limited extent. As Aileen McColgan explains in relation to provocation:

> 'However much the defence is tweaked and refined, the provocation plea is premised upon an angry loss of self-control; an explosion of rage ... It is not designed to serve those who act in panic or fear.' ('General Defences' in Donald Nicholson and Lois Bibbings (eds), *Feminist Perspectives on Criminal Law*, Cavendish (2000).)

We might also question the basis of provocation. Why is anger seen as less blameworthy than fear or despair? Is it morally better to kill in anger than for some other reason?

Finally, changes which have been made allow a woman's psychiatric condition to be attributed to the reasonable person. However, to establish such a characteristic, the defendant is likely to depend upon expert opinion, frequently based upon Battered Woman Syndrome. As we have discussed, the use of this defence brings its own difficulties.

A better option may be to extend the defence of self-defence. It fits much more closely with the perceptions of these women themselves. Susan Edwards points out: 'if we listen to the vocabulary of motives and justifications of battered women who kill, they talk in language of self-defence, not cumulative provocation and not of mental impairment'.

Aileen McColgan suggests that a correct interpretation of the existing law on self-defence should make it accessible to battered women who kill their abusers. For example, the use of fatal force could be shown to be necessary by providing evidence of how difficult it is for women to escape their abusers. Again, there could be some explanation of how the differing physical strength of men and women means that a woman's use of a weapon against an unarmed attacker can sometimes be proportionate. Her conclusion is that self-defence is rarely successful at present not because of the legal requirements but because of a mythical model of 'real' self-defence. We consider elsewhere how powerful such 'ideals' are in the law of rape (Chapter 8); McColgan argues that they operate similarly for self-defence, and again rarely match the reality of women's experiences. The problem is exacerbated in relation to self-defence by the fact that the ideal is based upon male behaviour.

However, there may be difficulties in persuading the courts to apply self-defence in a way which does not disadvantage women unfairly. In particular, because it is a complete defence the courts are concerned to keep it within strict limits. A process of education about the realities of domestic violence is required. Unfortunately, the most effective forum for such education may be the courtroom itself, and the only way to judge our progress is to see whether individual defendants succeed in their pleas of self-defence. However, with the current approach taken by the courts, it is unsurprising that many will prefer to take the less risky route of pleading diminished responsibility.

Should we create a new defence?

Kiranjit Ahluwalia was freed on the basis of diminished responsibility, not provocation. This need for reliance upon the defence of diminished responsibility has been strongly criticised by feminists. For example, Katherine O'Donovan argues that a woman subject to cumulative provocation might legitimately claim justification instead of having her own mental state – not the abusive behaviour of the victim – as the issue that is on trial.

Justice for Women (see: www.jfw.org.uk) is campaigning for a defence of self-preservation defined as follows:

'1. It shall be a defence to a charge of murder, reducing the charge to manslaughter, if:
(a) the deceased person had subjected the defendant or another person, with whom the defendant was at the time of the deceased person's death in a familial relationship, to continuing sexual or physical violence and
(b) the deceased person was at the time of their death or had at any time been in a familial or intimate relationship with the defendant or with the person as described in (a) above and
(c) the defendant believed that, but for their action, the deceased person would repeat the violence as stated above, so that their life or that of the person as described in (a) above was in danger.
2. In s1 above: "Familial" means related, cohabiting or living in the same household. "Continuing" means any act of violence as defined below on more than one occasion. "Violence" means any act that would constitute an offence under the Offences Against the Person Act 1861, the Sexual Offences Act 1976 (as amended), or the Protection from Harassment Act 1997. "Intimate" means any sexual relationship not included in the definition of "familial". "Belief" must be reasonable in the context of ongoing abuse and violence.
3. It shall be for the defence to raise the issue where the circumstances are as outlined in s1 above, and it will then be for the prosecution to prove that s1 does not apply.'

This defence is tailored to those who kill abusers. There are several advantages to such a defence.

1. It deals specifically with the circumstances: battered women are not forced to try to fit themselves into defences designed with other situations in mind.
2. The legal position of people who kill their abusers is improved without any corresponding benefit for people who kill for trivial reasons.

3. The history of the abuse is made directly relevant. The emphasis is upon that abuse, rather than the accused's mental reaction to it.
4. The reaction of the accused is characterised as a sane one, aimed at countering a threat to their own lives, rather than as irrational.
5. While the defence fully reflects women's experiences, it is gender neutral, so that it does not reinforce or depend upon stereotypes of women's behaviour.

The way forward for women, then, may be to campaign for the creation of new laws which incorporate their perspectives as central, rather than to continue the attempt to fit women within existing, male-centred definitions. However, feminist law reform is not without its own difficulties. In practice, the law has proved resistant to incorporating feminist perspectives and adept at reinterpreting laws to reinforce patriarchal attitudes. (For further discussion of these issues, see Chapter 8.)

Another possible reform would be to abolish the mandatory life sentence for murder. If judges were no longer obliged to sentence somebody convicted of murder to life imprisonment, then they could give lesser sentences in exceptional cases, such as those we have discussed. Advantages to this approach include the following.

1. Battered women would not have to fit themselves into any particular category or syndrome in order to receive appropriate sentences.
2. The focus would be placed upon the circumstances surrounding the killing (ie the background of abuse) rather than the mental state of the defendant. This might help challenge the labelling of such killings as irrational acts of 'madness'.
3. Leaving such consideration of the circumstances to the judge (through the sentencing process) rather than the jury (through the defence of provocation) might result in more consistency.

However, such reforms can be seen to pose their own problems.

1. A conviction for murder carries an exceptional degree of stigma. Should someone be labelled a murderer if we do not think they deserve the highest degree of blame for their actions?
2. Can we trust the judiciary? Judges have frequently failed to show understanding of such situations, and giving them more discretion might only exacerbate this problem.
3. Guidelines would be developed for which cases were 'exceptional', which may in themselves prove as limiting as the existing law.

8

Rape

8.1 Introduction

8.2 The law

8.3 The myth of 'real rape'

8.4 The criminal justice system in practice

8.5 Conclusion

8.1 Introduction

The development of the law on rape is particularly interesting as (like the defence of provocation) many of the reforms of the law have been in response to feminist criticisms. It therefore demonstrates both the benefits and the limitations of law reform in improving women's position. We will see that the wording of the offence is only part of the problem: the law does not exist in a vacuum, and social attitudes are just as important in affecting just how the legal rules operate in practice.

The most recent changes to the law are contained in the Sexual Offences Act 2003, which came into force in May 2004. However, in order to understand why those reforms were necessary, we must first look at the earlier definition of the offence and the criticisms of it. We will go on to consider the legal definition in its wider social context, analysing how the myths surrounding rape have had a very real impact upon what happens in court.

8.2 The law

Before the Sexual Offences Act 2003
The offence of rape was (until recently) defined in s1 Sexual Offences Act 1956, as amended by the Sexual Offences (Amendment) Act 1976 and the Criminal Justice and Public Order Act 1994. It stated:

'(1) A man commits rape if:
(a) he has sexual intercourse with a person (whether vaginal or anal) who at the time of the intercourse does not consent to it; and

(b) at the time he knows that the person does not consent to the intercourse or is reckless as to whether that person consents to it.'

The elements which needed to be proved were as follows.

1. That sexual intercourse had taken place. This was defined as the insertion of a man's penis into the vagina of a woman or the anus of a man or woman. Thus rape could only be committed by a man (although a woman could be guilty of, for example, aiding and abetting the rape), but the victim could be male or female.
2. The person with whom the man had sexual intercourse did not consent.
3. The man realised that there was a risk the other person did not consent to sexual intercourse, but continued regardless.

There were two parts of this definition which were heavily criticised by feminists, and which have now been changed by the 2003 Act. These were, first, the narrow definition of sexual intercourse, and second, the definition of recklessness.

First, sexual intercourse was defined from a male perspective: the legal definition centred upon penetration by the penis. Thus penetration with other objects, although equally or more serious from the victim's perspective, led to a conviction for the less serious offence of indecent assault (which had a maximum penalty of ten years' imprisonment, compared to life imprisonment for rape). In addition, forced oral sex was also considered to be indecent assault rather than rape. Feminists have argued that from the perspective of the female victim, this approach makes little sense. For the victim penetration with an object, or penetration of the mouth, can be just as serious and traumatic as penile penetration of the vagina or anus. However, there are several reasons why this classification does make sense from a male perspective.

1. The experience may be very different for the man if he is using some other part of his body, and even more so if he is using some other object.
2. Historically, rape was concerned with the loss of a woman's value to her father (loss of her virginity was likely to make her unmarriageable) or to her husband (if she had had intercourse with another man – in whatever circumstances – there could be doubt about the paternity of her children) rather than with the effect upon the woman herself.
3. Further, the definition reflects the enormous importance given by the law to the penis as a symbol, not just of masculinity, but of male power.

The second principal criticism concerned the definition of the mens rea for the offence. The relevant state of mind was recklessness, defined by a subjective test. In other words, what mattered was what went on in the defendant's own mind, however peculiar his reasoning or thought. *DPP* v *Morgan* [1976] AC 182 established that an honest but mistaken belief in consent would have the result that no offence had been committed, however unreasonable that belief was. The facts in that case were that Mr Morgan invited three other men home to have sexual intercourse with his wife. He claimed that if she resisted, that did not mean that she was not consenting: she liked to have sexual intercourse in that way. All four men did have sexual intercourse with her, although they had to use considerable violence against her, including dragging her screaming from her son's bedroom and holding her down forcibly during sexual intercourse. Nonetheless, the three visitors claimed that as a result of what her husband had told them, they believed she was consenting.

The House of Lords held that no offence was committed if the defendant honestly, but unreasonably, believed that there was consent. In other words, the issue was considered purely from the man's point of view. However unreasonable his state of mind, he would not have committed rape if he believed (even on some strange grounds) that the complainant had consented. The fact that the woman had not in fact consented, and that no reasonable person in that situation would think she had, made no difference. All that mattered was what the defendant's honest, albeit unreasonable, belief was. (Nonetheless, the convictions of the defendants in *Morgan* were upheld, on the basis that they did not have such an honest belief in Mrs Morgan's consent.)

The Sexual Offences Act 2003

Section 1 Sexual Offences Act 2003 provides a new definition of rape:

> '(1) A person (A) commits an offence if –
> (a) he intentionally penetrates the vagina, anus or mouth of another person (B) with his penis,
> (b) B does not consent to the penetration, and
> (c) A does not reasonably believe that B consents.
> (2) Whether a belief is reasonable is to be determined having regard to all the circumstances, including any steps A has taken to ascertain whether B consents.'

The most important changes made by the 2003 Act can be summarised as follows.

1. The definition of sexual intercourse has been widened to include penetration by the penis of the mouth. This change partly addresses feminist criticisms of the definition, but penetration by objects other than the penis remains a separate offence (although now with the same maximum sentence as rape).
2. The test for recklessness is now objective. In other words, *Morgan* is no longer good law: it is not enough that the defendant's belief in consent is honest. It must also be reasonable.

Section 75 of the 2003 Act also sets out a series of situations where it is assumed that there was no consent, unless the defendant can prove otherwise:

> '(2) The circumstances are that –
> (a) any person was, at the time of the relevant act or immediately before it began, using

violence against the complainant or causing the complainant to fear that immediate violence would be used against him;

(b) any person was, at the time of the relevant act or immediately before it began, causing the complainant to fear that violence was being used, or that immediate violence would be used, against another person;

(c) the complainant was, and the defendant was not, unlawfully detained at the time of the relevant act;

(d) the complainant was asleep or otherwise unconscious at the time of the relevant act;

(e) because of the complainant's physical disability, the complainant would not have been able at the time of the relevant act to communicate to the defendant whether the complainant consented;

(f) any person had administered to or caused to be taken by the complainant, without the complainant's consent, a substance which, having regard to when it was administered or taken, was capable of causing or enabling the complainant to be stupefied or overpowered at the time of the relevant act.'

While these changes are generally positive, there is real doubt how far such law reform alone can have an effect upon what happens throughout the criminal justice system. We shall now consider the stereotypes which underlie the law and conduct of rape cases, and see how they play as important a role as the definition of the offence in deciding whether a case goes to trial and results in a conviction.

8.3 The myth of 'real rape'

A recurrent theme throughout this book is the fact that law doesn't exist in a vacuum. Instead, social attitudes towards women, politics, etc all affect the way that women are treated in law. The law can both reflect and reinforce the inequalities, oppression and stereotypes that exist in the wider society. We are looking, then, at how cultural beliefs and attitudes work with the law, affecting how the law operates and how the law itself then reinforces those attitudes. In other words, we are analysing how the law and society work together – you can't separate the two and view law as an isolated subject unrelated to the rest of the world.

Particular myths which surround the offence of rape have been considered in detail by feminist theorists, and much campaigning has been done to change both the law and general attitudes. As well as law reform such as the Sexual Offences Act 2003 there have been campaigns aimed at changing popular views about rape, with slogans such as 'reclaim the night' and 'no means no'. Feminists emphasise that women have the right to personal autonomy: in other words, women have the right to say no to sex, and men should respect that refusal whether they are strangers, acquaintances, ex-boyfriends or even husbands.

Nonetheless, many stereotypes still exist. We will concentrate upon what is perhaps the central and strongest one – the idea of what a 'real' rape is. According to the mythology, rape 'really' means a violent attack by a stranger, on the street, upon a chaste and ladylike woman who struggles to defend herself and then reports the attack immediately afterwards. The reality is usually very different, as we will see. Although since 1994, the complainant can be male or female, we concentrate here upon cases where the victim is female, partly because these are the overwhelming majority of cases – 7,929 out of 8,593 in 2000/2001 – and partly because most research and criticism of the law is made in relation to female victims.

Violence

The first element of the myth is that rape is violent in the sense that force is used to cause injuries beyond the rape itself. In other words, it is expected that if a woman has really been raped, she will have cuts and bruises to show for it. Of course, some rapes are very violent indeed. However, not all are, nor is there any legal requirement for them to be. The legal definition of rape says nothing about the use of force: instead it refers simply to the lack of consent. The same was true of the definition under the old law, and we will begin by looking at the leading case prior to the Sexual Offences Act 2003, since nothing in the 2003 Act seems to require the courts to change their approach.

The Court of Appeal in *R* v *Olugboja* [1981] 3 All ER 1382 emphasised that force is not a requirement, so there is no need to show that any violence was used. Further, mere submission by a woman is not enough: there must be actual consent. So there is no need, in law, for the rape to be violent, involving weapons or injuries. In that case, two girls were forcibly taken to a house by two men and assaulted. One of the girls was raped by the first man, so when the second man ordered her to take off her clothes and then had sexual intercourse with her, she did not attempt to resist. He argued that she had therefore consented since there was no use of force. The Court of Appeal disagreed: the girl had merely submitted to sexual intercourse, because of the awful circumstances in which she found herself. Such submission was not the same as consent.

However, despite this clarification by the Court of Appeal, the myth of the rapist as violent remains powerful and routinely appears in trials. In most cases which go to court, the issue is whether the woman consented. In that situation, the lack of evidence of force is often used to suggest that the woman did consent. It is frequently suggested in trials that a man would not be able to commit rape if the woman really didn't consent unless the man used violence, leaving the woman with obvious injuries.

Section 74 Sexual Offences Act 2003 does now provide a statutory definition of consent: 'a person consents if he agrees by choice, and has the freedom and capacity to make that choice'. However, it is not clear that this new formulation takes us any further than *Olugboja*. Again, the question will usually be less about the boundaries of consent (which are still far from clear: what exactly is a free choice?) and more about whether the courts are reluctant to believe a woman when she says that she did not consent.

Another reason for the importance of showing that force was used is that the courts routinely assume that the complainants in rape cases cannot be trusted to tell the truth. Many lawyers and judges work on the assumption that women often lie about this, for reasons as varied (and often trivial) as revenge, fantasising the attack, embarrassment, to secure custody of children, to gain attention, to cover up an affair, or from emotional or psychological instability. Lord Lane CJ echoed remarks made by Sir Matthew Hale in the seventeenth century when he stated in the Court of Appeal that '[a]s everybody knows rape is an easy allegation to make and may be very difficult to refute' (*R* v *Goodwin* (1989) 11 Cr App R (S) 194).

In reality, the reasons not to make a false complaint are many and obvious, including the painful and unpleasant medical examination, the embarrassing personal questioning by police, the long and stressful court process and the difficult and distressing experience of giving evidence and being cross-examined (in great detail) about one's personal life. Unsurprisingly, the actual evidence doesn't bear out the myth: there is no convincing evidence to suggest that the rate of false reporting in rape is higher than in other offences, and some studies suggest that it is lower.

However, the assumption that the complainant may be a devious and lying woman has been highlighted in the court process. Until as recently as 1994, judges had to give a corroboration warning as part of their summing up in rape cases. This consisted of a special warning to the jury that they needed to exercise caution before convicting on the uncorroborated evidence of the complainant. In other words, because of the myth that women are somehow prone to lie about being raped, in a way men are not (and even female victims of other offences are not) juries were warned that they should be wary of convicting on the evidence of the woman alone. They should look for some supporting evidence, and a classic example of this supporting evidence was medical evidence of injuries suffered during the incident.

Section 33 Criminal Justice and Public Order Act 1994 removed the requirement for judges to give the corroboration warning. However, the warning is not dead and buried. Instead, judges now have a discretion to give the warning in cases where they feel it appropriate. This was confirmed by the case of *R* v *Makanjuola* [1995] 3 All ER 730, which also commented that the Court of Appeal would be reluctant to interfere with the judge's use of discretion in giving such a warning. Thus, if a judge feels that a woman is in some way unreliable, they are still free to give the warning.

The first element of the myth, then, is that real rape involves violence. The particular importance of this is twofold:

1. the absence of evidence of violence will often be used to suggest that the woman must have consented; and
2. given that there are rarely witnesses to the offence, evidence of injuries to the woman is a classic way of corroborating her version of events. Without any corroboration, she is vulnerable to insinuations that she has lied and made the whole thing up for (often trivial) reasons of her own.

It is unsurprising that the presence or absence of violence has a significant impact upon conviction rates: researchers Grace (et al) found that trials where the victim was injured were almost twice as likely to end in conviction than those where there was no physical injury (cited in Jennifer Temkin, *Rape and the Legal Process*, Oxford University Press (2002)).

Strangers

The next facet of the myth is that rape is classically committed by a stranger. In reality, most rapes are committed by somebody known to the complainant. They may be a slight acquaintance, a friend, an ex-partner, somebody with whom the complainant has flirted or a current partner or spouse. Unfortunately, the closer the relationship between the complainant and the accused, the less likely an allegation of rape is to result in a conviction. Indeed, the closer the relationship prior to the alleged rape, the less likely the case is to even to reach court. This myth of the stranger as rapist has a very real impact upon convictions.

What if the case does actually make it as far as trial? During the trial, any relationship between the complainant and the accused is likely to come under intense scrutiny. For example, even if there was no previous sexual relationship, it may be suggested that the woman flirted, showed that she was attracted to the accused or gave clear signals that she wanted to have sex with him. If there was a previous sexual relationship between the complainant and the defendant, that can be used to suggest consent on this occasion, subject to the legal rules on previous sexual history.

One of the most extreme examples of an accused who is not a stranger is where the complainant and the accused are married. Unbelievably, until 1990 a man could not be convicted of raping his wife (a rule known as the 'marital rape exemption'). A wife was assumed to give her consent to sexual intercourse with her husband by marrying him, and she could not withdraw that consent. In the words of Sir Matthew Hale, 'by their mutual matrimonial consent and contract the wife has given up herself in this kind unto her husband, which she cannot retract' (*Pleas of the Crown*, 1678). The courts did create some exceptions: the consent was withdrawn when she divorced him, and later, when she legally separated from him. However, these mitigations did nothing to alter the fact that while the marriage remained in existence legally and in fact, a man could force his wife to have sex with him against her will without committing an offence in criminal law.

It had been argued that this interpretation of the law was supported by the definition in Sexual Offences Act 1976: s1(2), which was inserted by the Sexual Offences (Amendment) Act 1976, had originally defined rape as unlawful sexual intercourse without consent. The courts had argued that 'unlawful' sexual intercourse was sexual intercourse with somebody to whom the accused was not married (*R v Chapman* [1958] 3 All ER 143). It therefore followed that when he and the complainant were married, the intercourse was lawful and so outside the legal definition of rape. In other words, it was by definition lawful sexual intercourse which in turn, by definition, could never be rape.

This remained the legal position until 1990. The law was then changed not by parliament but by the House of Lords. They did explain the decision on the technical ground that in interpreting the statute, the word 'unlawful' was meaningless padding and did not mean 'outside marriage' at all, so that all sexual intercourse without consent could be rape whether or not the parties were married to each other. However, more important than that rather technical argument (which was slightly dubious since it directly contradicted a very long line of other case law) was the Law Lords' attention to changing social attitudes. The House of Lords accepted, and explicitly acknowledged, that it is no longer acceptable for the law to say that a woman can never refuse sexual intercourse with her husband. This is a positive example of how the relationship between the law and social attitudes can result in a change of the law for the better.

Unfortunately, while the technical law changed, the reality for complainants has not. It remains extremely difficult to obtain a conviction where the complainant knew the accused prior to the rape. The closer the previous relationship, the more difficult it is to prove that rape has occurred, with cases of marital rape perhaps the most difficult of all. Thus, whatever the legal position, the practical reality is that convictions for marital rape are very rare and very difficult to obtain.

The final issue in relation to the myth of the 'true' rapist as a stranger is the courts' approach to sentencing. The fact that the accused was known to the complainant is, incredibly, viewed as mitigation, effectively making the offence less serious. The leading case on sentencing for rape, *R v Billam* [1986] 1 All ER 985, indicated a starting point of five years' imprisonment. *R v Billam* did not give specific guidance upon the effect of a pre-existing relationship: it left open the question of whether such a relationship made the offence more or less serious. The case which did seem to answer that question, *R v Berry* (1998) 10 Cr App R (S) 13, suggested that the effect of a prior relationship between the rapist and the victim was to make the offence less serious: 'in some instances the violation of the person and defilement that are inevitable features where a stranger rapes a woman are not always present to the same degree when the offender and the victim had previously had a longstanding sexual relationship' (per Evans LJ). Despite the qualifications in that judgment suggesting that a pre-existing relationship was not always a mitigating factor, in practice later cases have generally treated it as such. For example, in *R v Diggle* (1995) 16 Cr App R (S) 163, the Court of Appeal referred to 'the two extremes of violent rape or attempted rape between strangers and intercourse without the girl's consent on a particular occasion after she had consented previously or indicated that she might consent' (per Evans LJ). This comment is a stark illustration of the idea that the mythical rape scenario we have described is 'real rape', while rape between acquaintances is some lesser thing, 'intercourse without consent'.

In reality, factors such as the breach of trust and sense of betrayal that stem from rape by an acquaintance mean that for many women, it is as serious as rape by a stranger. This fact was eventually recognised in recommendations issued by the Sentencing Advisory Panel in 2002, which were adopted by the Court of Appeal in *R* v *Millberry; R* v *Morgan; R* v *Lackenby* [2003] 1 WLR 546. The Court specifically accepted the Panel's conclusion that 'cases of "relationship rape" and "acquaintance rape" are to be treated as being of equal seriousness to cases of "stranger rape"'. However, it went on to set out specific aggravating factors which could apply in a case of 'stranger rape' but not where the parties were known to each other, such as the fact that rape in a public place could cause fear to other members of the public as well, and the fear that the rapist might be a murderer too (although, in fact, this would be a realistic fear even in the case of some marital rapes, given that over a hundred women are killed by their partners every year). It also suggested the possibility that mitigating factors may apply specifically to marital rapes, although these were not set out.

On the street

If the myth has it that the rape is committed by a violent stranger, it is therefore hardly surprising that it is also expected to be committed outside. Again, any deviation from that scenario is used to suggest that the complainant must have been consenting. If she went into a house with the defendant, it is often suggested that she must have wanted to have sex with him. Even if the complainant and the defendant are staying the night at the same place, such as a friend's home after a party, that can all be used to suggest that some kind of expectation had been raised by her that she would consent to sexual intercourse with him.

In real life, inviting someone into your home – even in the evening, even late at night – is not the same as inviting them to have sexual intercourse with you. Equally, accepting an invitation into someone else's home is not the same as an acceptance of an invitation to have sexual intercourse. It can be difficult to travel home late at night by public transport, for example, and a completely innocent invitation can be made and accepted to stay overnight and travel home when public transport is working again the next morning. Ironically, one might accept because it seems much safer to stay over with a friend than to travel at home using scarce and unreliable public transport or an unlicensed minicab in the dead of night. However, that is not the way such decisions tend to be viewed in court. Situations can be twisted so that where a woman invites a man to her home, or goes to his because he is a platonic friend whom she trusts, that is used to suggest that she clearly intended to have sex.

A chaste victim

We have already considered how women's previous relationships with the accused are used to suggest consent. We will now look in more detail at the ways in which a woman's sexual history is used to suggest that she was not raped. The myth of the 'real rape' requires the victim to be a chaste woman: she should be either a virgin, or a married woman whose only sexual relationship is with her husband. If a woman does not conform to that stereotype (and most women do not) then her previous sexual history is likely to be used to suggest that she consented. This can be done in one of several ways.

First, if there has been any previous sexual relationship with the defendant that will be used to suggest she must also have consented on this occasion. It may even be suggested that the previous relationship provides a motive for fabricating an allegation of rape, such as spite or revenge.

Second, whoever her previous relationships were with, it can be suggested that the fact a complainant has had sexual intercourse previously makes it more likely that she consented on this occasion. There is an assumption that a woman who consents to sex with one man in one situation is likely to consent both to any other man in a similar situation, and to that man in any situation. This isn't the way that most women conduct their sex lives, but it remains a very potent myth.

The myth is at its most powerful if it can be suggested that a woman is promiscuous. The courts' threshold of what type of behaviour constitutes promiscuity can be very low. In *R v Brown* (1989) 89 Cr App R 97, the Court of Appeal described the facts that the complainant had sex with her boyfriend and had had a child with another man as being 'near the borderline' of relevant promiscuity. Little consideration is given to the reality that even if one has a large number of one-night stands with people one finds attractive, one is still highly unlikely to consent to a one-night stand with somebody one does not find attractive, or on an occasion when one simply does not want sexual intercourse.

The power of this stereotype is illustrated by Zhusanna Adler's research, 'The Relevance of Sexual History Evidence in Rape: Problems of Subjective Interpretation' [1995] Crim LR 769. She found that in trials where the complainant came across as 'chaste and virginal', the conviction rate was 98 per cent. By contrast, if the complainant's sexual reputation was discredited in court, the conviction rate dropped by half to 48 per cent.

Because of concerns about the way that women's previous sexual history was being used inappropriately in rape trials, s2 Sexual Offences (Amendment) Act 1976 sought to limit the situations in which such history was used. Such questioning was only to be allowed with leave of the judge, and the judge was only to give leave where to refuse would be to cause unfairness to the defendant. However, the emphasis upon the defendant's interests, coupled with the attachment of many judges to the stereotypes we consider here, meant that leave was usually given. Given the powerful effect of such evidence (as demonstrated by Adler), it was almost always likely to make a significant and arguably unfair difference to the defendant not to allow it. The provision made little difference in practice, with most applications for leave to cross-examine being successful.

A new, and hopefully more effective, provision is now in force: s41 Youth Justice and Criminal Evidence Act 1999. This limits the situation in which such evidence is admissible. Previous sexual history must now be excluded except where:

1. it is relevant to an issue other than consent; or
2. it is relevant to an issue of consent and the alleged sexual behaviour occurred at or about the same time as the alleged offence; or
3. it is relevant to an issue of consent and is alleged to have been so similar either to sexual behaviour which took place as part of the alleged event or to other sexual behaviour that took place at or about the same time as the event that it cannot reasonably be explained as coincidence; or
4. the evidence relates to evidence adduced by the prosecution about the complainant's sexual behaviour and would go no further than is necessary to rebut or explain that evidence;

and a refusal of leave might render unsafe a conclusion of the jury on any relevant issue in the case. Except where the issue is raised by the prosecution, such evidence cannot be used if its main purpose is to attack the witness's credibility.

However, the effectiveness of this provision will depend upon the courts being willing to strictly apply it. In *R* v *A* [2001] 3 All ER 1, the House of Lords used the Human Rights Act 1998 to extend the exceptions under which such evidence is admissible. In that case, they ruled that evidence that the complainant had had a sexual relationship with the defendant should have been admitted despite the fact that it did not fit into any of the statutory exceptions. They thereby ensured that evidence of a past sexual relationship with the defendant is likely to be admissible even if it appears to be excluded under the statutory rules.

The courts appear to accept the myth that if a woman has consented to sexual intercourse with somebody on one occasion, she is more likely to do so on any other given occasion. The truth is rather different. Although sometimes a previous sexual experience with a particular man may make a woman more likely to agree on a future occasion (the obvious example being where it took place in the context of an ongoing relationship), often that will not be true. For example, the sexual intercourse may have been no more than a single incident; she may have fallen out with the man since; the relationship may have ended; or, of course, she might simply not feel like it at that time or in that situation. Under the legal definition of the offence, all that matters is that the woman did not consent on that occasion, regardless of whether she consented an hour, a day or a month earlier.

A ladylike victim

The complainant's best chance of seeing her rapist convicted may be to present herself as a chaste woman who is not sexually active. However, that alone may not be sufficient. She would do well to also show herself to be ladylike (in the sense of conforming to middle class norms of femininity), since all aspects of her life may come under scrutiny to suggest that she is not trustworthy and so should not be believed.

A fundamental principle of the law of evidence is that only relevant evidence is admissible. However, judges routinely admit evidence which has no obvious relevance unless one accepts that all aspects of a woman's behaviour can be used to decipher whether or not she consented to sexual intercourse on one specific occasion. In particular, the situations used to suggest that she is not a credible witness are not limited to ones which have an obvious bearing on her truthfulness, or indeed her likeliness to consent to or to lie about sexual intercourse with the accused. Sue Lees (*Ruling Passions: Sexual Violence, Reputation and the Law*, Hamish Hamilton (1996)) has noted that cross-examination is allowed on areas of the complainant's life such as her financial situation, her role as a mother (including whether she is a single mother, and the childcare arrangements she has made), her past drug-taking and alcohol use, and any past abortions.

A number of other researchers have noted cross-examination upon details related to the time leading up to the incident, with a focus upon such points as how the complainant was dressed, including intrusive and apparently irrelevant details such as the colour of her underwear, what she had had to drink, and whether she had engaged in any flirtatious behaviour, or behaviour open to interpretation as flirtatious (whether with the defendant or with anyone else). This is often used to suggest that she was in effect 'asking for it': that her behaviour suggested her sexual availability. There is no concept of contributory negligence in the legal definition of rape – the crucial issue is the complainant's consent – but the defence can put forward a stereotype of women as 'making themselves available', as 'leading men on' or being a 'prick tease'. The woman's right to say no and to have that refusal accepted, the fact that 'no means no' even if the woman saying no is wearing a short skirt, are regularly overlooked by the courts.

Furthermore, the woman's behaviour can be taken into account in sentencing the defendant. The fact that she behaved in a way which, in the court's (usually the middle aged, upper middle class male judge's) opinion suggested that she was likely to consent is considered to be a mitigation which will result in a lower sentence.

A struggle to defend herself

The chaste and virtuous woman will, when facing this violent attack from a probably armed stranger, struggle to defend her chastity, according to the myth of 'real rape'. Again, the reality is rather different. Many people, faced with a sudden and frightening attack, will simply freeze: this is a natural reaction, but means that the victim will be unable to scream or resist. In court, this reaction, which is the result of deep fear, is open to reinterpretation as evidence that the complainant did not resist or complain, and therefore may have consented; or at the least, that the defendant believed that she was consenting since she did not demonstrate otherwise.

Even a complainant who is able to react may make a reasoned decision not to. If faced with a violent attacker, she will be aware that resistance may well provoke further violence. Thus she may choose not to struggle believing this to be the only realistic way to survive the attack. However, again this is open to misinterpretation by the court who will measure her behaviour against that of the mythical victim who resists to the best of her ability and suffers injury as a result.

It is important to note that verbal refusal is not necessarily enough. The attitude of some judges was demonstrated by Judge Raymond Dean: 'As the gentlemen on the jury will understand, when a woman says no she doesn't always mean it' (*The Times*, 11 April 1990). This comment is revealing not only in its attitudes towards women, but also in its assumption that men (the gentlemen on the jury) can know women's true intentions better than the women themselves.

An immediate report of the attack

There is an assumption that if the complaint of rape is genuine, it will be made at the first opportunity. This ignores the reality that after such a traumatic event, it may be some time before a victim feels able to talk to anyone else about it. The problem is particularly serious where the defendant is known to the complainant. The myth already discussed, that women are prone to lie about being raped, is put together with the law's emphasis upon spontaneity as being equivalent to accuracy, and delay allowing premeditation (an idea also central to the defence of provocation). There is an assumption that if a woman does not report a rape immediately, it suggests that she has invented the incident for reasons of her own.

So concerned is the law with evidence of a recent complaint as supporting the truthfulness of a rape allegation that it has created a special rule for it. Usually, evidence of a previous consistent statement would not be admissible: in other words, a witness cannot give evidence of having given the same version of events in the past. So, if my car was allegedly stolen, the fact that half an hour later I said to a friend, 'Somebody's just stolen my car' would not be admissible. This is because it would serve no purpose: the evidence comes from me both times, and repeating my lie twice doesn't make it more likely to be true; repeating the truth twice doesn't make it any truer.

However, the rule is different for rape. If a rape victim tells somebody at the first available opportunity that she has been raped, then that is admissible as a so-called 'recent complaint'. It is used to suggest that her allegation is more likely to be true, because she made it at the first possible chance. The rule also has the effect of carrying the opposite implication: that if there was no recent complaint, the allegation is less likely to be true. Thus although many women are not able to report a rape immediately, because of the trauma and distress it causes, the law sees that delay as suggestive of invention and lies. Further, the existence of this special rule (which applies only to sexual offences) draws attention once more to the underlying assumption that women are prone to lie about being raped, and so evidence which helps the court to assess their truthfulness is particularly significant.

8.4 The criminal justice system in practice

Perhaps the best way to summarise the effect of these myths about rape upon the legal process is with a statistic. Only one in 13 – or just 8 per cent – of cases reported to police end in conviction. Ninety two per cent of women who report a rape to the police don't see their rapist convicted (HM Crown Prosecution Service Inspectorate, *Report on the Joint Inspection into the Investigation and Prosecution of Cases Involving Allegations of Rape*, 2002). That figure does not include any rapes which aren't reported to the police at all: here we must pause to consider the fact that rape is a very under-reported crime. A recent Home Office study suggests that only one fifth of rapes are reported to the police (Andy Myhill and Jonathan Allen, *Rape and Sexual Assault of Women: The Extent and Nature of the Problem*, Home Office Research Study 237, 2002).

Some of those 12 out of 13 cases which don't end in conviction will be the result of a not guilty verdict in court. However, many more will never have reached trial at all. There are two reasons for this: either the complainant does not proceed with the complaint, or the police or the Crown Prosecution Service (CPS) make the decision not to prosecute.

The decision not to prosecute

The police and the CPS decide whether a suspect should be charged with an offence, and once charged, whether the case should proceed through the court system to trial. The police make the initial decision on whether to charge a suspect so that the case begins the prosecution process, but in a serious offence such as rape the police will often consult the CPS about that decision. Once the suspect has been charged, the court proceedings are in the hands of the CPS, who can discontinue them at any stage if they believe either that there is not a sufficiently good prospect of conviction, or that it is not in the public interest to proceed.

In making these decisions, both the police and the CPS will base their conclusions upon the match of the particular case to the 'real rape' stereotype we have already analysed. The problem is that once either the police or the CPS decide not to proceed with a prosecution, the case comes to an end. Thus even if the police change their practices, for example through the use of specially trained officers, that in itself won't be sufficient if the CPS continue to rely upon these stereotypes. Another difficulty is that a conviction is less likely if the case does not match the myth of the 'real rape': remember that the CPS test focuses upon prospects of achieving a conviction. However, not to continue with the prosecution in such cases is to reinforce the myth rather than challenge it, thereby creating a vicious circle.

Withdrawal of complaints

A large number of cases do not go to court because the complainant decides not to pursue the case. There are many reasons for this. She is more likely to decide not to pursue the case if she and the accused are well known to each other: this may be a result of various factors such as pressure from the accused, other family members or friends, or some kind of reconciliation between them. In particular, where there is a history of domestic violence it is often difficult for the complainant to pursue a complaint (whether of assault or of rape) as far as trial.

However, sometimes women do not proceed with allegations of rape because they cannot face the prospect of giving evidence in court. A Home Office study (Jessica Harris and Sharon Grave, *A Question of Evidence? Investigating and Prosecuting Rape in the 1990s*, Home Office Research Study 196, 1999) confirmed that one of the main reasons given by complainants for not pursuing a case is that it would be too traumatic to go to court. This is not an unrealistic fear. First, while most criminal cases end in pleas of guilty, the position is different for rape. Where a case does proceed as far as court, only 39 per cent of cases end with a guilty plea (compared to 93 per cent for drugs possession cases, for example). Thus, if the case does go to court, there is more or less a two in three chance that the case will go to trial and that the complainant will have to give evidence at that trial.

Second, giving evidence is traumatic. We have looked at some of the ways women are attacked in cross-examination, and the highly personal and intimate details of their lives upon which they are likely to be cross-examined. That cross-examination may be long and go into minute detail about the offence and the surrounding circumstances, as well as many other apparently unrelated and highly personal areas. In a Victim Support survey in 1996 (*Women, Rape and the Criminal Justice System*), women described the cross-examination as 'patronising', 'humiliating' and 'worse than the rape'. Many women refer to the experience as being as bad as the original crime, and feel that they are on trial, rather than the defendant.

The Bar Code of Conduct theoretically provides some protection for witnesses. It states that a barrister must not 'ask questions which are merely scandalous or intended or calculated only to vilify, insult or annoy either a witness or some other person'. However, Sue Lees monitored a number of rape trials and found that defence counsel routinely broke the Code without any complaint being made by prosecution counsel or the judge. It seemed to be accepted as part of the culture of the Bar that that part of the Code is secondary to the duty to do one's best for the client (*Ruling Passions: Sexual Violence, Reputation and the Law*, Hamish Hamilton, 1996).

However bad that experience can be, one of the worst cases – and one which did cause public outrage – was that of Ralston Edwards, who was tried for rape in August 1996. The accused represented himself and personally examined the complainant in minute detail, making her re-live the original rape, for six days. At the end of the trial he was convicted, and as a result of that case the law was changed. The Youth Justice and Criminal Evidence Act 1999 provides that in sexual offences cases, cross-examination of the complainant must be carried out by an advocate, not the defendant in person. Thus a repeat of this situation is now avoided. However, even where examination is carried out by a barrister, research by David Brereton ('How Different are Rape Trials? A Comparison of the Cross-Examination of Complainants in Rape and Assault Trials' (1997) 37 Br J Crim 242) established that rape victims tend to be cross-examined for longer, and find that cross-examination more traumatic, than complainants in other cases. The awful experiences that complainants have in cross-examination can be said to contribute to the very low conviction rate for this crime.

8.5 Conclusion

It is vital to remember that the fact that a particular mythology is ingrained within the system does not mean that it cannot change. We have considered some of the progress made through feminist campaigning. Another important factor has been the growing awareness, among the police in particular, that these myths are not reliable guides to assessing complaints. The presence of specially trained officers (and even special units) within many police stations has made a real and important difference, with the result (hopefully) that less cases will be thrown out at a very early stage by the police simply because the offence is not reported immediately. However, important as this development is, provision across areas is not even: some police stations still do not have such specialist expertise and training available. Further, improved police attitudes can only go so far if they are not matched by changes in the CPS and the courtroom. The CPS recognises that it has an ongoing problem in this area; the courts appear more resistant to change.

This situation can be contrasted with the work of a specialist unit in New York City. That unit prosecutes rapes even in cases where the prospects of success seem low, such as where the victim is a prostitute or drug addict, and has achieved huge improvements in the conviction rate (*The Guardian*, 10 April 2002). Such schemes could provide an important model for the English prosecution authorities to follow. However, such legal initiatives can only go so far. The problems inherent in the criminal justice system reflect wider cultural stereotypes, and so it is the culture as a whole – the attitudes of those who will sit on juries, for example – which needs to be changed if there is to be a real difference. That kind of deep societal change is necessary for substantive equality in any area of the law, and this recognition is a central theme of radical and socialist feminisms. The indifferent success of changes to legal rules such as those on sexual history provide a good example of the limitations of a liberal feminist approach.

9

Defining Women's Sexuality

9.1 Introduction

9.2 Prostitution

9.3 Lesbianism and the criminal law

9.1 Introduction

The criminal law is popularly seen as having moral as well as legal importance. If people engage in behaviour that is considered morally wrong, there will be calls for the courts to punish them. On the other hand, if conduct is not morally objectionable there may be campaigns against it being categorised as a crime (consider changing attitudes to the possession of cannabis, for example).

There is real debate concerning how far the criminal law should reflect morality (and if so, whose?). Most textbooks on jurisprudence analyse this debate in some detail, and we will not debate the arguments here. However, we will look at what the law does (or does not do) to regulate one aspect of morality: women's sexuality.

We have already seen in Chapter 8 that the criminal law passes judgment on what it considers acceptable sexual behaviour for all women. It does this through the medium of the rape trial. This chapter looks at two more specific examples. One is prostitution, which the law has considered as an example of women's sexuality (although many women dispute this, arguing that it is instead an example of women's employment or abuse). The other is lesbianism, where the law has tried to hide or deny any sexual element, at least for white, middle and upper class women.

9.2 Prostitution

Prostitution has generated a great deal of feminist debate. In essence the issues raised by prostitution can be divided into three central themes:

1. what effect (if any) does prostitution have on women's lives;
2. should prostitution be decriminalised or legalised; and
3. how does the current law treat women who are prostitutes?

Prostitution is the provision of sexual intercourse for payment. However, we will see that it is not the act of selling sexual intercourse that the law is concerned with, but rather the activities connected with it, such as loitering in order to find work or living off the earnings of a prostitute. Despite this attention to the surrounding activities rather than the sexual conduct itself, prostitution is labeled a sexual offence in a series of Sexual Offences Acts (most recently the Sexual Offences Act 2003).

The current law

The introduction of the Sexual Offences Act 2003 on 1 May 2004 effected many significant changes in the law on prostitution. We will discuss each of them in turn.

The meaning of 'prostitute'

The definition of a prostitute is complicated, and depends on whether the prostitute is a child or an adult. If the person is a child under the age of 18, they may fall within ss48, 49 or 50 Sexual Offences Act (SOA) 2003 (a child who has been incited or caused to become a prostitute, or is being controlled by another person whilst a prostitute, or who has been brought into prostitution by another person). In these situations, s51(2) SOA 2003 defines 'prostitute' as:

> '... a person (A) who, on at least one occasion and whether or not compelled to do so, offers or provides sexual services to another person in return for payment or a promise of payment to A or a third person ...'

However, if the prostitute is an adult (of either sex) then prostitution is defined by the old common law. A 'common prostitute' was a woman (but now is also a man: Sch 1 and s56 SOA 2003) who has been cautioned on two previous occasions for loitering or soliciting. On the third and subsequent occasions of loitering or soliciting, the prostitute will be labeled as 'common' and prosecuted in the magistrates' court. Thus, the court will be fully aware of the defendant's previous criminal record: the defendant would not be before the court on these charges if they had not already been cautioned twice before.

Prostitution is not confined to acts of sexual intercourse

R v *de Munck* [1918] 1 KB 635 concerned a mother who was charged with attempting to procure her daughter to become a common prostitute. However, a police surgeon gave evidence that the girl was still a virgin. The judge sought to define what prostitution actually involved. He held that 'common prostitute' does not just mean someone who permits sexual intercourse, but also a woman who offers her body commonly for lewdness in return for payment. 'Lewdness' was not defined in that case, but since there was no evidence as to what the girl actually did, arguably that word covered any sexual act.

Further, it was held in *R* v *Webb* [1964] 1 QB 357 that acts such as the masturbation of the client also amounted to 'offering her body commonly for lewdness': in other words, a prostitute does not need to passively 'offer her body'. It is enough that she offers herself as a participant in physical acts of indecency, whether taking an active or a passive role.

In *R* v *McFarlane* [1994] 2 All ER 283 a man was charged with living on the earnings of prostitution. The defendant did live with the woman, but they denied that she was a prostitute. Rather she claimed to be a 'clipper' (a woman who offers sexual services and then runs off without delivering). In the Court of Appeal Lord Taylor held:

> '[T]he distinction between "clippers" and "hookers" is immaterial ... For a man to live off the earnings of a woman who offers sexual services, takes the money and then reneges on the offer, if she does, is in our view to live off the earnings of prostitution, or, as it used to be termed, immoral earnings. Indeed, most people would consider such earnings doubly immoral.'

The offences

As already explained, the law does not criminalise prostitution itself. Instead, it has created a number of offences which make the activities connected with prostitution illegal. The principal offences are summarised below.

Soliciting or loitering. Section 1 Street Offences Act 1959 (as amended by para 2 of Sch 1, and s56, Sexual Offences Act 2003) provides that:

> 'It shall be an offence for a common prostitute whether male or female to loiter or solicit in a street or public place for the purpose of prostitution.'

Section 32 Sexual Offences Act 1956, which created an offence where a man persistently solicits or importunes in a public place for an immoral purpose, is now an offence which can be committed by a woman or a man (Sch 1 and s56 Sexual Offences Act 2003).

Kerb crawling. A person commits an offence if he or she solicits another person or different persons for the purpose of prostitution either: from a motor vehicle while it is in a street or public place; or in a street or public place while in the immediate vicinity of a motor vehicle he or she has just got out of or off, persistently or in a way like to cause annoyance to the person solicited, or nuisance to other persons in the neighbourhood (s1 Sexual Offences Act 1985, as amended by Sch 1 and s56 Sexual Offences Act 2003).

Brothel keeping. Under s33 Sexual Offences Act 1956 (and s33A of that Act as inserted by the Sexual Offences Act 2003) it is an offence to keep a brothel. 'Keeping' includes managing or assisting in the management of the brothel.

Child prostitution. Sections 47–50 Sexual Offences Act 2003 deal with children involved in prostitution.

Exploitation of prostitution. Section 52 Sexual Offences Act 2003 makes it an offence for anyone to cause or incite a person to become a prostitute in any part of the world. Further, s53 makes it an offence to control a prostitute for financial gain. Both offences have a maximum penalty of seven years' imprisonment. The 2003 Act also deals with trafficking for sexual exploitation inside or outside the United Kingdom in ss57–59.

History

From our brief examination, it can be seen that the present law is concerned with keeping prostitution off the streets. The act of prostitution is not illegal; rather, the way prostitutes seek clients is criminalised. However, why is the law concerned with prostitution at all?

In the past, venereal disease was a major concern for legislators. Prostitution itself was seen as 'a necessary evil'. Society operated a system of double standards, condemning the women but not the men involved, and the law concerned itself with keeping prostitute women 'clean' for men to use, rather than keeping men from using prostitute women.

Between the reign of Kings Henry II and Henry VIII, England tolerated prostitution. Brothels were allowed in Southwark, provided that they held a licence under the authority of the Crown. These were called the 'Bankside Stews' and were in fact under the jurisdiction of the Church. However, from the end of the fifteenth century public opinion changed as venereal disease began to be associated with prostitution. The Southwark brothels were closed in 1546 by Henry VIII as a result of that association with the spread of venereal disease.

The Protestant Reformation of that time and Oliver Cromwell's Puritan regime in the following century both emphasised personal religiousness and Puritan morals. The interests of public health and personal morality therefore came together to require the legal regulation of prostitution. Since this period, England has continued to regulate prostitution.

Many new laws were enacted during the nineteenth century (for example: the Vagrancy Act 1824; the Town Police Clauses Act 1847; and the Metropolitan Police Act 1839). The Victorians operated a system based upon double standards (which still persists today): all of the above-mentioned Acts tried to regulate prostitution without making the actual selling of sexual acts illegal. Prostitution was seen as a necessary evil which protected the virtue of middle and upper class women by allowing men a sexual outlet. However, prostitute women were regarded as 'fallen': sinful, blameworthy and dirty. No sympathy was granted to prostitute women. Instead, they were blamed for the increase in crime and disorder associated with the Industrial Revolution (though the real causes included a rising population and a growth in urban dwelling).

The law changed radically with the Contagious Diseases Act 1864. In total there would be three such Acts (1864, 1866 and 1869). These Acts operated for nearly 20 years until they were suspended in 1883 and finally repealed in 1886. The ideology behind them was to ensure that the military and navy were free of venereal disease by keeping women 'clean' for soldiers and sailors. Military men below a certain rank were not allowed to marry and therefore prostitutes were seen as necessary for these men. Generally, society as a whole viewed prostitution as:

1. necessary to meet men's sexual needs;
2. a way of prolonging marriages; and
3. a way of ensuring that property was passed without difficulty because there were no broken inheritance lines.

There was a double standard in operation whereby young men were encouraged to sow their wild oats, while women were supposed to be coldly feminine and chaste; if they were not then they were considered to be 'fallen'.

In 1862 a committee was set up to consider the question of venereal disease within the army and navy. This arose as a result of public concern over the military after the Crimean War (1854–1856), and specifically the numerous reports on the incidence of venereal disease within the forces. Though there were some dissenters who favoured compulsory measures, the committee decided that the compulsory examination of prostitute women was not required, but that women should voluntarily submit themselves for examination and hospital treatment.

In accordance with the dissenting view, Parliament passed the first Contagious Diseases Act (CDA) 1864. This Act shared the name of a previous bill dealing with cattle: as a result, there was virtually no one in Parliament to hear its reading, and no debate. The Act sought to enable men to use prostitute women without the fear of catching venereal disease (though there were no similar provisions enacted to prevent men from passing on venereal disease to the prostitute women). Its provisions:

1. covered eleven garrison towns;
2. provided for the compulsory examination of any woman believed to be a diseased common prostitute;
3. established a special taskforce of the Metropolitan Police, answerable only to the Admiralty and War Office, to enforce the Act;
4. established special 'lock hospitals' to detain and treat women;
5. required a woman found to be diseased to be admitted to a lock hospital for a maximum of three months;
6. created a procedure whereby, if a woman refused to be examined, then she was taken before the magistrate and ordered to submit: if she still refused then she was sent to prison.

There was no requirement in the Act that men can be so examined or treated. If the woman did not have venereal disease when she was examined then she may have been given it as a result of the examination, as instruments were often not cleaned.

These were painful and humiliating examinations, carried out by male military surgeons.

Two years later the Contagious Diseases Act 1866 was passed, extending the original Act in time and geography and providing for the registration of prostitutes. Once on the register, a woman had to submit to an examination once every three months or go to prison. This resulted in women being detained in a hospital for up to six months on the word of a surgeon alone.

In 1869 the third Contagious Diseases Act 1869 was passed which again extended the geography of the original Act to another six towns and allowed for the detention of prostitute women for up to nine months.

In 1869 both men and women began to organise opposition to the Contagious Diseases Acts (CDAs), and the National Anti-Contagious Diseases Association was born. In their 1869 Report the Association stated the reasons for their opposition to the CDAs:

1. the passing of the CDAs under the name of a previous cattle Act meant that many MPs were unaware of its true content;
2. the original Act was ultimately to be extended to the whole of the civilian population, which was unacceptable;
3. the CDAs were set up to make 'fornication easy';
4. the CDAs encouraged adultery;
5. the CDAs 'diminish[ed] the shame of sin' and publicly sanctioned the use of prostitutes;
6. the CDAs 'lessen[ed] the obligation of private morality', increased the crime of seduction, 'spread cynicism and heartlessness in society, increased conjugal infidelity, wrung parents' hearts; further degraded and brutalised prostitute women and rendered their rescue impossible';
7. the women within the hospitals were slaves of the system and were 'riotous' and 'insubordinate': lock hospitals were not curative as the women just kept returning;
8. '[i]t is legislation which simply aims at securing these women be kept in health, secured solely for the sake of those resorting to their company'.

The Association believed that the CDAs were designed for the men who used prostitutes and that prostitute women were victims. It published a weekly circular, *The Shield*, devoted to the repeal of the legislation. Within the circular it was argued that the CDAs were based upon sex discrimination, for example by placing burden of proof on the woman to show that she was not a common prostitute. *The Shield* protested:

> 'It is unjust to punish the sex who are the victims of the vice, and leave unpunished the sex who are the main cause, both of the vice and its dreaded consequences.'

Further, the Nottingham female branch declared:

> 'The disease which they [the CDAs] are designed to suppress being shared in by both sexes, it becomes an act of cowardice to arrest women only.'

Doctors joined the Association with their support and delivered their own protests, particularly stating that the examinations were futile in discovering disease and possibly spread it as the instruments used were often not sterilised. Perhaps the most celebrated campaigner for the abolition of the CDAs was Josephine Butler, who stated that the law punished only women, maintaining their position as chattels, and concluded that:

> '[If] chastity is the law for woman, it must be so for every woman without exception, and if it is a law for every woman, it follows necessarily that it must be equally so for every man.'

There were also supporters of the CDAs, such as Frederick W Lowndes and William Acton. Frederick W Lowndes was a surgeon to the Liverpool Lock Hospital and believed that the CDAs should be spread to the rest of the civilian population. He argued that they were good for women and that the women were treated well. He did suggest that merchant seamen should also be examined (but apparently on racial grounds rather than those of sexual equality).

Lowndes asserted in his book *Prostitution and Venereal Diseases in Liverpool* (J A Churchill (1886)) that the police were very courteous. In fact, the police inspector that he specifically mentioned (Inspector Anniss) was, in that same year, charged with molesting a shop girl. More generally, it was common for detectives to make every effort to discover 'prostitutes' and bully or force them into signing a voluntary submission form. The majority were local girls who had no education and could not read or write, and who had no idea what they were signing.

The surgeon William Acton believed that the CDAs had happy results as regards the army and navy, and that the sanitary and moral condition of prostitute women was much improved. He did address the fact that men spread venereal diseases too, suggesting that soldiers should have weekly inspections (which should consist of parading in their underwear!), and should wash and 'apply lotions' after sex with a prostitute. He further questioned why the armed forces could not marry and suggested that married soldiers should have their wages increased, as lack of money could drive their wives into prostitution.

Although the CDAs were eventually repealed, it is rather worrying that in times of war this type of legislation is recreated. For example in 1918, Regulation 40d of the Defence of the Realm Act 1918 empowered the authorities to submit a prostitute to medical examination if accused by any member of the armed forces of infecting him with venereal disease. It was repealed within a year of its adoption as a result of its openness to abuse.

Again in 1942, the Ministry of Health introduced Regulation 33b which provided that, in the event of two patients with venereal disease naming the same individual as the source of infection, that individual should be ordered to undergo examination and submit to treatment until free from disease. Failure to do so could result in a fine or imprisonment. This measure was aimed at professional prostitutes and could in theory be applied equally to men and women. It expired in 1947, and had been a poor attempt at regulation as it left the law open to abuse.

Historically many campaigners have sought the total abolition of prostitution; others have been concerned with venereal disease; whilst yet others have focused upon the sex discrimination aspect of the legislation. Indeed, to this day we are no further forward in solving the moral dilemmas that surround prostitution. To understand the range of explanations and solutions offered, we will now consider a few of the countless reports that have been published since the Sexual Offences Act 1956 was drafted (which still forms the basis of the current law).

1. The Progressive League, in 1955, submitted evidence to the Home Office arguing that:

   a) legal discrimination against prostitutes should be abolished;
   b) the legal term 'common prostitute' should also be abolished; and
   c) street offences should be treated under general (not specific sexual) laws.

   They considered it better that sexual intercourse should take place under decent social conditions.

2. The British Medical Association Report on Homosexuality and Prostitution 1955 stated that prostitution was a social ill. However, the man was virtually excused of any blame for this 'ill':

   > 'It is still true that the prostitute's client is most frequently an unaccompanied male who has taken alcohol and who probably has no intention of seeking a sexual partner until solicited. Nevertheless, it is also important to regard prostitution as a matter of supply and demand, and not to consider it only from the angle of the female partner. We are persuaded that a genuine and serious demand does exist and must be taken into account.'

   It further described the alleged reasons why a man resorts to prostitutes:

   a) he is unable to find a partner;
   b) he is unable to find a companion;
   c) he is unable to have sex with his wife because conditions make her unable temporarily/permanently, or unsuitable, or unwilling to be a sexual partner (ie it's portrayed as the fault of the wife, not the husband);
   d) he is not risking the emotion of an ordinary relationship (men are allowed sex without commitment);
   e) he is perverted; or
   f) he has an inadequate personality.

Compare this to the Report's profile of a female prostitute:

a) she is from an unsatisfactory home background or broken home and subjected to too much discipline or 'allowed too much licence';
b) she is lazy or self indulgent;
c) she wants an easy way to earn money;
d) she has a desire for glamour and excitement;
e) she suffers from emotional immaturity;
f) she has a failure to accept reality;
g) she is an adolescent rebel; or
h) she suffers mental deficiency or mental subnormality.

The Report concluded that the solution to the problem was a combination of improved social conditions and heavy fines for women prostitutes in order to drive them off the streets and stop them tempting men. The suggested law reform was therefore designed to target the women prostitutes and not the men who used them.

3. The Wolfenden Report on Homosexual Offences and Prostitution 1957 was perhaps the most significant Report since it led to the 1959 Act. This Report must be put in its social context: during the post-war period, male jobs were in short supply and women were being encouraged back to the home after their wartime independence. The government was concerned about post-war family breakdown and wanted to encourage women to rear children and confine their sexuality within the nuclear family. It was therefore seen as important to regulate women prostitutes.

The Wolfenden Report did not ignore society's double standards, and in fact only attempted to take prostitution out of the public eye, not to eradicate it. Paragraph 257 of the Report speaks for itself:

> 'The law should confine itself to those activities which offend against public order and decency or expose the ordinary citizen to what is offensive or injurious; and the simple fact is that prostitutes do parade themselves more habitually and openly than their prospective customers, and do by their continual presence affront the sense of decency of the ordinary citizen. In doing so they create a nuisance which, in our view, the law is entitled to recognise and deal with.'

4. The Report of the Working Party on Vagrancy and Street Offences 1976 considered that the law was necessary to keep prostitutes off the street and that the conclusions of the Wolfenden Report were still valid.

5. The Sixteenth Report of the Criminal Law Revision Committee ('Prostitution on the Street') 1982 suggested that the present law be maintained. It made a variety of suggestions which failed to really address the problems with the current legislation. However, its recommendation that kerb crawling be criminalised was enacted in the Sexual Offences Act 1985.

Until the Sexual Offences Act 2003, solicitation was an offence that could be committed by prostitute women only, even though it was originally believed that the section would cover men too. *DPP* v *Bull* [1994] 4 All ER 411 confirmed that s1(1) Street Offences Act 1959 applied only to women: it was sex-specific. *Crook* v *Edmondson* [1966] 2 QB 81 established that soliciting by a man did not constitute an 'immoral purpose' and men therefore could not be guilty of the offence. There was a direct inequality here: if a man solicited women it was not immoral, but if a woman solicited men it was. As Susan Edwards highlights:

> 'The law clearly demonstrates its differential treatment of women in the interpretation of the statute and its predilection to turn its attention away from the activity which is the object of the legislation, to the person doing it, so to speak.' (In Graham and Anette Scambler (eds), *Rethinking Prostitution: Purchasing Sex in the 1990s*, Routledge (1997).)

Until 1985, the law continued to operate on a double standard, with primarily women being convicted of prostitution offences. This began to change with the Sexual Offences Act 1985 which created a law against men kerb crawling. This law has now been amended by the Sexual Offences Act 2003 to include women kerb crawlers. However, a Home Office circular offered guidance to the police to caution offenders rather than charge. In fact, in order to prosecute a kerb crawler, the police have to prove persistent solicitation. Compare this to the Street Offences Act 1959 which created a procedure of cautioning women on their first two arrests and then prosecuting them in court. Edwards states:

> 'This gender politics of selective enforcement of the law extends further, even into the difference in evidential requirements to prove the offence of solicitation (a female only offence) and the offence of kerb crawling (a male only offence) whereby a prostitute woman commits a crime by one act of solicitation whilst the male kerb crawler must be cited on several occasions to satisfy the "persistent" requirement ... It is as if the state is setting its face against the weakest and most vulnerable who are selectively victimised by the law and the full force of its might.'

The English Collective of Prostitutes (ECP) argue that kerb crawling legislation has added to prostitute women's vulnerability to violence by:

> '... forcing working women further underground: curtailing the time available for women to sus out clients, committing more police time and resources to prostitution rather than rape and violent crimes.' (*No Bad Women, Just Bad Laws*, ECP, London (1997).)

They argue that not only is the law discriminatory, but it also has an overall effect on how prostitute women are generally treated.

Kathleen Barry claims that the laws surrounding prostitution are sexist and promote inequality. She says prostitution and the laws that govern its activities are made by men for men:

> 'All legal approaches to prostitution are masculinist systems that yield to the male market demand and concede to the misogynist myth that prostitution is a necessary

and inevitable sexual service required by men. States' laws promote men buying women for sex and support social hatred of women for doing it.' (*The Prostitution of Sexuality*, K Barry, NYU Press (1995).)

Why is this a feminist issue?

The rule against previous convictions

There very few offences where the defendant's previous convictions are automatically laid before the court before a judgment as to guilt or innocence has been passed. The ECP argue that the law regarding solicitation is grossly unfair and breaches prostitutes' human rights. Since women prostitutes are given two cautions and then prosecuted, this denies the prostitute the fundamental right under the law to be considered innocent until proven guilty. Unlike other defendants, who are not tried on the basis of their past convictions, a prostitute woman is judged first on her record and not the present evidence against her. The cautions 'stamp and condemn her'. A woman prostitute's guilt has never been established, but it will be confirmed at her first trial and will prove her further guilt: the ECP claim that this 'presumption of guilt is the basis of every arrest and conviction of prostitute women'.

Double standards

The Wolfenden Report claimed that no change in the law would eradicate prostitution. But why has prostitution itself never been criminalised?

Barry argues that prostitution is not illegal because men will never criminalise it. She says that prostitution is a form of sexual exploitation by male dominance and that the law will only protect women when women have set new standards. Further, she claims that prostitution is sexual exploitation that is depoliticised and neutralised by men. As Joplin states ('On the Backs of Working Prostitutes: Feminist Theory and Prostitution Policy' (1994) 40(1) *Crime and Delinquency* 69), prostitution never becomes a topic of great social debate in itself; rather, it is discussed only in the context of large reforms. The Sexual Offences Act 2003 provides a good example of this. While the changes to other sexual offences were widely discussed, little attention was paid to prostitution.

The law still presumes that prostitution cannot be eradicated. Indeed, the Home Secretary, David Blunkett, launched a Consultation Paper in 2004 suggesting the creation of legalised brothels. However, this is not a view shared by all. Just because prostitution is assumed to be 'the oldest profession', does that necessarily mean that it can be condoned in the present or future? Ila Gannon and Jack Gannon (*Prostitution – The Oldest Male Crime*, Jig Publications (1980)) state that this is equivalent to saying that if something has existed for a long time, then it must always be with us. This is clearly absurd. The phrase is more a comment on traditional sexual attitudes than a historical observation and serves as a convenient excuse for the men who exploit prostitutes. If social power were presently distributed in favour of women the common phrase concerning prostitution might well now be that it is the oldest male crime. What a different perspective that phrase offers.

Margaretha Jarvinen (*Of Vice and Women: Shades of Prostitution*, Oxford University Press (1993)) is of the same opinion as Gannon and Gannon:

'In fact it is a myth that prostitution is the oldest profession, because without demand there would be no supply.'

The disproportionate number of convictions for (women) soliciting and (men) kerb crawling

There are more men frequenting prostitutes than women working as prostitutes (Eileen McLeod, *Women Working: Prostitution Now*, Croomhealm (1982)) and yet the number of women convicted for solicitation is grossly disproportionate to that of men convicted for kerb crawling. In 1993, 7,912 women were prosecuted for loitering and soliciting, as against 857 men who were prosecuted for kerb crawling (Susan Edwards, *Rethinking Prostitution: Purchasing Sex in the 1990s*, Routledge (1997)). Home Office figures show that, in 1996, 112 male kerb crawlers were cautioned, 1,239 were prosecuted and 1,092 were convicted. Compare this with the same year's figures for female prostitutes, of whom 3,342 were cautioned, 5,660 were prosecuted and 5,312 were convicted.

The differences between the sexes is remarkable, although not unexpected. Sex discrimination, in some form, is quite clearly taking place. Various explanations have been put forward to explain the difference between these figures, some of which are listed below.

1. The police are unwilling to prosecute men whose only error in their view was to consort with a prostitute. The practice of men using a prostitute is acceptable in our society. By contrast, when a woman works as a prostitute it is unacceptable because society believes:

   a) that prostitution undermines marriage;
   b) that it spreads venereal disease;
   c) that it is better to have sex within marriage than outside it;
   d) that sex within marriage is good but female sex outside marriage is not.

2. Until 2003, only women could be common prostitutes, further constructing women as sexual objects. The law seeks to control women's bodies and encourage them to stay within the family as wives and mothers.
3. Women are blamed for prostitution. They are made scapegoats who take the blame for prostitution to satisfy the criminal justice system and the public's hypocritical morality.
4. Once prostitute women are before the court, they are subjected to patriarchal bias from the magistrates who see women in traditional roles. They are then fined, which pushes them further into prostitution in order to pay off those fines.

5. The law places prostitute women in a position where they are open to violence because they are seen as second class citizens. Carol Smart argues that this prototyping of 'normal women and prostitutes symbolises a very decisive moral division in patriarchal societies: of all conceivable classifications applied to women, the designation of "prostitute" has the most degrading connotations'. She further states that the legislation and the way that it is enforced 'serves to construct women as mere sexual objects; which therefore preserves their status as denigrated legal subjects and helps to preserve the legislation which by most standards, must be regarded as unusually harsh and oppressive'. The 'legislation identifies a special class of woman and therefore gives her fewer rights than other citizens'.

Sex discrimination

The ECP state that 'most women do not complain about being arrested when they are breaking the law. What they object to is the sexist and – if they are not white and English – racist police behaviour, false arrests, insults, threats and violence, double standards and demands for free sexual services or for information on other women or clients as a condition of not being arrested.'

This is reiterated by Eileen McLeod when she remarks that police officers have admitted to her off the record that they entrap prostitutes, and that she has evidence of violence, abuse and insulting remarks made by the police to women prostitutes. She argues that this police behaviour stretches the law regarding women prostitutes' civil liberties.

The inequality within the criminal justice system as regards prostitution does not just affect women in terms of arrest and conviction but also has a knock-on effect as to how they are forced to live, the violence that they are exposed to and has the effect of infringing their human rights. It also affects 'other' women, that is non-prostitute women, in that they retain higher status only if they are seen as chaste and as existing within a traditional patriarchal world. All women are affected by this legal division of 'good' and 'bad' women.

Legalisation or decriminalisation?

There have been numerous debates on the issue of prostitution, but the heart of the matter over the last 20 years has centred on its:

1. legalisation (the passing of legislation which would permit prostitution subject to licensing and controls); or
2. decriminalisation (the removal of the criminal element through the abolition of the laws surrounding prostitution).

A recent study noted that women prostitutes were of the opinion that prostitution should be legalised, but feared that this would encourage young women on to the street, which they saw as dangerous and also viewed as possible competition. They were keen to work in brothels for reasons of safety and were willing to pay tax (S V

Carr, D Goldberg and S T Green 'Prostitution: Would Legalisation Help?' (1994) 308 *British Medical Journal* 538). The ECP argue the contrary: if prostitution was legalised the state would become a pimp and tax would replace the fine system (see *The Guardian*, 6 May 1995).

Ila Gannon and Jack Gannon (*Prostitution – The Oldest Male Crime*, JIG Publications (1980)) can see no difference between legalisation and decriminalisation as they believe that prostitution is the pure exploitation of women, of their labour and of part of their sexuality, and can and should be ended.

Interest in decriminalisation or legalisation is seen not just as a feminist issue, but also a medical one. If prostitution were legalised, certain doctors fear that some prostitute women would not register with the state and would therefore be outside the protection of the law, further disempowering them and adversely affecting not only their health but also their human rights. The medical profession appear to believe that decriminalisation would restore prostitute women's human rights and promote safe sex (Basil Donovan and Christine Harcourt, 'Prostitution: to Decriminalise or to Legalise' (1996) 348 *The Lancet* 1962).

Other people believe the opposite: that legislation is needed to protect women prostitutes from violence and exploitation, to protect street residents from nuisance and to promote health care for all (Phil Hubbard, 'Red-light Districts and Toleration Zones': Geographies of Female Prostitution in England and Wales' (1997) 29(2) *Area* 129).

Women as sex objects

Further controversy is raised with the argument that prostitution uses women as sex objects – it objectifies them into this traditional role. Prostitution is sex in exchange for money. Feminists are uneasy with the idea of a woman's body being seen as a commodity for sex. Indeed, prostitution has been regarded as sexual slavery.

Feminists are torn between the idea that prostitution can be seen as a woman's right, with her exercising her freedom to work as she wishes, and the fact that it reflects a particular view of women within society. Prostitution is seen as a male institution that reduces women to a sexual commodity to be bought and sold.

Reinforcement of women's traditional role

A further debate concerns the fact that prostitution reinforces the idea of women having a proper, traditional role. Margaretha Jarvinen (*Of Vice and Women*, Scandinavian University Press (1993)) argues that from a feminist perspective, the concept of prostitute women is directly related to a gender system in society. She argues that the supply side of commercial sex reflects the traditional role assigned to women and the demand side reflects a male role. The English Collective of Prostitutes agree, but suggest that there is the potential to challenge those roles:

'Counting prostitute women's work unveils the sex work that all women are forced to do – at home, on the job, on the street – gratifying men's sexual demands and egos, with understanding and encouraging smiles, words and acts. Counting all women's work, including sex work, is a strategy for examining the division between sex work and other women.'

Maggie O'Neil comments that prostitution shows heterosexual sex without the trappings of romance or romantic attachment and reveals the inequalities within traditional gender relations, particularly relating to masculinity and the interrelated structures of work, sexuality and in contemporary society (Graham and Anette Scambler (eds), *Rethinking Prostitution: Purchasing Sex in the 1990s*, Routledge (1997)).

A form of male domination

Prostitution, it is claimed, is also a further form of male domination. Sheila Jeffreys sees prostitution as the only form of labour constructed solely for the oppression of women – they are used by men solely to satisfy their sexual urges. It is a form of male domination, 'a political construction arising out of male supremacy' (*The Idea of Prostitution*, Spinifex Press (1997)).

Jeffreys answers sexual libertarians' arguments that men should have access to prostitutes and that there is demand for it by stating that using a prostitute is a privilege created out of men's ruling class status and therefore would not exist without a subordinate class of women.

Feminists are in agreement that the social and economic forces that allow men to set aside women for sex are a form of inequality that has a negative effect for all women. How to reform the current situation is a more difficult question that is currently under debate (Joplin, 'On the Backs of Working Prostitutes: Feminist Theory and Prostitution Policy' (1994) 40(1) *Crime and Delinquency* 69).

Hypocrisy

Prostitution has also been seen as an illustration of society's hypocrisy. In our society it is more socially acceptable for a man to use the services of a prostitute than for a woman to do the same. Why does society still continue to have these double standards? A possible answer is that prostitution is bound up with social processes and assumptions of how men and women should behave within our society at large. Patriarchal society has a set of double standards:

'... there is a cultural contradiction that men want to have sex with different women but want women to have sex with only one man. Men's practical solution to this theoretical impossibility is that they set aside women, that is they use prostitutes.' (Joplin, 'On the Backs of Working Prostitutes: Feminist Theory and Prostitution Policy'.)

A form of empowerment?

It is ironic that although women prostitutes are very much under the control of men, women can equalise their economic status by becoming prostitutes (Eileen McLeod, *Women Working: Prostitution Now*, Croom Helm (1992)). Indeed Maggie

O'Neil ('Prostitute Women Now' in Graham and Anette Scambler (eds), *Rethinking Prostitution: Purchasing Sex in the 1990s*, Routledge (1997)) states:

> 'In contemporary society prostitution, for some women, offers a good enough standard of income for shorter working hours and some degree of autonomy and independence for those working for themselves. Sex work has always been an alternative form of work for women. But sex work also brings fear, violence, criminalisation, stigmatisation and reduced civil liberty rights of human dignity, as well as the risk of disease and, for some death.'

However, the picture of economic autonomy through prostitution is not true for all prostitute women. Many street prostitutes 'trade' to pay off fines, and become trapped into a cycle of going to court, paying off fines and going out to work on the streets (Roger Matthews, *Kerb-Crawling, Prostitution and Multi-Agency Policing*, Crime Prevention Unit (1993)). Thus the idea that women can work in this manner to obtain financial parity with men is untrue for many. Further, male violence against women prostitutes is endemic (O'Neil, 'Prostitute Women Now'): they are subjected to violence from their clients and sometimes the police (Prostitutes Collective, 1997). So prostitute women are open to physical abuse and may be economically trapped.

Conclusion

As Carol Smart says (*Law, Crime and Sexuality*, Sage (1995)) there are no simple solutions to prostitution, but law reform will stop any further deterioration of the situation and the law must therefore be confronted. Prostitution carries a message to women about how they are seen within society, hence it is debated by feminists.

Could it ever be eradicated? This is not a question which can be answered in isolation. It does exist: therefore we need, as a society, to honestly look at the causes of prostitution (poverty, sex discrimination, double standards and male domination). Certainly until some form of positive action is taken women will continue to be abused. The law needs to take a positive stand, listen to prostitute women themselves, and seriously tackle negative and traditional stereotypes. The law hasn't tried to prevent prostitution. Rather it has concentrated on preventing the spread of venereal disease or the social nuisances that prostitution causes.

Despite the inclusion of prostitution in the Sexual Offences Act 2003, the law is still in need of reform. The new legislation simply makes minor modifications to a law that is dishonest and outdated. Society and the law need to look at prostitution honestly and address the issues. There is no consensus as to whether prostitution ought to be legalised or decriminalised. Some form of control may be needed, but not in a way that forces women underground and subjects them to abuse. The law never intended to stop prostitution and it does not prevent prostitution. Feminists, however, see the law as in urgent need of reform. The challenge is to frame proposals which will best serve women's interests, but there is no single position on how this might be achieved.

9.3 Lesbianism and the criminal law

Introduction

In contrast to prostitution, lesbianism has been virtually invisible in English criminal law. Such invisibility is not a sign of either ignorance or endorsement: in other words, parliament and the criminal courts have both known that lesbianism exists and disapproved of it. However, they have chosen to say very little about it. We will look both at why there has been such silence and at how the criminal law nonetheless has an effect upon lesbians.

History

English law has never had a criminal offence directly aimed at lesbianism. Contrast this with the regulation of male homosexuality, which was illegal until 1967 and remained subject to discriminatory criminal laws until the Sexual Offences Act 2003 came into force.

However, it does not follow that lesbians have never been prosecuted for their relationships. Although such prosecutions were not common, we are aware that some were made. For example, in the eighteenth century various women were prosecuted for fraud when they married other women by disguising themselves as men. The fraud was against the 'wife' because, as we saw in Chapter 2, upon marriage a husband gained ownership of all the wife's possessions, even the clothes she wore. Thus by becoming her 'husband', the other woman obtained everything she owned (however little). Although the real motive behind such marriages was probably rarely financial – indeed, many of the women involved were poor – using a property offence hid the real issue, the relationship between two women.

At the beginning of the nineteenth century, the House of Lords considered the case of two schoolmistresses accused of lesbianism by one of their pupils. The pupil's grandmother had told other parents of the allegation, with the result that the school was forced to close. The teachers sued her for libel in the case of *Miss Marianne Woods and Miss Jane Pirie Against Dame Helen Cumming Gordon* (published in facsimile by Arno Press, 1975; discussed in Lilian Faderman, *Scotch Verdict*, Quartet (1985)). The court accepted that lesbianism existed (although perhaps not among white, middle class women such as Marianne Woods and Jane Pirie), but was clear that it should not be publicly acknowledged: the transcripts of the proceedings were available only to the judges and parties, and were ordered to be destroyed.

These cases illustrate that the courts wanted to keep knowledge of lesbianism away from women, but only a certain class of women. The prosecutions which took place were of working class women, while the court in *Woods and Pirie* accepted that a half-Indian schoolgirl might have known about lesbianism simply because of her Indian background. What the courts did, therefore, was not as simple as denying that lesbianism existed: rather, they denied that it existed among their own wives and daughters. Lesbianism was seen as 'other': as something only women of different races or classes engaged in.

Such secrecy continued into the twentieth century. In 1921, a proposal to criminalise lesbianism was rejected by parliament. MPs argued that making it a criminal offence would merely publicise it, encouraging more women to become lesbians.

This legal silence therefore appears to have been designed to keep knowledge of lesbianism away from women. This was important for a number of reasons.

1. Lesbianism posed a threat to patriarchal society, since women living in lesbian relationships were not under the control of a husband or father.
2. (White, middle and upper class) women were supposed to be sexually passive, lacking sexual desire. However, lesbianism contradicted this myth: a sexual relationship between two women could only occur if women were in fact capable of active sexual desire.
3. Consider how marriage is voidable if no sexual intercourse has taken place, and how rape is narrowly defined. These are examples of the myth that sexual intercourse (defined as penetration of the vagina by the penis) is the only 'real' sex. The fact that lesbian relationships function despite the absence of a penis contradicts this myth.

The current law

Since 1934 (*R* v *Hare* [1934] 1 KB 354) the courts have accepted that a woman can commit indecent assault. It therefore followed that a woman who sexually touched another woman who either did not consent, or was under 16 and therefore unable, legally, to consent, committed the offence of indecent assault on a woman (s14 Sexual Offences Act 1956). Recently, the law on sexual offences was altered by the Sexual Offences Act 2003. The two (previous) offences of indecent assault on a man and indecent assault on a woman are now combined in one offence, known as sexual assault, as defined in s3:

> '(1) A person (A) commits an offence if –
> (a) he intentionally touches another person (B),
> (b) the touching is sexual,
> (c) B does not consent to the touching, and
> (d) A does not reasonably believe that B consents.'

There is also a separate, more serious offence of 'assault by penetration' under s2. This is defined in similar terms as rape, except that the penetration can be by any body part or object, not necessarily the penis. It can therefore be committed by both men and women, against male or female victims.

Both the new offences have been written in gender neutral terms. Thus, although they do apply to lesbians, that fact is not specifically acknowledged in the legislation.

More importantly, throughout the extensive discussions and consultations on the Sexual Offences Bill before it became law, almost no attention was paid to the position of lesbians. Instead, most discussion focused upon heterosexuals or gay men. Thus although the legal position of lesbians is the same as that of other people, they remain barely acknowledged by parliament.

Feminist perspectives

The legal invisibility of lesbianism serves both to limit women's sexual autonomy and to reinforce patriarchal family structures. First, the silence surrounding, and the devaluation of, lesbianism and the implication that it is not a 'real' option or something that matters, all add to the pressures on women to be heterosexual. Sexual autonomy requires not just the ability to engage in sexual activity at times when one wants to but also the freedom to do so with a partner of one's choice, male or female. Legal recognition of this, however, would undermine the idea that nice women do not take an active role in sexual activity or even particularly enjoy sex.

Second, heterosexuality is a central institution of patriarchy. By tying women to men, it ensures that women continue to be in a position where they serve men's needs. This is not to suggest that women stay in heterosexual relationships only because they know no better, or that all heterosexual relationships are necessarily oppressive. Rather, it is the social, political and legal institution of heterosexuality that is the problem: the way that heterosexual relationships are given a value and level of recognition not available to other family structures. Women face a range of disadvantages (social, cultural, economic, etc) if they choose lesbian relationships. Again, we must recognise that women are not making a free choice: instead, that choice is constrained by its wider context.

We should not be surprised that lesbian relationships have been a source of real concern to the law, or that lawmakers should prefer their wives and daughters to remain in ignorance if possible. The idea of women living independently of men, using their energies for each other rather than on caring for men, is a threatening one to patriarchy.

Of course, a policy of silence is less realistic today. Cultural changes, especially lesbians' own demands for greater visibility, mean that women are aware of lesbianism in a way they may not have been decades, or centuries, ago. This change is reflected in new legal approaches, such as the gender neutrality of the Sexual Offences Act 2003. What is happening now is less a policy of general silence, than one of portraying lesbianism as a less attractive choice, or else one which need not threaten patriarchy. Representations may concentrate upon very feminine lesbians, having a girlfriend as a form of 'experimentation' rather than a permanent choice, or upon lesbianism as a sort of sub-category of male homosexuality.

Conclusion

We have seen in this chapter that the law's regulation of women's sexuality even defines what counts as sexual. Thus prostitution is treated as a sexual activity, although most women work as prostitutes for economic reasons rather than sexual ones. By contrast, lesbianism is not portrayed in the criminal law as a possible sexual choice for women: again, the experiences of women themselves are discounted. We have already discussed how the criminal law defines and interprets the offence of rape from a male perspective. Here, we have seen that the same is true of lesbianism and prostitution, even though in both activities, women are the (potential) offenders.

10

Culture, Women and the Law

10.1 Introduction

10.2 Pornography

10.3 Anorexia nervosa

10.4 Cosmetic surgery

10.1 Introduction

Feminists have been very concerned about the portrayal of women in advertising, television programmes, drama, magazines, newspapers and other mediums. Here, we consider two aspects of such portrayals of women: pornography, which is concerned with representations of women; and anorexia nervosa and cosmetic surgery, often understood as women's responses to these representations.

For pornography, the particular question feminists have asked is: should we attempt to change the law? Some feminists say 'yes', as it is a constructive way of addressing the harm done by pornographic depictions of women. Others say 'no', either because they do not accept that pornography does such harm, or because they do not trust the law to forward feminist goals. However, both statute and common law deal with pornography very differently: as a matter of public morality.

For anorexia and cosmetic surgery, the question is rather: should the law interfere? Of particular concern is the way that the law reinforces the medicalisation of these issues and ignores the role of the wider culture. By treating anorexia as a purely medical (mental health) issue, and implicitly equating cosmetic surgery with medically-indicated surgery, the courts have accepted that doctors (male and rational) are able, like lawyers, to regulate anorexics and those who choose cosmetic surgery (overwhelmingly female, hence irrational).

The common theme linking these topics is the law's failure to recognise that they are fundamentally concerned with women's position in society. In particular, feminists have identified the ways in which they make us consider the representation of women as (sexual) bodies rather than as people whose minds are also of value. The law, however, has determinedly avoided such insights.

10.2 Pornography

Introduction

The subject of pornography is one of the most controversial among feminists. It has given rise to a great quantity of literature, much of it addressing jurisprudential issues. The legal approach and the opinion of the writer towards pornography are usually very closely linked: those who declare themselves in favour of pornography generally favour little or no legal intervention, while those who oppose it may seek legal remedies or else produce arguments for the ineffectiveness or undesirability of legal intervention given the current system.

The first issue is how we define pornography. This has been problematic: as Susan SM Edwards comments:

> 'For sexual liberals, pornographers, producers and consumers of pornography, it is about sex ... To feminists, the term misleads, "pornography" functioning as a prefix, a headnote, a sub-text, constructing expectation and levelling all that is subsumed within it, as of the same ontology ... The answer may be that all this "pornography" has the potential to arouse a physiological response in a male audience. Pornography thus describes the reaction to it, the response, but only the response of those who are sexually aroused by its content.' (*Sex and Gender in the Legal Process*, Blackstone Press (1996).)

Edwards highlights the difficulty of the word, and the very male bias contained within it. However, feminists have used the term and attempted to arrive at a feminist definition of it. For Gloria Steinem, the word:

> '... begins with a root "porno", meaning "prostitution" or "female captives", thus letting us know that the subject is not mutual love, or love at all, but domination and violence against women ... It ends with a root "graphos", meaning "writing about" or "description of", which puts still more distance between subject and object, and replaces a spontaneous yearning for closeness with objectification and voyeurism.' ('Erotica and Pornography: A Clear and Present Difference', cited in Hilaire Barnett (ed), *Sourcebook on Feminist Jurisprudence*, Cavendish (1997).)

Andrea Dworkin goes further, stating that:

> 'The word "pornography", derived from the ancient Greek "porne" and "graphos", means "writing about whores". "Porne" means "whore", specifically and exclusively the lowest class of whore ... The word "pornography" ... means the graphic depiction of women as vile whores.' (*Pornography: Men Possessing Women*, The Women's Press (1981).)

While Steinem's definition makes clear that pornography is the depiction of women as sexual objects for men's sexual gratification, Dworkin goes farther in emphasising pornography's implicit hatred of and contempt for women. The problem is not just that the viewer is distanced from the women depicted, but that the depiction itself encourages the viewer to see women as both sexually available and as vile for their availability. By encouraging its viewers to despise the image of women which it has itself created, pornography directly encourages the hatred of women.

However, many people reject the idea of pornography as necessarily sexist or exploitative of women, and accordingly reject these definitions. In fact, many pro-pornography feminists have paid little attention to producing a definition, since it is unimportant to them to differentiate pornography from other material. For example, an anthology produced by Feminists Against Censorship activists Alison Assiter and Avedon Carol (*Bad Girls and Dirty Pictures: The Challenge to Reclaim Feminism*, Pluto Press (1993)) rejects anti-pornography feminists' definitions, but does not propose any of its own beyond quoting the *American Heritage Dictionary of the English Language* (1973) definition: 'Written, graphic or other forms of communication intended to excite lascivious feelings'.

The current law

English law does not discuss or define pornography as such. Instead, it relies upon the concept of 'obscenity'. The definition of obscenity is given in s1 Obscene Publications Act 1959:

> '(1) For the purposes of this Act an article shall be deemed to be obscene if its effect or (where the article comprises two or more distinct items) the effect of any one of its items is, if taken as a whole, such as to tend to deprave and corrupt persons who are likely, having regard to all relevant circumstances, to read, see or hear the matter contained or embodied in it.'

It is an offence under s2 to publish or have for publication or gain an obscene article. Section 4 provides a defence where 'the publication of the article in question is justified as being for the public good on the grounds that it is in the interests of science, literature, art or learning or of other objects of general concern'.

Thus the essential characteristic of the material is not its content but its effect upon the viewer: they must be likely to be depraved and corrupted by it. *R* v *Hicklin* (1868) QB 360 explained this as matter which would 'deprave and corrupt those whose minds are open to such immoral influences, and into whose hands a publication of this sort may fall'. Part of the aim of the 1959 Act is to 'protect the less innocent from further corruption, the addict from feeding or increasing his addiction' (*DPP* v *Whyte* [1972] 3 All ER 12). As to how many people must be so corrupted, they must amount to 'a significant proportion' (*R* v *Calder and Boyars Ltd* [1969] 1 QB 151) of 'persons who are likely ... to read, see or hear the matter' (*DPP* v *Whyte* [1972] 3 All ER 12).

There is also a common law offence of conspiracy to corrupt public morals. In *Shaw* v *DPP* [1961] AC 220, the House of Lords held that:

> 'There remains in the courts of law a residual power to enforce the supreme and fundamental purpose of the law, to conserve not only the safety and order but also the moral welfare of the State.'

The leading cases do not concern pornography in the traditional sense, but are rather concerned about 'immoral' behaviour being promoted or faciliated: *Shaw* was concerned with a 'directory' providing details of prostitutes, while *Knuller* v *DPP* [1973] AC 435 involved the prosecution of a magazine which carried contact advertisements from gay men.

In practice, convictions for obscenity have proved very difficult to obtain and the criminal law is rarely used to prosecute for these offences. However, s3 Obscene Publications Act 1959 allows material to be searched for, seized and forfeited without the requirement of a criminal trial, and this provision does remain in use.

Jo Bridgeman and Susan Millns point out that while English law treats pornography as a moral issue, for the European Union the focus is economic (*Feminist Perspectives on Law: Law's Engagement with the Female Body*, Sweet & Maxwell (1998)). Thus the European cases (which also form part of English law) focus upon the free movement of goods. Leo Flynn has identified this approach as indicating the masculine nature of EC law. He argues that the European Court of Justice's deference to the market results in it treating a broad range of things, including human bodies, as market objects (*Feminist Perspectives on Law: Law's Engagement with the Female Body*).

Article 28 EC prohibits restrictions on imports between Member States. Article 30 EC does allow restrictions justified on public interest grounds, including public morality, public policy and the protection of health and life of humans. The European Court of Justice (ECJ) applied these articles in two leading cases. In the first, *R* v *Henn and Darby* Case 34/79 [1981] AC 850, the defendants had been convicted of importing indecent or obscene article from the Netherlands. The particular articles were films and magazines depicting rape, buggery with animals and gross indecency with children. They appealed, arguing that the conviction was a restriction on the free circulation of goods within the European Community.

The ECJ concluded that restrictions upon imports of pornography would be a breach of art 28 EC unless one of the justifications in art 30 EC applied. In principle, a Member State could prohibit the importation of obscene articles on the ground of public morality, provided that there was no lawful trade in such goods within that Member State. It was for each Member State to determine the requirements of public morality 'in accordance with its own scale of values'. Importation of these films and magazines could therefore be prohibited.

The second case, *Conegate Ltd* v *Customs and Excise Commissioners* Case 121/85 [1987] QB 254, concerned the same articles. Inflatable rubber dolls designed for sexual use were imported from Germany. However, they were seized by Customs and Excise on the basis that they were obscene. Again, the prohibition on importation was argued to be justified on the ground of public morality. However, this time the materials could legally have been manufactured and sold within Britain. The ECJ concluded that since there were no measures preventing the distribution of such goods within the Member State, public morality could not be used to justify preventing their importation.

The emphasis in these cases was entirely upon the materials being 'goods', and upon the consistency of Member State restrictions. There was no consideration of the issues which feminists would consider important, such as the harm which such materials may do to women. While the English law focuses entirely upon ideas of community standards, European law takes an even narrower, purely economic view of the material. In the words of Leo Flynn '[t]he Court in *Henn and Darby* finds women as a set of two dimensional figures to be seen and not heard, and it leaves them in that position as well'.

Criticisms of the law

Listed below are some of the principal criticisms levelled at the law by the anti-pornography feminists.

1. The Obscene Publications Act 1959 is concerned with regulating morality rather than with the depiction of sexual violence (S Eason, 'A Plea for Censorship' (1991) 141 New LJ 1478).
2. Judgments are to be based on existing social norms and community standards, while feminists criticise and seek to change these (particularly in relation to attitudes to women).
3. The law is drafted from a male perspective, aimed at protecting patriarchal morality, rather than from the feminist perspective of resisting the subordination of women. 'Obscenity ... is a moral idea, an idea about judgments of good and bad. Pornography, by contrast, is a political practice, a practice of power and powerlessness' (Catherine MacKinnon, 'Francis Biddle's Sister: Pornography, Civil Rights and Speech' in *Feminism Unmodified: Discourses on Life and Law*, Harvard University Press (1987)).
4. Contrast the legal definition with MacKinnon's own definition. We can see that the materials feminists consider to be pornographic, and the materials the law considers to be pornographic, are very different. Jennifer Mather Saul gives the example of 'a sexually explicit depiction of egalitarian, loving lesbian sex'. This would not be pornography under feminist definitions, but might be considered obscene under the legal definition. (Jennifer Mouther Saul, *Feminism: Issues and Arguments*, Oxford University Press (2003)). On the other hand, 'page three' photographs of partially-naked women might fall within the feminist definition, but are certainly not considered obscene under English law.
5. Liberal feminists opposed to pornography argue that it ought to be regulated where it breaches the liberal harm principle (ie that one person's freedom should only be restricted where it causes harm to another person). The particular harm done by pornography is that it dehumanises women.
6. Catherine MacKinnon argues that this individualistic liberal notion of harm is inadequate: the harm is social, affecting women as a social group rather than affecting particular individual women.

These are some of the main criticisms levelled at the law by the pro-pornography feminists.

1. The law breaches liberal principles since it represents an unjustified interference by the state in private conduct. It is not the state's role to regulate personal morality.
2. Notions of what can 'deprave and corrupt' are subjective, and aim at imposing one notion of morality upon all individuals.
3. The idea that pornography is harmful is rejected by some feminists. In particular, studies that have aimed either to show or to disprove a direct link between viewing pornography and committing violent acts have proved controversial, with none settling the debate.
4. The courts' interpretation of 'deprave and corrupt' forces pornography to be male-oriented, for example by prohibiting depictions of the erect penis. This legal attitude is compounded by custom, such as the refusal of newsagent chains to stock material showing couples, which means that mutuality cannot be represented but pictures of women aimed solely at men can be (Avedon Carol, *Submission By Feminists Against Censorship To The Home Affairs Inquiry Into Computer Pornography*, Feminists Against Censorship (1994)).

Almost all feminists agree that the current law is unsatisfactory: what they differ about is how the law should be changed.

History

There have been several attempts to change the law. The most infamous of these was probably the Labour MP Clare Short's Bill, which aimed to prevent newspaper pictures (such as *The Sun's* 'page three' photographs) of partially-naked women. Her Indecent Displays (Newspapers) Bill 1986 failed to achieve a second reading; it was introduced again in 1988 but still failed to progress further. In both cases, this lack of progress was due to the fact that the Bills were introduced under the 'Ten Minute Rule' Bills procedure rather than with government support and time.

The Bill would have created a simple offence:

> 'It shall be an offence to publish in newspapers pictures of naked or partially naked women in sexually provocative poses.'

'Page three' is often seen as the least explicit, and therefore least harmful, type of sexual representation of women: why try to prohibit it? For many feminists, there are a number of important reasons why these types of picture should be banned.

1. Such pictures are disseminated widely: they are in homes, workplaces, cafes, trains, etc.
2. They are used by men, especially in the workplace, to harass and demean women (for example by comparing them to the women in the photographs).

3. Their wide availability, including to children, instils and reinforces the objectification of women (they portray women as objects to be judged, fantasised about and made demands of rather than as full human beings with the same range of mental, physical and emotional characteristics and the same right to respect as men).

Internationally, the most influential legal response from feminists to the challenge of legislating upon pornography was the Dworkin/MacKinnon ordinance of 1983. This began with a very specific and detailed definition of pornography as 'the sexually explicit subordination of women, graphically depicted, whether in pictures or in words, that also includes' any one of a series of instances of women being dehumanised, subjected to pain, mutilation or humiliation, presented as sexually submissive, etc.

Such material would not be forbidden or subject to criminal prosecution under the ordinance. Instead, those harmed directly or indirectly by it could bring a case in the civil courts. Thus the focus would be placed firmly upon the effects of pornography on women, both in its making and as a result of the images it depicts. The material would be judged upon whether it amounted to the practice of sexual discrimination. For material meeting the definition of pornography, the ordinance set out four potential causes of action.

1. Anyone coerced into pornography could seek both damages and an injunction preventing distribution of the material.
2. Anyone could sue for violation of a right not to have pornography forced upon her.
3. Damages could be sought for injury directly caused by pornography.
4. An action could be brought against anyone trafficking in pornography.

These causes of action clearly concentrate upon the harm caused to women by being involved in the making of, or subjected to the viewing of, pornography. This is in contrast to England's obscenity laws, in that there is no reference to community standards or likely viewers: instead, the focus is firmly upon those harmed by pornography.

The ordinance was welcomed by many anti-pornography activists, not only (or even necessarily primarily) for the causes of action which it would give to women: radical feminists tend to be very aware of the limitations of legal reform. In the case of pornography, any requirement to prove harm would pose great difficulty, particularly given the contradictory scientific evidence relating to pornography and sexual violence. However, despite these problems, the proposed legislation is valuable for its potential to alter the terms of debate surrounding pornography: the emphasis is taken away from 'obscenity' and refocused firmly upon the harm to women, individually and collectively.

There has been feminist opposition to the Dworkin/MacKinnon ordinance on the basis that while pornography is problematic, we should not assume that the law can be made to fit feminist goals. According to Carol Smart:

> 'The legal framework (whether civil or criminal) requires that we fit pornography, or the harm that pornography does, into existing categories of harms or wrongs. Hence we are left with a focus on degrees of actual violence or the traditional (non-feminist) concern with degrees of explicitness which are the mainstay of obscenity laws.' (*Feminism and the Power of Law*, Routledge (1989).)

We will now look in more detail at the views of different feminists upon the legal regulation of pornography. As already discussed, this is an issue upon which feminists are very divided, so there is a particularly wide range of views. We touch on just a selection of them here.

Anti-pornography feminism

Pornography's role in women's oppression – both in its methods of production and in its content – has been analysed at length. Opponents of pornography argue that it is instrumental in women's abuse on a number of levels: its making, its explicitly misogynist portrayal of the abuse and subordination of women and its underlying messages denoting women as objects, as sexually available and as colluding in and deserving or enjoying sexual assaults against them. Pornography eroticises patriarchal relationships of (male) dominance and (female) submission. Women are portrayed as always welcoming men's sexual approaches and always seeking to fulfil male desires. When women are viewed as inferior, as existing for men's use in this context, they are likely to be viewed as inferior in other contexts too. The question, then, is what the law's role should be in addressing this problem.

There is a dilemma for feminists in deciding how far the law can be made to work in ways which are positive for women. Should feminists trust judges to make appropriate decisions about pornography? We have seen that in other areas of law, the courts have been able to defuse reforms which ought to help achieve feminist aims (think of the rules on previous sexual history in rape cases, for example). As Smart points out in *Feminism and the Power of Law*, 'using the law requires compromise and collaboration from feminists'. The question is, should feminists make this compromise? Can the results be worthwhile?

The answer of feminists arguing for law reform is that by setting out detailed definitions of pornography, harm and so on (in the way that the Dworkin/MacKinnon ordinance does), limits can be made to the discretion given to the courts. By using legislation, notions of harm can be added or expanded upon. There may be more scope for this in England and Wales than in the USA, where the Dworkin/MacKinnon ordinance has been declared unconstitutional on the ground that it breaches the constitutional right to free speech. However, the law may prove resistant to expanding its definitions: Emily Jackson suggests that the Dworkin/MacKinnon ordinance 'would only work for women who were able to prove that a specific image interfered with a specific right of theirs' ('The Problem with Pornography: A Critical Survey of the Current Debate' [1995] *Feminist Legal Studies* 49).

The process of attempting to enact such legislation can be valuable in itself. By focusing discussion upon feminist-inspired legislation, the very terms of the debate can perhaps be redefined. Despite the risks in seeking to use the legal system to enact feminist reforms, Susan SM Edwards describes refusing to make the attempt as 'a pragmatic surrender, it is unsatisfactory and nihilistic' (*Sex and Gender in the Legal Process*, Blackstone Press (1996)).

Pro-pornography feminism

Not all critics simply doubt whether truly feminist law reform is possible. Some do not seek such reform at all, since they are in favour of pornography. Some support the availability of most pornography, while others do not want any 'censorship' which might affect materials produced by women. These arguments are frequently made from either a liberal or a postmodern perspective.

Liberal critiques

Liberals emphasise the 'right to free speech', which is part of English law both through the common law and under art 10 European Convention on Human Rights. To many liberal feminists, pornography amounts to speech and so is protected by the right to free speech. Thus attempts to legislate against it are violations of the freedom of speech and unjustifiable censorship.

This argument has been criticised because it ignores the fact that not everybody has equal access to speech (in this wider sense of publications and the media). Catherine MacKinnon argues that there is an assumption among liberals that the important issue is the avoidance of restrictions rather than access to speech for those, such as women, to whom it has been largely denied ('The Sexual Politics of the First Amendment', *Feminism Unmodified*, Harvard University Press (1987)).

The emphasis upon pornography as 'speech' also ignores the way that pornography is produced. Rather than simply coming from one person's mind or imagination, it is created by the actions of many people. The way in which pornography is produced is one of the concerns for anti-pornography feminists, and is one of the issues that the Dworkin/MacKinnon ordinance would address.

Not all liberal feminists argue that pornography should be protected as a form of free speech. An important element of liberal philosophy is the 'harm principle' set out by philosopher John Stuart Mill (*On Liberty* (1859)): we only have freedom to act in ways which do not harm others. The law's role is (only) to prevent harm to people. Thus the state would be justified in intervening to regulate pornography if its purpose was not censorship, but the protection of women from harm. The crucial issue for liberal feminists is therefore: does pornography harm women? As we have already seen, there is not agreement on the answer.

Some liberals argue that the increasing availability of pornography is not a problem for women. On the contrary, it has made it possible for women to explore their sexuality and to feel less guilt about doing so. What is needed is not less pornography, but rather more pornography targeted at women. However, there are important criticisms of this position. First, pornography (being largely made by men, for men) does not offer a neutral or supportive view of female sexuality. Instead, it portrays this in a way which supports male fantasies and patriarchal attitudes rather than women's liberation. Second, women themselves have not proved the huge market for pornographic material which this argument would suggest they should: publications targeted specifically at women, particularly heterosexual women, have generally failed commercially.

Postmodern critiques

Some feminists arguing from a postmodern perspective, particularly 'queer theorists', argue that pornography has a positive role to play in women's liberation. They argue that pornography is a text capable of multiple readings (different viewers can interpret it in different ways, including ways which are positive for women). The problem is effectively shifted from the materials themselves and instead becomes an issue of how we 'read' them.

There is an emphasis upon pornography as fantasy: the connection between the viewing of pornography and real-life behaviour is denied. It can have multiple meanings, because it is part of our fantasy lives rather than 'real' lives. Through these many and various readings, pornography can have a special role in undermining ideologies about sexual relations. Carol J Clover says that 'pornography is ... different, set apart by its status as a second-order practice or a fantasy of practices rather than itself a "practice"' (Pamela Church Gibson and Roma Gibson (eds), *Dirty Looks: Women, Pornography, Power*, British Film Institute (1993)).

However, this argument has been criticised on several grounds. First, while the contents of pornography may be used as fantasy, they were created using real people. In the words of Renate Klein, 'The bodies ... in postmodern feminist writings do not breathe, do not laugh, and have no heart. They are "constructed" and "refigured" ... They are written about in the third person ... Women are absent' (Diane Bell and Renate Klein (eds), *Radically Speaking: Feminism Reclaimed*, Zed Books (1996)).

Second, postmodernists perhaps overestimate the potential of multiple readings. Most materials are produced to obtain a specific response from their audience. This is particularly true of pornography, which mostly has the single aim of sexually arousing its (overwhelmingly male) target audience.

Conclusion

We have seen that feminists disagree on many issues. However, those differences are perhaps most intense and polarised on the issue of pornography. One's attitudes on the basic issue (whether pornography is sex discrimination or sexual liberation) fundamentally affect the choice of definition, critique of the existing law and proposals for reform. However, the one point on which the majority of feminists do agree is that the current English law is unsatisfactory, and does little to advance women's interests.

10.3 Anorexia nervosa

Introduction

The word anorexia literally means 'loss of appetite'. This is misleading, since many sufferers do not lose their appetite at all. Instead, they use enormous self-discipline not to eat. Such a wilful refusal poses legal problems at the point where that self-starvation becomes life-threatening. Should the courts intervene to order anorexia sufferers to be fed against their will? To examine this question, we will begin by discussing what anorexia is and some of the causes of the condition, before going on to examine the law's response to it.

What is anorexia?

Anorexia is considered a psychiatric illness, and has the highest mortality rate of any psychological illness. It is defined by the World Health Organisation (World Health Organisation, *International Statistical Classification of Diseases and Related Health Problems*, 10th edition) as being present when all the following criteria are met:

'(i) Body weight maintained at least 15 per cent below that expected ...
(ii) The weight loss is self-induced by avoidance of "fattening foods" and one or more of the following: self-induced vomiting; self-induced purging; excessive exercise; use of appetite suppressants and/or diuretics.
(iii) There is body-image distortion in the form of ... a dread of fatness ... as an intrusive, overvalued idea ...
(iv) A widespread endocrine disorder involving the hypothalamic-pituitary-gonadal axis is manifest in women as amenorrhoea [absence of menstruation] and in men as a loss of sexual interest and potency ...
(v) If onset is pre-pubertal, the sequence of pubertal events is delayed or even arrested ...'

What causes anorexia?

There are potentially many causes of anorexia, although nobody is absolutely certain what causes it. The World Health Organisation acknowledges that the causes are unknown, but that there 'is growing evidence that interacting sociocultural and biological factors contribute to its causation, as do less specific psychological mechanisms and a vulnerability of personality'.

We will consider a selection of suggested factors. This is not an exhaustive list; nor would these suggested causes apply to every sufferer. None of them work in isolation: it is fairly certain that there is no single cause for the condition. However, they do give an idea of the complexity of the condition and the difficulty of finding a single answer (medical or legal) to the problems which it causes to sufferers and those involved in treating or caring for them.

1. The desire to literally disappear: for example, to remove oneself from abusive situations. One sufferer, Natalie, recalls:

   'I remember having intense feelings of self-hatred and wanting to disappear (very common amongst anorexics).'

2. The desire to avoid developing a woman's body: this can be linked to fears about adulthood and to sexual abuse. The Royal College of Psychiatrists' leaflet *Changing Minds: Anorexia and Bulimia* (2003) suggests that anorexia is a refusal to become woman-sized and thus expected to live up to cultural expectations of women ('mature, responsible, motherly, caring, supportive, submissive, strong, reliable, successful, sensual, compassionate, kind, sensible …').

3. The desire to have control over one area of one's life: for young women in particular, their body and eating may be the only thing over which they do feel they have control. This need to be in control of oneself is an important factor to be considered in the legal and medical treatment of anorexia sufferers, as we discuss below.

4. As a response to cultural pressures on women to be thin. Anorexia is more common in cultures which value thinness (Royal College of Psychiatrists' leaflet, *Changing Minds: Anorexia and Bulimia* (2003)).

5. There also appear to be genetic factors (Royal College of Psychiatrists' leaflet, *Changing Minds: Anorexia and Bulimia* (2003)).

The current law

Just as with forced caesareans, the main legal issue which arises in the treatment of anorexic patients is that of consent, and in particular the refusal of consent to medical treatment. The courts have generally become involved in decisions concerning the treatment of anorexics when clinics have wished to treat them against their will. Such treatment can take various forms, but one in particular is that of naso-gastric feeding.

We have seen that anorexia can often be fatal, and it is in that context that the courts have had to make their decisions. The women and girls concerned have often been in danger of dying from starvation, but have refused to take in nourishment which would save their lives. The question for the courts is: must these women's refusal of treatment be respected? Questions of competence are arguably more complicated than for forced caesareans, since the patient is suffering from a serious psychiatric illness. At the same time, the patient's need for control over her own life means that forced treatment can seriously damage her prospects of improvement or recovery.

Hilde Bruch (a psychiatrist) has argued that anorexia is an attempt by the patient to assert and define herself, assuaging self-loathing by becoming thin. Thus treatment must focus upon creating patient autonomy, allowing her to restore her sense of self. Forcing the patient to accept treatment and focusing upon weight gain rather than patient choice is therefore damaging: even if the anorexia is life-threatening, forced weight gain can be equated with giving up the reason for living (Margery Ganns and William B Gunn Jr, 'End Stage Anorexia: Criteria for Competence to Refuse Treatment' (2003) 26(6) *International Journal of Law and Psychiatry* 677).

We will consider the law's approach to these issues in two parts: first the position of patients under 18, who are legally minors, and then that of adults. However, before considering these cases, we first have to establish what the legal status of artificial (naso-gastric) feeding is: do we consider it to be simply a way of nourishing the patient, as part of their ordinary care, or is it a medical procedure to which the law governing medical treatment applies?

Feeding as medical treatment

Airedale NHS Trust v *Bland* [1993] AC 789 first held that naso-gastric feeding is medical treatment and can therefore be withheld as part of medical treatment. The facts of this case did not concern a sufferer of anorexia. Anthony Bland was 17 when he was seriously injured in the 1989 Hillsborough Disaster, where a large number of Liverpool Football Club fans were crushed and suffered injury or death. Anthony Bland's injury caused him to be in a persistent vegetative state, where all the higher functions of the brain were destroyed. He had no prospect of recovery or improvement, and he was unaware of anything happening around him: he could not see, hear, feel or communicate.

Part of the treatment which kept Anthony Bland alive consisted of artificial feeding by naso-gastric tube. The hospital treating him (supported by his family) sought a court order allowing them to discontinue this feeding, and withhold antibiotics for any infections, with the result that he would die in ten–14 days. One of the questions for the court was whether the naso-gastric feeding amounted to medical treatment (in which case it could be lawfully withheld in certain circumstances) or ordinary care. Normal feeding, of course, is not medical treatment, but the House of Lords held that naso-gastric feeding does amount to medical treatment: 'the administration of nourishment by the means adopted involves the application of a medical technique' (Lord Keith of Kinkel) and is 'no different from life support by a ventilator' (Lord Goff of Chieveley).

Patients under the age of 18

Many of the cases involve sufferers under the age of 18. These cases are complicated by the parental right to consent on their child's behalf. The *Gillick* rules (*Gillick* v *West Norfolk and Wisbech Area Health Authority* [1985] 3 All ER 402) apply here: a girl can make her own decisions on treatment provided that she has sufficient understanding and intelligence. Nonetheless, the courts have taken the view in this context that her right to make the decision does not necessarily extinguish the rights of her parents. In *Re W (A Minor) (Medical Treatment: Court's Jurisdiction)* [1992] 4 All ER 627, the Court of Appeal held that treatment could lawfully proceed with the consent of either a competent young person or the young person's parents. Where the two parties differ, the parental consent will override the refusal of the young person. *Gillick* was distinguished on the basis that it referred to the child's consent; here, the issue was a refusal of consent. Lord Donaldson did not accept that a child's refusal of treatment recommended by doctors could be binding in the same way that her consent was. They further held that the court's inherent jurisdiction was wider even than the powers of a parent.

W was a 16-year-old anorexic who was receiving in-patient treatment in her local area. She had already consented to have her arms encased in plaster to prevent her from self-harming, and to previous naso-gastric feeding, but refused to transfer to another treatment centre. There was medical opinion which supported her continuing with her current course of treatment, as well as medical opinion supporting the transfer. The Court accepted that W was legally competent, but nonetheless upheld the decision to transfer her against her wishes.

It would appear from the facts that W, as a competent person, had chosen a medically valid option. The decision by the Court to intervene and overrule that choice is therefore difficult to justify. As Jo Bridgeman commented ('Old Enough to Know Best?' (1993) 13 *Legal Studies* 69), '[W] wanted some degree of self-determination and control over her own life … The law should have respected this.'

The impact of *Re W* also extends to situations other than the treatment of anorexia: it applies to all such questions of the medical treatment of minors. According to Margaret Brazier and Caroline Bridge ('Coercion or Caring: Analysing Adolescent Autonomy' (1996) 16 *Legal Studies* 84), *Re W* undermines the autonomy of all minors. Doctors are given the power to determine the competence of minors on the basis of outcome. In other words, if they make the decision the doctor approves of, it will be respected, but if they do not, someone else is able to override that decision. Lord Donaldson saw consent as important because it provided legal protection (a 'flak jacket') for the doctor, not because it provided personal autonomy for the patient. We should recognise such legal deferral to medical paternalism from other contexts, particularly abortion, as previously discussed. Once again, the figure of the rational male doctor is opposed to that of the irrational female patient.

Re C (A Minor) [1997] 2 FLR 180 confirmed that the court had an inherent jurisdiction to order compulsory treatment. A 16-year-old girl (C) with anorexia nervosa had received treatment at a specialist clinic, but had repeatedly absconded. The director of the clinic refused to readmit her without a court order allowing her to be detained there. C argued that she was willing to attend voluntarily, and that there was no need for such an order. The High Court nonetheless ordered her to be detained against her will (by reasonable force if necessary) for the purpose of treating her eating disorder. They said that in exercising their inherent jurisdiction they were bound to treat the child's welfare as the paramount consideration. The threshold for exercising the jurisdiction in order to detain a child would be 'significant harm'. Here, her presence at the clinic was an essential part of her treatment, but she would probably leave (and consequently suffer significant harm) if free to do so.

Patients over the age of 18

A competent adult has the right to refuse medical treatment, and psychiatric illness is not in itself a bar to competence (*Re C (Adult: Refusal of Medical Treatment)* [1994] 1 All ER 819). There are therefore two issues to consider in relation to the forcible feeding of anorexic women: first, if the patient is detained under the Mental Health Act 1983, is force feeding treatment for the mental disorder (for which consent is not required)? Second, if the person is not so detained then how should competence be assessed: is the *Re C* test adequate?

Feeding as treatment for a mental disorder. *Fox* v *Riverside Health Trust* [1994] 1 FLR 614 concerned F, a 38-year-old anorexic woman who was detained in hospital under the Mental Health Act 1983. Under such detention, medical treatment can be given without consent if it is treatment for the mental disorder, but not otherwise. F's condition was critical, and she may have died if unfed. An order was made allowing her to be fed without her consent, on the basis that '[u]ntil there is steady weight gain no other treatment can be offered for the respondent's mental condition so ... forced feeding if needed will be medical treatment for the mental disorder'. Although the order was discharged by the Court of Appeal on grounds of jurisdiction, they did not dispute that forced feeding could amount to treatment under the Mental Health Act 1983. On the contrary, it was indicated that if the patient's condition deteriorated a fresh application could be made.

In *South West Hertfordshire Health Authority* v *KB* [1994] 2 FCR 1051, the High Court held that naso-gastric feeding amounts to medical treatment, rather than food. It is treatment of a mental disorder since it is necessary both to treat a symptom of mental illness and to make psychiatric treatment of the underlying cause possible. Bridgeman & Millns (*Feminist Perspectives on Law*) note that this significantly extends the treatment which can be given under the Mental Health Act 1983.

The following year, this issue was fully considered by the Court of Appeal for the first time in *B* v *Croydon Health Authority* [1995] 1 All ER 683. B had a psychopathic disorder and when prevented from self-harming, refused to eat. The only treatment for her condition was psychotherapy, but this was suspended as the health authority felt she should gain weight before continuing. B then resumed eating when threatened with naso-gastric feeding, but later stopped eating again and sought an order prohibiting the health authority from using naso-gastric feeding without her consent. That order was initially made, but was then refused at a full hearing where it was held that the Mental Health Act 1983 allowed her to be fed without her consent.

On appeal, it was argued that since the only treatment for B's disorder was psychotherapy, forced feeding could not amount to treatment for the disorder, as s63 of the 1983 Act requires: at most, it was treatment of a symptom of that disorder. The Court of Appeal disagreed: treatments ancillary to the core treatment fell within the definition, and therefore naso-gastric feeding ancillary to the psychotherapy constituted medical treatment for a mental disorder and could be carried out without B's consent. This would not apply where the forced feeding was the only treatment being given: there must also be a core treatment. Further, art 8 European Convention on Human Rights (the right to private life) is not breached since s63 creates a sufficiently precise exception.

The courts are therefore willing to authorise the forced naso-gastric feeding of anorexia patients. However, naso-gastric feeding itself poses serious health risks including pneumonia and over-hydration. It may even damage the patient's long-term prospects for recovery from the anorexia itself (Kirsty Keyward, '*B* v *Croydon Health Authority* 1994, CA: Force-feeding the Hunger Striker under the Mental Health Act 1983' [1995] 3 Web JCLI). As already discussed, the capacity for controlling her own life is vital to the anorexic, yet to force this treatment upon her denies her that capacity. The consequences for her trust in the treatment and those providing it can be very negative.

Anorexia and competence. Just as the process of childbirth has been held to render a woman not competent to refuse a caesarean, the condition of anorexia is also seen as undermining sufferers' competence by its very nature. The Mental Health Act Commission emphasise this viewpoint in *Guidance Note 3: Guidance on the Treatment of Anorexia Nervosa Under the Mental Health Act 1983* (1999): 'capacity to consent may be compromised by fears of obesity or denial of the consequences of their actions, notwithstanding the retention of intellectual capacity to understand the nature, purpose and likely effect of treatment'.

However, the legal test for competence may itself be inadequate to deal with these cases. Anorexia poses very specific problems:

> '[A]n account of capacity based on understanding and reasoning does not capture the difficulties in decision-making that these patients experience ... The problems with alternative approaches, which do not use capacity, are that the use of compulsory treatment can be experienced as very difficult and can further compromise the ability of patients to make their own treatment decisions and to accept treatment.' (Jacinta O A Tan, Tony Hope, Anne Stewart and Raymond Fitzpatrick, 'Control and Compulsory Treatment in Anorexia Nervosa: The Views of Patients and Parents' (2003) 26(6) *International Journal of Law and Psychiatry* 627.)

Margery Ganns and William B Gunn Jr discuss a (medical) decision on competence for a patient in the US. Special criteria were developed to test both cognitive and emotional competence; the family of the patient was deeply involved; and the fact that her anorexia was 'end stage' (chronic, without remissions and with significant, irreversible medical problems) itself made a finding of competence more likely ('End Stage Anorexia: Criteria for Competence to Refuse Treatment' (2003) 26(6) *International Journal of Law and Psychiatry* 677). This complex test, devised in response to the particular patient's circumstances, is very different to the simple, three-stage test used by the English courts.

Of course, the competence test does not apply where a patient has been sectioned under the Mental Health Act 1983 and the treatment is for the mental disorder itself. However, the test described by Ganns and Gunn implicitly suggests that there may be a point where treatment will have limited effect as a result of irreversible medical complications. This point might be significant for cases under the Mental Health Act 1983. Given the difficulties of treating anorexia, is it realistic to say that feeding a patient with a view to long-term weight gain and mental treatment is a realistic option where the patient has reached the 'end stage'? In that situation, ought the court take a different approach to whether forced feeding is genuinely part of the treatment of this mental disorder? That issue is one which the English courts have not yet addressed.

Feminist perspectives

The first question in analysing the approach taken by the courts is: why are they so keen to order treatment? The obvious answer is that, like the doctors who wish to carry out naso-gastric feeding, the judges are keen to save the lives of starving patients. However, this response does not tell the whole story. First, the issues previously raised in relation to forced caesareans and abortion, such as deference to the medical profession (assumed to represent rationality) and suspicion of decisions taken by women (viewed as embodying irrationality), also apply in this instance.

Second, the behaviour of anorexic women itself induces strong responses. Susie Orbach suggests that the rebellion and strength inherent in rejecting food call forth a strong desire in observers to control and overpower that force (*Hunger Strike*, Penguin (1993)). Rebecca Dresser makes a similar point:

> 'The specter of anorexia nervosa evokes uneasiness in its observers. The legal system should be reluctant to ease this discomfort by broadly sanctioning forcible treatment that may temporarily remove the condition's obvious symptoms, but too often ignores the needs of the individual who suffers from them. Strict legal limits on the involuntary treatment of anorexics could encourage a more widespread examination of the cultural context of anorexia nervosa.' ('Feeding the Hunger Artists: Legal Issues in Treating Anorexia Nervosa' [1984] Wisconsin Law Review 297.)

Many feminists take a similar approach to Dresser, and suggest that treating anorexia as a mental illness like any other is itself incorrect. Anorexia cannot be separated from its social context, particularly the portrayal of women's bodies as something which they ought to control and change; the widespread sexual abuse of girls and young women (an apparent trigger for many cases of anorexia); and the emphasis upon dieting and body size in the media, women's magazines, within families and by peer groups. This is reflected in the hugely disproportionate number of women sufferers.

The pressure upon most women to diet begs the question: is anorexia a psychiatric illness at all, rather than an extreme form of normal female behaviour? Many symptoms originally thought unique to sufferers have been found among large proportions of non-anorexics. Incidence of anorexia has increased since the 1960s: at the same time the dieting and exercise industries have expanded (Kim Chernin, *Womansize*, The Women's Press (1981)).

'[B]ody-image distortion in the form of ... a dread of fatness ... as an intrusive, overvalued idea' is both one of the diagnostic criteria for anorexia and a common frame of mind among non-anorexic women. Dieting is certainly a normal part of women's (and teenage girls') behaviour in contemporary Britain. Research undertaken by the University of Glasgow in 2002 indicated that, at the age of 15, 26 per cent of girls were dieting compared to 5 per cent of boys. Between the ages of 11 and 15, the number of boys worried about their weight fell, but 70 per cent of 15-year-old girls worried about their weight.

However, it is not simply a dread of fatness which is common among women. Body-image distortion (not being able to see one's body, and in particular to assess one's weight, as it really is) is also incredibly widespread. Susan Bordo discusses a survey of 53,000 women undertaken by the American *Glamour* magazine in 1984. In that survey, 75 per cent of those surveyed considered themselves 'too fat' although only 25 per cent were overweight according to standard weight tables; in fact, 30 per cent were underweight (*Unbearable Weight: Feminism, Western Culture and the Body*, University of California Press (1993)). The measure women routinely take to control their (real or imagined) excess weight – dieting – further exacerbates the problem. An obsession with food and the development of eating rituals can themselves be triggered by low-calorie diets. The Minnesota Studies, which examined the effects of semi-starvation upon fit, healthy men, are perhaps the most famous evidence of this.

We have seen in other contexts how women are associated with the body, men with the mind. Often in law, the effect of this dichotomy is that men are seen as rational, in contrast to women who are stereotyped as irrational. However, the association of women with the body also focuses women's and men's attention onto female bodies, which are given an importance greater than either men's physical appearance or women's minds. Thus the cliché 'you are what you eat' has greater resonance for women, whose weight, body shape and eating habits are under continual scrutiny: media scrutiny, the scrutiny of lovers, family and friends, and above all, self-scrutiny.

If the idea that unhealthy eating habits and unsustainable body shapes are praised in our culture seems an over-statement, think of women such as Jordan, who has based her career on having surgically-enlarged breasts. We will consider the pressure upon women to have cosmetic surgery in a moment, but anorexia is also seen as having a kind of glamour, even in mainstream culture. Susan Gilbert comments (in *Womansize*): 'It is now a glamorous cross between two Victorian favourites, consumption and hysteria, but updated for a modern audience'.

Florence Nightingale, best known for her reform of nursing in Britain and in the British Army, also concerned herself with feminist issues. Her comment upon the attention given to women's bodies (but denied to their minds) was written in the nineteenth century, but still rings true today:

> 'If we [women] have no food for the body, how we do cry out, how all the world hears of it, how all the newspapers talk of it, with a paragraph headed in great capital letters, DEATH FROM STARVATION! But suppose one were to put a paragraph in *The Times*, "Death of Thought from Starvation or Death of Moral Activity from Starvation", how people would stare, how they would laugh and wonder! One would think we had no heads or hearts, by the indifference of the public towards them. Our bodies are the only things of any consequence.'

10.4 Cosmetic surgery

Introduction

The attention given to women's bodies, and the identification of women as 'body', men as 'mind', do not only encourage women to diet. Cosmetic surgery is also, according to Kathy Davis:

> 'Symptomatic of a culture where it is possible to view one's body as separate from who one is or would like to become and as a site, particularly for women, to negotiate their identities in a context of structured hierarchies of power. Cosmetic surgery becomes both an expression of the objectification of the female body and of women's struggles to become embodied subjects rather than mere bodies.' (*Reshaping the Female Body: The Dilemma of Cosmetic Surgery*, Routledge (1995).)

The current law

Technically, all medical treatment (including surgery) involves the committal of criminal assaults under the Offences Against the Person Act 1861. Surgery will usually involve wounding, and either actual or grievous bodily harm. However, surgeons are not prosecuted every time they operate on a patient. This is because the consent of that patient serves as a defence for surgeons carrying out 'proper medical treatment' or 'reasonable surgical interference' (*R v Brown* [1993] 2 All ER 75).

We cannot consent to injury in every situation. The leading case on consent to assaults causing injury, *Brown*, established that consent was no defence to such assaults committed in the course of sadomasochistic sexual activity. Their Lordships suggested different situations where consent would be valid.

1. Consent is not a defence to activities which are not otherwise lawful (Lord Templeman).
2. The infliction of bodily harm without good reason (eg organised sporting contests and games, parental chastisement or reasonable surgery) is unlawful (Lord Jauncey of Tullichettle).
3. 'Proper medical treatment' is in a category of its own (Lord Mustill).

There is no case law on consent to cosmetic surgery. *Brown* would suggest that the answer depends upon whether cosmetic surgery is a 'good reason' either because it is 'proper medical treatment' or for some other reason. Usually, of course, surgery is a 'good reason' because it improves our health or even saves our lives. When we think of 'proper medical treatment', it is such surgery that we are likely to have in mind, rather than cosmetic surgery.

It is not clear, therefore, whether or why cosmetic surgery falls within the exception preventing the surgery from being an assault. The Law Commission, in its report *Consent in the Criminal Law* (Consultation Paper 139 (1995)), suggests that 'it would not be possible to identify a therapeutic benefit in every case [of cosmetic surgery], and it may be that this is a field in which English law unconsciously recognises that the criminal law has no acceptable place in controlling operations performed by qualified practitioners upon adults of sound mind with their consent'.

However, this answers only part of the question. While our legal system may recognise that the criminal law should not intervene to prevent the practice of cosmetic surgery, it does not take the same approach regarding sadomasochistic sex. Why the distinction? The answer must be that the courts believe there is some benefit or justification for cosmetic surgery which does not apply to all sexual activity. One possibility is that cosmetic surgery is viewed as an extension of the 'personal adornment' exception. Consent is a defence in relation to body piercing and tattoos, for example (although the risks involved in those procedures are very different to those involved in some cosmetic surgeries).

The answer may lie in part in the law's acceptance of patriarchal norms. Within a system where women are valued for their bodies – their appearance – it makes sense that women will try to improve those bodies as far as they are able. Cosmetic surgery may appear a desirable activity despite the risks, and hence be a 'good reason' for the infliction of injury. If conforming to cultural norms of beauty is accepted as a valid pursuit for women, then assisting them (and men, although fewer men seek cosmetic surgery) through the application of medical expertise can be viewed as 'proper medical treatment'.

It is important to realise that the law's approach to injury is highly gendered. The apparent exception for cosmetic surgery is by no means the only example of this. Other situations include the following.

1. 'Rough and undisciplined horseplay': in *R* v *Jones* (1986) 83 Cr App R 375, two boys were thrown into the air by fellow pupils and suffered serious injuries (a ruptured spleen and a broken arm) on landing. The Court of Appeal accepted

that 'rough and undisciplined horseplay' forms an exception; consent to such activities is a defence. The reasoning for this exception is that such behaviour is normal and acceptable for boys, and men, since the defence was also held applicable to adult RAF officers in *R v Aitken* (1992) 95 Cr App R 304 (this is an instance of the law's reliance upon gender stereotypes which are insulting, not to say damaging, to men).

2. 'Manly sports' such as boxing. Although the purpose of boxing is to inflict severe injury upon one's opponent, and the benefit to society is far from obvious, the courts have refused to criminalise the infliction of grievous bodily harm involved.

3. Sexual diseases: in *R v Clarence* (1889) 22 QB 23, where a husband who knew that he had gonorrhoea had sexual intercourse with his wife and infected her, the court held that consent to sexual intercourse was a defence to a charge of assault. The Court of Appeal recently overruled *Clarence* on that point in *R v Dica* [2004] 3 All ER 593, but did find that consent to the risk of contracting a sexual disease was a defence to charges of inflicting grievous bodily harm. In other words, consent to sexual intercourse is not enough: there must be consent to the risk of disease. The Court thought it undesirable that the criminal law should interfere in 'private and essentially personal relationships', illustrating the point by reference only to heterosexual couples. *Brown* was distinguished on the basis that in that case, the harm was deliberate rather than reckless.

4. Activities between couples involving deliberate injury have caused the courts some difficulty. We have seen that in *Brown*, the House of Lords rejected consent as a defence where injuries were inflicted in the course of sadomasochistic sexual activity. In that case, all the participants were gay men. However, a rather different approach was taken in the case of *R v Wilson* [1997] QB 47 where a man branded his initials onto his wife's buttocks, using a hot knife. The Court of Appeal accepted her consent as a defence. The Court treated this as a matter of personal adornment which the woman wanted, and which was assumed to be no more painful or dangerous than tattooing. They accordingly held the consent to be valid on that basis. However, they also suggested that as a general principle, the heterosexuality of the participants was relevant:

> 'Consensual activity between husband and wife, in the privacy of the matrimonial home, is not, in our judgment, normally a proper matter for criminal investigation, let alone criminal prosecution.'

Only in *R v Emmett* (1999) The Times 15 October several years later was the approach in *Wilson* rejected. There, the defendant had asphyxiated his fiancée on one occasion, causing subconjunctival haemorrhages, and on another burned her breast using lighter fuel for their sexual pleasure. The Court of Appeal now declined to follow *Wilson*, instead holding that there was no reason in principle 'to draw any distinction between sadomasochistic activity on a heterosexual basis and that which is conducted in a homosexual context'.

Feminist perspectives

We could question how far consent to cosmetic surgery is in fact valid. This is not to say that women are passive victims of patriarchal ideologies, submitting to cosmetic surgery because they cannot make rational decisions for themselves. On the contrary, as Susan Bordo argues, many women who have cosmetic surgery are making a rational decision since they see that living up to feminine norms is important for their goals in life (cited in Jennifer Mather Saul, *Feminism: Issues and Arguments*, Oxford University Press (2003)).

Nonetheless, that rational decision is not a free choice. Instead, it is made in the context of a society that puts enormous pressure upon women to change their appearance in a wide range of ways, from wearing make-up and high heels, through to dieting and surgery. While women may see themselves as making an individual decision to achieve their personal ideals, in fact cosmetic surgery involves conformity to a specific, racist, ageist and anti-Semitic ideal of beauty, defined in relation to attractiveness to men. Thus women are not choosing freely how to appear: they are doing so in the context of a society that sees certain white, heterosexual women as ideals of beauty all women should aim to live up to. Women almost invariably have surgery which makes their features look more, not less, Western European; more, not less, appealing to men.

The result of the growth of cosmetic surgery is that patriarchal control over women's bodies is increased. First, there is direct dependence upon overwhelmingly male 'experts': most cosmetic surgeons are men. In consultations, they will suggest to their clients what would and would not be desirable alterations to those women's appearance. Their description of the risks and benefits of the procedure are likely to influence the woman's final decision whether or not to undergo the surgery.

Second, there is not just a possibility of changing one's body: there is growing pressure to do so. Women's normal bodies, in all their variety, are no longer seen as natural. Instead, they are reinterpreted as a series of problems. To take one example, Eugenia Kaw describes how many Asian women have surgery to make their eyes look more Western. These operations are carried out by doctors whose textbooks use descriptions such as 'absent or poorly defined superior palpebral fold'. Thus the language used is that of a problem, a lack (by comparison to a white norm), rather than a recognition of the huge variation in women's eye shapes.

Conclusion

Women may have cosmetic surgery for rational reasons, and be pleased with the results. Feminists would not argue that they are stupid, deceived or deserving of condemnation for doing so. What is problematic is a society which encourages or pressurises women to take these expensive, risky measures. While a very narrow range of facial and body shapes are presented as 'attractive', and women face judgment upon and criticism of their appearance (to an extent which men do not), we can query whether there is an autonomous choice in these circumstances. We can also question why the law is so ready to endorse cosmetic surgery, and to assume that there has been valid consent.

11

Employment

11.1 Why is this a feminist issue?

11.2 Equal pay

11.3 Pregnancy

11.4 Harassment in the workplace

11.5 Harassment outside the workplace

11.1 Why is this a feminist issue?

One source of female subordination is women's economic dependence upon men. When women are unable to earn enough to support themselves and their families, and when welfare provision is inadequate, they may be forced into dependence upon male partners or relatives.

There are various ways in which workplace discrimination can prevent women from achieving equality. One is to pay women less than men doing similar work. When women earn less than male partners, their independence is threatened indirectly as well as directly. Social norms and prejudices dictate that it should be the woman who stays at home to look after the children. These factors can be reinforced and obscured by women's lower earnings: if the mother of a child earns less than the father, it seems simple common sense that she should stay at home while he continues his paid employment.

Equal pay also has a symbolic function. How can women be paid less if they are viewed as being of equal value to men? In other words, women's lower pay is not just economically damaging to their interests: it is also a potent symbol of their subordinate, undervalued status in society.

Another form of discrimination against women is to fail to accommodate the needs of pregnant women. Both women's autonomy and society's interests require that women are able to have children if they so wish. However, they are not free to choose motherhood if the consequences include losing their job, losing career prospects or having the impossible task of combining full-time work with childcare.

Finally, a further difficulty encountered by women in the workplace takes the form of sexual harassment. Such conduct can affect a woman's employment, promotion, health and wellbeing. This chapter will consider each of these areas of discrimination in turn.

11.2 Equal pay

The current law

The basis of the comparison

We will begin by considering how women's pay compares to that of men. We have already seen that overall, women earn less than men. The law appears to forbid such discrimination, but we will see that it has a number of weaknesses. The first area of difficulty has been determining the best way to compare the pay of individual women to that of individual men. Women's pay can be compared to men's in two different ways.

1. Do women and men doing the same work receive the same wage for it?
2. Where men and women have been given different kinds of jobs to each other, does different work of the same value receive the same rate of pay?

The first approach is obvious, but rather unfair as women frequently do different kinds of work to men. Use of the second approach as well as the first is much fairer to women, since typically women have been kept in lower-paid occupations, with the more lucrative types of work going to men.

Originally only the first type of comparison was made by the law governing equal pay. The Equal Pay Act 1970 required a comparison between a woman and a man simultaneously employed by the same employer, doing the same or broadly similar work (unless the work had been the subject of a job evaluation exercise which rated it at the same value). Further, a defence of 'justification' allowed the employer to argue that the pay difference was justified by something other than the woman's sex. Women who did different jobs to men (such as sewing machinists, typists and others doing work which few or no men did) therefore could not benefit from the legislation (unless a job evaluation exercise had been carried out), even if equally or less-skilled men were being paid more by the same employer.

However, in 1972 Britain joined the European Economic Community and signed up to its founding treaty, the Treaty of Rome (now the EC Treaty). Article 119 (now art 141 EC) required Member States to legislate to provide women with equal pay. There was uncertainty as to whether the first approach, comparing men and women doing the same work, was sufficient. The matter was clarified by the Equal Pay Directive 1975, which required equal pay for work of equal value. In other words, what mattered was the value of the work done, not whether it was exactly the same job. This point has now been incorporated into art 141 EC, which states:

> '1. Each Member State shall ensure that the principle of equal pay for male and female workers for equal work or work of equal value is applied.

2. For the purpose of this article, "pay" means the ordinary basic or minimum wage or salary and any other consideration, whether in cash or in kind, which the worker receives directly or indirectly, in respect of his employment, from his employer.'

With effect from 1999, the Treaty of Amsterdam made equality between men and women one of the tasks of the European Community, thus strengthening the EC's role in this area. Article 3 EC now states:

'In all the activities referred to in this article, the Community shall aim to eliminate inequalities, and to promote equality, between men and women.'

English law and European law therefore both now require that women receive equal pay for work of equal value. The comparison can be either to a man doing the same job, or to a man doing a different job which is of equal value to the employer.

Applying European law

Although European law required Member States to ensure that equal pay was received for work of equal value, few had fully enforced this principle. How could women enforce that right without going through the long and expensive process of applying to the European Court of Justice?

The case of *Defrenne v Sabena (No 2)* Case C–43/75 [1976] ECR 455 established that art 119 (now art 141 EC) had horizontal direct effect: that is, it gave individuals rights which they could enforce between each other, in their own national courts, even if their government had not brought in the relevant national legislation to protect those rights. Those rights could also be enforced against the government of the Member State that had failed to implement the appropriate national measures. The individual concerned could bring such an action before the European Court of Justice. Gabrielle Defrenne was a flight attendant for the Belgian airline Sabena. As a woman, she was paid less than male cabin crew. *Defrenne* not only ruled that this discrimination was unlawful, but also confirmed that this article of the Treaty was directly effective.

The Equal Pay Directive 1975, as a mere explanation of the article, is also horizontally directly effective (*Jenkins* v *Kingsgate (Clothing Productions) Ltd* Case C–96/80 [1981] ECR 911). Though the equal pay provisions had direct effect, it did not follow that Britain's failure to pass legislation applying the law did not matter. The European Commission brought proceedings against the United Kingdom in *European Court of Justice (Commission of the European Communities)* v *UK* Case C–165/82 [1984] ICR 192), as a result of which the Equal Pay Act 1970 was amended to create a right to equal pay for work of equal value.

European case law further expanded the right to equal pay in other ways. *Macarthys Ltd* v *Smith* Case C–129/79 [1980] ECR 1275 ruled that while there had to be an actual male comparator (rather than a hypothetical one), he need not work in the company at the same time as the claimant. In that case, the woman had replaced a male employee who had been paid £60 per week; she was only paid £50 per week. The European Court of Justice ruled that this was unlawful.

Garland v *British Rail* Case C–12/81 [1982] ECR 359 closed a significant loophole by interpreting 'pay' to include benefits, such as reduced rail fares for workers' families. British Rail had given this benefit to the families of male workers after retirement, while the families of female workers lost the benefit when they retired. The European Court of Justice held that the perk of reduced rail fares amounted to pay, with the result that there was a breach of art 119. The later case *Arbeiterwohlfahrt der Stadt Berlin* v *Botel* Case C–360/90 [1992] ECR I–3589 defined pay as 'all consideration, whether in cash or in kind, whether immediate or future, provided that the worker receives it … in respect of his employment'.

The right to equal pay also applies to pensions, provided that they are part of the worker's pay rather than state-provided social security. Thus in *Barber* v *Guardian Royal Exchange Assurance Group* Case C–262/88 [1990] ECR I–1889, a policy which entitled female employees to an immediate pension at the age of 50 while men had to wait until they were aged 55 was discriminatory. The ECJ confirmed that any pension wholly financed by the employer (and worker) but not the state will amount to 'pay'. However, the ruling did not apply retrospectively.

The expansion of the definition of 'pay' to include other benefits and pensions was significant. *Jenkins* v *Kingsgate (Clothing Productions) Ltd* Case C–96/80 [1981] ECR 911 was also important, confirming that different rates for part-time and full-time workers were discriminatory if considerably less women than men performed the minimum number of hours to receive the full hourly rate, because women have more difficulty arranging to work the minimum number of hours. However, if the difference can be objectively justified on grounds other than sex, then that difference will not be discriminatory. Since the majority of women who work part-time do so because of family commitments, different pay for mostly female part-time workers will usually be discriminatory where most full-time workers are male. This ruling was therefore a very important one in improving women's rights to equal pay.

Limitations on the right to equal pay

Unfortunately, there are also important limitations to the right to equal pay. For example, *Angestelltenbetriebsrat der Weiner Gebeitskrankenkasse* v *Weiner Gebeitskrankenkasse* Case C–309/97 [1999] ECR I–2865 held that (mostly female) graduate psychologists who worked as psychotherapists could be paid less than (mostly male) medical doctors doing the same work. The difference was held to reflect the higher qualifications of the doctors. In other words, if an employer can find a good reason for paying female workers less than their male colleagues (provided that the reason is not that they are women), the courts will allow the different rates of pay.

There are also difficulties for claimants who cannot find a direct comparator, as *Evesham* v *North Hertfordshire Health Authority* [2000] IRLR 257 highlighted. The claimant's male comparator was junior to her. She argued that as she had more years of service than him, she should be on a higher rate of pay. However, the Court of Appeal would not accept the comparison: they said that the Equal Pay Act 1970 requires equality of treatment, while she was asking for more favourable treatment than her comparator. The 1970 Act did not allow for this, it only enabled her to establish that she was entitled to the same pay. Such a narrow interpretation will make equal pay claims difficult for women who cannot find a comparator who is truly their equal (for example in length of service, qualifications or some other relevant factor).

Another difficulty arises where comparators have different employers, although they work at the same establishment. This situation is likely to arise frequently now that many services are contracted out by state employers (local councils, the NHS, etc). In one case where female workers had previously worked directly for a council as school cleaners and catering staff, but were then employed by private contractors to do the same jobs, they were not entitled to use men still employed directly by the council as comparators (*Lawrence* v *Regent Office Care Ltd* [2002] IRLR 822). Since different contractors are often used for different jobs (one contractor for cleaning, another for security, yet another for running the canteen, and so on), it will now be difficult – if not impossible – for many female employees in low-paid work to find a comparator.

History

Women's pay was lower than men's throughout the nineteenth and twentieth centuries, and is still lower than men's today. It was not until 1970 that the law prevented women being paid less than men on the basis of their sex. In the nineteenth century, the dominant political approach was to avoid interference in the labour market. The government was not prepared to set minimum wages or other regulations governing how much employers paid their employees. Additionally, most of those involved in making legislation saw nothing wrong with women being paid less than men.

Sandra Fredman suggests a number of reasons why people accepted women's lower pay (*Women and the Law*, Oxford University Press (1997)).

1. Women were seen as worse workers than men.
2. Women worked in different jobs and those jobs were seen as less valuable.
3. Men were assumed to need a 'family wage' while women worked for 'pin money'. In reality, of course, many families were dependent upon the woman's wage as well as (or instead of) the man's, and many families had no male wage-earner at all.
4. Women had less bargaining power. Many women were homeworkers, who didn't meet their fellow workers, making it very hard for them to organise unions or pay campaigns. A lot of trade unions did not allow women to become members.
5. Some women trade unionists worried that equal pay would make women employees too expensive, increasing female unemployment.

The courts actively supported different pay rates for men and women. In *Roberts* v

Hopwood [1925] AC 578, the House of Lords described Poplar Borough Council's decision to pay their lowest-grade male and female workers at the same rates as motivated by 'eccentric principles of socialistic philanthropy, or by a feminist ambition to secure the equality of the sexes in the matter of wages in the world of labour'. It was held to be unreasonable to fix the same minimum wage for women as for men, without regard to 'the nature of the work to be done by the women, or their fitness for it'.

There were campaigns for equal pay. Trade unions often supported these because they saw equal pay as also being in men's interests: if women and men were paid the same rate for a job, employers could not use women to undercut men's wages. It was for this reason that the Trade Union Congress passed a resolution supporting equal pay in 1888. However, little progress towards equal pay was made. In particular, the main political parties of that time did not believe that it was the role of the government to interfere in the market, certainly not by introducing legislation which dictated what wages employers should pay their employees. Until the government accepted that it was entitled to interfere in the setting of wages, equal pay legislation could not be enacted.

Progress was made first with the Trade Boards Act 1909. This was a response to concerns about low pay, particularly for 'sweated labour' (where workers endured long hours and poor conditions in factories and workshops in return for very low wages). This humanitarian concern combined with the belief that low pay was a real problem for society as a whole, not just individual workers. It was argued that it discouraged progress since low wages meant that employees had little incentive to improve themselves and their work.

The Trade Boards Act 1909 created boards to control wages in certain occupations. Each board contained employers, trade union representatives and independent members. Women were involved in the boards, and where the workers covered by a board were mostly female, it was a requirement that a female independent member be involved on the board. However, the 1909 Act applied only to a small number of industries (just wholesale tailoring, box-making, machine lace-making and chain-making initially, although by the 1950s this had increased to 66 industries) and so the majority of workers were not affected. There were only a few inspectors to enforce the law, and wages were still set at quite low levels. Crucially, the 1909 Act actually made equal pay less likely, because the boards generally set women's wages at a much lower rate than men's.

During the First World War, equal pay became a reality – but only briefly. Men who went to fight insisted that women taking over their jobs should be paid the same wages as they had been. They were worried that otherwise, women would under-price them and they would be paid less – or even be unemployed – after the war. The government enacted the Treasury Agreement 1915 in March of that year, giving women equal pay. However, this was a temporary measure: when the war ended, women were returned to low-paid and traditionally female occupations, or left paid employment altogether.

The Second World War brought more progress. The issue was not originally one of pay, but of compensation paid to civilians injured by enemy action. This compensation was paid at a lower rate to women. Following campaigning by the feminist Equal Compensation Campaign Committee, the government equalised the rates for women and men in 1943. This rejection of different rates for women and men led to further campaigning on equal pay, which almost succeeded for women teachers. The Education Bill 1944 contained an equal pay amendment for teachers which was initially passed. However, the government, led by Winston Churchill, required a second vote, which it treated as a vote of confidence in the government. As a result, the amendment was defeated. Instead, a Royal Commission on equal pay was established but it did not have the power to make recommendations.

After the war there were a number of significant developments. First, both major parties accepted the principle of equal pay. However, they were happy to implement it very slowly. It was only in 1955 that the Conservative government said they would introduce equal pay in the public services, but this process would not be completed until 1961.

Second, there was increasing international pressure and progress on equal pay. The International Labour Organisation created a Convention (No 100 of 1951) which required equal pay for work of equal value, but Britain refused to ratify it. It was with Britain's entry to the European Economic Community in 1972, which required Member States to ensure 'equal pay for equal work', where real progress was made. This principle of equality had been incorporated into what was then a primarily economic organisation because France had such a principle in its domestic law, and had feared that it would be at a competitive disadvantage if the principle were not also part of Community law (Malcolm Sargeant (ed), *Discrimination Law*, Pearson Longman (2004)).

Third, feminists and trade unionists actively campaigned for equal pay. In 1968 there were a number of strikes organised by female workers for equal pay, beginning with the Ford sewing machinists in Dagenham. Women sewing machinists making car seat covers were put on a lower grade than men doing less skilled work. They went on strike in protest, and were joined by workers at other Ford plants in Britain. The strike gathered enormous publicity and support, and the Employment Secretary, Barbara Castle, invited the women leading the strike to tea at Whitehall. The outcome was the passing of the Equal Pay Act 1970.

The culmination of all these factors was the creation of a legal right to equal pay in the Equal Pay Act 1970 (which came into effect in 1975). This 1970 Act required equal pay for men and women doing the same work. We have seen how this principle has continued to develop (largely as a result of EC law), particularly through the concept of 'equal pay for work of equal value'.

Feminist perspectives

The law regulating equal pay has been important in remedying the most glaring injustices, such as different pay scales for men and women doing the same job. However, their effect has been limited in practice: women still earn less than men in general, not only when considering the employment market as a whole but also when looking at individual professions.

There are many reasons why women have not yet achieved equal pay. One important factor is job segregation. While some jobs are commonly done by both men and women, others involve employees who are overwhelmingly of one sex. Consider these occupations: a lorry driver, a bricklayer and being the chairman of a multinational company (all overwhelmingly male occupations – to use one example, in 1991, 90 per cent of construction workers were male: Sandra Fredman, *Women and the Law*, Oxford University Press (1997)). Now consider these occupations: a dinner lady (try to think of an equivalent male term in everyday use), a home help and a secretary (all overwhelmingly female occupations – for example, 96.6 per cent of secretarial workers were women in 1991: *Women and the Law*).

Now compare typical wages for each of these jobs. The predominantly male jobs tend to be higher paid than those usually undertaken by women, with ethnic minority women concentrated in the lowest grades of female occupations. It is easy to assume that women's work is less skilled than that of men, but jobs such as typing, factory work and domestic labour often require complex skills. However, the courts are not interested in improving women's pay generally: the law's aim is 'to eliminate sex discrimination in pay not achieve fair wages' (*Strathclyde Regional Council* v *Wallace* [1998] IRLR 146).

Another reason for women's lower pay is their concentration in part-time work, which is typically less valued and less likely to lead to promotion. In 2002, the Equal Opportunities Commission reported that just over five million women worked part-time, compared to 1,125,000 men. Over half of these women were in part-time work for family or domestic reasons, compared to just one in 20 men.

Women also face a very practical difficulty in attempting to implement the law: they may not know what their colleagues earn. Many employers do not have clear pay structures, and they may encourage a climate of secrecy concerning individual salaries. While recognised trade unions can secure information about pay rates, many women are not members of unions or are employed in workplaces without a recognised union. The Employment Act 2002 has improved the position by introducing a questionnaire procedure, allowing the claimant to request relevant information from their employer. However, employers are under no legal duty to answer the questions: the only remedy where an employer provides either no answers, or unhelpful answers, is for an employment tribunal to draw inferences (Malcolm Sargeant (ed), *Discrimination Law*, Pearson Longman (2004)).

As important as equal pay for work of equal value is in the employment sphere, there are other forms of work that should be considered. Many women do a lot more work than they are paid for. Housework, childcare, cooking, looking after relatives, volunteering at the local playgroup or school, all of these have enormous social value. However, this extra work – women's 'domestic' labour – is economically invisible. Thus many women do not do equal work for equal pay, even if they receive the same wages as male colleagues: the law ensures only equal paid work receives equal pay.

The effect of this devaluation of women's domestic work is not only the obvious one, that many hours of labour are worked without economic reward. A woman's unpaid responsibilities will often impact negatively upon her earning capacity. Caring responsibilities may mean that she has to work part-time, drastically cutting her earnings, or cannot undertake overtime work at short notice as her male colleagues can. More subtly, the need to be home in time to do the housework, cook dinner, collect the children from school or provide care for an elderly relative may mean that she cannot complete the extra training needed to earn promotion. Thus she remains on a lower, worse grade not because of her abilities (or lack of them), but because of her responsibilities. At the same time, because this domestic work is typically done freely, paid work involving the same tasks (think of cleaners, cooks, care assistants) is less valued. Most of the employees doing such work tend to be women.

Finally, gender does not operate in isolation from other issues, yet the law on sex discrimination does tend to do so. Thus the comparisons are simply between female and male employees: there is little scope for analysing the intersections between race and gender, for example, in relation to ethnic minority women's wages. Sandra Fredman points out that the gap between men's and women's wages is narrower for ethnic minority workers, and 'the greater the disadvantage based on race, the smaller is the gender gap' (Sandra Freeman, *Women and the Law,* Oxford University Press (1997)).

The existing law aims to provide formal equality: women and men doing paid work of equal value should receive equal pay. However, it does not address the subtler inequalities caused by the way women's domestic responsibilities undermine their earning power. Thus women have not achieved substantive equality in this area of law.

11.3 Pregnancy

Introduction

Only women can become pregnant. The foetus grows inside the woman's womb and she must give birth, an event that varies for all women in length, duration, pain and after effects. It is an event that has been used to stigmatise and discriminate against women in the workplace. Pregnancy has been a central issue to feminist debate.

On the one hand, women have striven for employers and the government to recognise the particular problems that women have in the workplace because of their biological (women are at present the only sex able to bear children) and social (child rearing/nurturing) roles. On the other hand, women have fought to be viewed not just as mothers with the negative stereotype that has been attached to motherhood (that women are hormonal and only useful for child-bearing). This is a difficult debate. Child-bearing has been devalued in our society because it is difficult for women to strike a balance between child nurture and work. Employment is the giver of status in our society. Paid work is valued in our society, yet staying at home to bring up children is not. What is required is a revaluation of pregnancy and child rearing by providing equal rights for both parents once the child is born, thus emphasising that as a society we value children, but also recognise that their upbringing is not just a role for women alone.

The current law

The law has recently been altered by the Employment Act (EA) 2002. It has attempted to reflect the image of the government in 2002 as 'family friendly'. However, as we shall see, the legislation's 'family friendliness' is limited and inconsistent.

Time off for antenatal care
Under ss55–56 Employment Rights Act (ERA) 1996 a pregnant employee has the right to take time off for antenatal care during working hours and is entitled to be paid for that time off.

Right not to be subjected to any detriment
Under s47(c)(1) and (2) ERA 1996 (as amended by s53 EA 2002), an employee has the right not to be subjected to any detriment by her employer if that detriment relates to pregnancy, childbirth or maternity.

Maternity leave
Entitlements to maternity leave apply to employees (people working under a contract of employment). Employees are potentially entitled to three types of maternity leave.

1. Compulsory Maternity Leave (CML): a woman may not return to work within the two weeks following the birth of her child. It is an offence for an employer to allow her to work at this time (s72 ERA 1996).
2. Ordinary Maternity Leave: under the Maternity and Paternity Leave (Amendment) Regulations 2002 women are now entitled to 26 weeks of ordinary maternity leave. This is available to all women from the first day of their employment, and can start any time between 11 weeks before the expected date of birth and the actual birth. During this period, most women will be entitled to statutory maternity pay or maternity allowance (currently £100 per week). Some employment contracts will provide higher benefits (eg full pay).
3. Additional Maternity Leave: this is only available to a woman who:
   a) is entitled to Ordinary Maternity Leave; and
   b) has been continuously employed by her current employer for at least 26 weeks by the fourteenth week before the expected week of birth.

Paternity leave

Section 1 EA 2002 amends the ERA 1996 by inserting s80A. This section gives fathers a right to paternity leave in order to care for the child or to support the mother. Section 80A(3) ERA 1996 provides that fathers have a statutory right to two weeks' paid leave if they are working. Fathers have the right to take this paternity leave only after the child is born but 'before the end of a period of at least 56 days beginning with the date of the child's birth' (s80A(4)). However, they only have the right if they have worked for 26 weeks continuously, ending with the fifteenth week before the baby is due. During the leave, the father is entitled to statutory paternity pay (currently £100 a week).

Who is a father? The Paternity and Adoption Leave Regulations 2002 provide that a man is entitled to paternity rights if he expects to have responsibility for the upbringing of the child and is:

1. the biological father; or
2. a person married to the mother or to the adopter; or
3. a person who is the partner of the mother or a partner to the adopter; and
4. is in an enduring relationship: what this means is not yet clear, but it does include lesbian and gay partners.

Parental leave

Traditionally, English law has concentrated upon pregnancy as the critical point where the interests of employers must cede to the needs of parents. The result has been to disregard both the realities of parenting and to limit the recognition of (or indeed, possibility for) men's active parenting role. However, such an approach is neither inevitable nor universal. There are two recent measures that have granted rights to the parents of young children after the end of maternity leave: parental leave and flexible working. Unfortunately, both of these measures are subject to notable limitations which severely limit their practical effect.

The European Community's Directive on the Framework Agreement on Parental Leave reflected the existing rights of parents in many Member States. However, the concept of parental leave (except for maternity leave) was new to English law. It was brought into effect by the Maternity and Parental Leave Regulations 1999, which have since been amended by the Maternity and Parental Leave (Amendment) Regulations 2001 and the Maternity and Parental Leave (Amendment) Regulations 2002.

The new rights created only apply to employees who have completed at least one year's continuous employment, and the leave is unpaid. A total of 13 weeks' leave (but no more than four weeks per year) can be taken before the child's fifth birthday. The employer has considerable discretion to specify when the leave can be taken, to avoid undue disruption. This package of rights has been described as 'the most minimal possible' to comply with the European Directive (Erica Neustadt in Malcolm Sargeant (ed), *Discrimination Law*, Pearson Longman (2004)).

Flexible working

The lack of suitable, affordable childcare during working hours, and the desire to spend time with their children, mean that many women do not wish or feel able to continue working full-time after having a child. Flexible working provisions aim to enable women (and men) with young children to continue with their jobs while fulfilling these caring responsibilities. While the provisions apply to both women and men, in practice most parents seeking to take advantage of them are likely to be women. This reflects the lower status and pay of women's employment, and the most usual allocation of caring responsibilities within families.

Section 80F ERA 1996 (as amended by the EA 2002) allows an employee to make an application to their employer for changes in their terms and conditions of employment if these are needed to enable them to care for a child (the child must be either under the age of six, or, if disabled, under the age of 18). The employee must have 26 weeks' continuous employment, and agency workers are excluded. Typical changes might include time working at home or different hours of work.

Section 80G ERA 1996 states that an employer can refuse to grant such a change in terms and conditions if:

1. as a result of that change they would incur additional costs; and/or
2. the change would be detrimental to customer demand; and/or
3. they are unable to reorganise work among existing staff; and/or
4. the changes would have a detrimental impact on quality; and/or
5. they are unable to recruit additional staff; and/or
6. the change would have a detrimental impact on performance; and/or
7. there is insufficient work during the periods the employee proposes to work.

Should the request be refused, there are provisions relating to appeals and tribunal complaints. Regardless of the outcome of the request, the employee must not be subjected to any detriment as a result of making it.

Time off for dependants

Under s57A ERA 1996, an employee upon whom a dependant relies is entitled to take time off work:

1. if the dependant falls ill, gives birth or is injured or assaulted; or
2. to make arrangements for the care of a dependant; or
3. because of the death of a dependant; or
4. because of an unexpected disruption or termination of arrangements for the care of a dependant.

Section 57A(3) defines dependant as:

1. a spouse;
2. a child;
3. a parent; and

4. a person living in the same house as the employee (not an employee, tenant, lodger or border).

A dependant can also, under s57A(4) ERA 1996, include a person who reasonably relies on the employee in relation to illness or injury. The employee must inform the employer as soon as reasonably practicable, and is then allowed reasonable unpaid leave.

History

Employment is generally considered to be within the public sphere, while child-bearing and child rearing take place within the private sphere. The law has historically supported this division, accepting the belief that child-bearing was impossible to reconcile with the workplace. For working class women in particular, child rearing was assumed to be a matter for the woman and was of no concern to the employer (a view which, to a large extent, continues today, despite some overlapping of the public and private spheres through the provisions for flexible working and parental leave).

Section 17 Factory and Workshop Act 1891 stated that no employer could employ a woman who had, within four weeks, given birth to a child. Such a provision might appear to have given valuable protection to pregnant women. However, it should not be confused with maternity leave: there was no right for the woman to return to work, nor was there any provision for maternity pay. Thus child-bearing women were relegated firmly to the private sphere, with no guarantee that they could return to the public sphere at any future date.

The National Insurance Act 1946 provided a maternity grant for non-medical expenses, provided the woman didn't take any paid work during the period of the maternity payment. Again the law created a division between public employment and private child-bearing, with disincentives for attempting to combine the two. While the Employment Rights Act 1966 began to improve matters by giving rights to pregnant women, it also provided the employer with many exceptions and imposed a qualification period upon the worker of two years' employment.

Matters became more complicated when the Sex Discrimination Act (SDA) 1975 made it unlawful to treat a woman less favourably than a man on the ground of her sex. Under s1(1)(a) SDA 1975 it is unlawful for an employer to treat a woman differently on the ground of her sex. The notion of 'different' treatment requires comparison with a man. Who then should the male comparator be?

In pregnancy no (male) comparator can be found – obviously. Therefore discrimination on grounds of pregnancy appeared to be legal, a view articulated in *Turley* v *Allders Stores Ltd* [1980] ICR 66. In the now infamous words of Bristow J:

'In order to see if she has been treated less favourably than a man in the sense of the section you must compare like with like, and you can not. When she is pregnant she is no longer just a woman. She is a woman ... with child and there is no masculine equivalent.'

The search for a direct comparison with a man in the same situation could only ever be fruitless. Thus the law took a different approach: it looked instead at the woman's ability to work. Since pregnancy required women to take time off work, a comparison was made with a sick man. In *Hayes* v *Malleable Men's Working Club and Institute* [1985] ICR 703 a woman was dismissed after telling her employers that she was pregnant. She brought a case under the SDA 1975. Waite J commented that 'if you dismiss a woman on the ground of her pregnancy, no one can say that you have treated her less favourably than you would a man, because nature has ensured that no man could ever be dismissed upon the same ground'. However, he suggested it was not the pregnancy that she was being dismissed for, but rather the consequences of her pregnancy (the necessity for time off work). The appropriate comparison was therefore with a man who needed to take time off in analogous circumstances, eg a sick man. If the sick man was treated more favourably than the pregnant woman, there would be sex discrimination. Conversely, if he would have been treated no better, then the pregnant woman was left without legal recourse for the loss of her job.

This comparison of the pregnant woman to a sick man was approved by *Webb* v *EMO Air Cargo (UK) Ltd* [1992] 2 All ER 43 (CA); [1992] 4 All ER 929 (HL). A woman was employed to cover another woman's maternity leave, but shortly after starting the job found that she herself was pregnant. She would therefore need to take maternity leave at the same time as the woman whose job she had been employed to cover. When she told her employers, they dismissed her. The Court of Appeal and the House of Lords held that she was not dismissed because of her sex, but because she wasn't available for work at the right time: a sick man in the same position would have been treated in the same way. The European Court of Justice, however, disagreed with this argument. They held that the reason that she would not be able to work on the dates required was because of her pregnancy: that pregnancy was therefore the real reason for her dismissal. The comparison with a man medically incapable of working was rejected.

The result in that particular case may seem difficult to justify: the employee had been employed specifically to cover another woman's maternity leave, after all. (Note, though, that the ECJ did make specific reference to the fact that her employment contract was indefinite: the company had intended to continue employing her beyond the period of maternity cover.) However, the principle is a vital one if women are to receive fair treatment. Pregnancy is not an illness, nor should it be compared to one. Only if it is accepted as a natural and healthy condition can pregnancy be viewed as compatible with continuing employment, thus securing women's legal right not to be discriminated against.

The shift from comparing pregnancy to illness, to treating pregnancy as a separate condition, is an ideologically significant one. The law has moved to creating specific rights rather than simply enforcing equal treatment. The fact that such a move has been necessary is a potent example of the limits of formal equality: laws that set out a single rule for women and men can have a very different practical impact upon women than upon men, particularly in relation to child-bearing. Only in those instances where the need for different treatment was recognised could a truly fair result be obtained.

It is important to be aware that this new approach was pioneered not by the English courts but by the European Court of Justice, which first established that discrimination on the grounds of pregnancy was linked to gender (because only women could become pregnant) and therefore breached the Equal Treatment Directive which required 'the protection of women, particularly as concerns pregnancy and maternity'. In *Dekker* v *Stichting Vormingscentrum voor Jonge Volwassenen Plus* Case C–177/88 [1990] ECR I–3941, an employer refused to employ a pregnant woman as its insurance company would not reimburse the maternity payments: therefore it could not afford to employ maternity cover. Since there were no male candidates for the job, there was no male comparator available. The ECJ held that only women could be refused employment on the grounds of pregnancy and therefore it was direct discrimination on the grounds of sex, in contravention of the Equal Treatment Directive. They did not compare her to a sick man because pregnancy is unique to women. A general principle was articulated:

> '… whether the refusal to recruit a woman constitutes direct or indirect discrimination depends on the reason for that refusal. If that reason is to be found in the fact that the person concerned is pregnant, then the decision is directly linked to the sex of the candidate.'

The EC Pregnancy Directive 92/85/EEC set out rights for workers who are pregnant, breast-feeding or have recently given birth. Member States must provide maternity leave and protect against dismissal during such leave. However, the emphasis of the Directive is upon ensuring health and safety at work, rather than preventing discrimination (Penny English in Malcolm Sergeant (ed), *Discrimination Law*, Pearson Longman (2004)).

It is worthy of note that if a woman is part of a redundancy scheme operating within her workplace or has been guilty of some gross misconduct (as in *Shomer* v *B & R Residential Lettings Ltd* [1992] IRLR 317, where the dismissal of a pregnant woman for allegedly serious misconduct was upheld), there can be no sex discrimination of the woman on the ground that her dismissal/redundancy does not relate to her pregnancy. This approach has been used in the English courts to find that an applicant has not been dismissed because of her pregnancy, but rather because of another cause. However, such allegations can be a mere screen for dismissing because of pregnancy, as Ms Shomer alleged in her case.

Why is this a feminist issue?

It is obvious why pregnancy is a feminist issue: quite simply, it is something which fundamentally affects women since they alone become pregnant. However, the interest and importance of this topic goes far beyond that biological fact. Pregnancy and employment also raise the difficult question of whether women should be seeking equality or special treatment from the law.

Feminists are very wary of special treatment. In the past, arguments based upon difference were used as a method of excluding women from the public sphere. However, formal equality has a crucial weakness, as it is based upon treating women as equal to men. Thus a dilemma exists: rely upon equality, and an experience unique to women is inadequately addressed. Rely upon the differences, and risk reinforcing the myths and stereotypes surrounding motherhood – and thereby risk excluding women from the public sphere.

Perhaps the real issue is that pregnancy should not be seen purely as a problem. While it challenges our thinking, it also forces the law and society to face up to the fact that traditional divisions of labour are not as hard and fast as we assume. If the public and private spheres were truly separate, then the issue of pregnancy would never intrude into the workplace. The fact that it does serves to emphasise how women's and men's lives bridge both spheres. Men potentially have as valuable a role to play in the private sphere as women do in the public sphere.

Lucinda M Finlay comments that the confinement of child rearing to the private sphere has been a mechanism for subordinating women, because nurturing has been devalued and assigned to women without comment. This has not only been the largest impediment to women's participation in the workplace; it has denied men the opportunity of proper participation in the home, since most employers expect employees to work to a rigid work pattern that does not fit in with most employee's lives. Such a work pattern, however, can be, and perhaps ought to be, challenged: 'there is nothing inevitable or natural about this' ('Transcending Equality Theory: a Way Out of the Maternity and then Workplace Debate' (1986) 86 Columbia L Rev 1118).

The issue of pregnancy and employment law therefore raises further questions concerning the very way we work. It also forces us to analyse society's attitudes towards motherhood: in deciding what rights pregnant women and mothers have, we are deciding who should bear the cost of child-bearing and child rearing. If women have little protection, then they bear those costs; the more rights they have, the more the costs are borne by employers or the state.

Vitally, a reallocation of rights to both women and men allows for those costs to be shared by men. The further extension of these rights to people other than the legal parents offers an even more fundamental change: an opportunity to define the family as wider and more flexible than the patriarchal model of the heterosexual nuclear family unit.

Unfortunately, despite important changes in recent years, the law in this area takes a confused and contradictory approach to parenting. The length of maternity leave compared with the very short period of paternity leave actually reinforces, rather than challenges, the existing social expectation that women will bear primary responsibility for childcare. A wider view is taken in relation to parental leave, but still only people with parental responsibility (in the legal sense) are entitled to it; yet wider – and thus better – definitions are used for flexible working and time off for dependants.

There is some evidence of positive change. However, the progress made to date is uneven. Further, the emphasis upon parenting and childcare as the only ground for such leave ignores important realities such as the caring responsibilities of women (and men) in relation to other relatives and friends. Generous provision for parents is always liable to be resented both by employers and by childless employees who have no similar benefits. It reinforces notions of childcare as somehow natural and desirable for women in a way that other valuable activities are not. A better answer may, then, be to move away from the equal versus special treatment dilemma of pregnancy, and instead seek more flexible working practices (including paid sabbaticals, flexible hours and so on) for all workers.

11.4 Harassment in the workplace

Introduction

We will end this chapter by seeking to highlight the connection between workplace discrimination and the subordination of women in other areas of their lives. In other words, we reject the division of our lives into public and private spheres, and suggest that many of the issues are not discrete, confined to one or the other. The particular area we focus on is harassment. Sexual harassment in the workplace tends to be conceptualised as completely separate to harassment in the private sphere (frequently termed 'stalking'). The law thus has different provisions for the two scenarios, as we shall see. However, we suggest that the two are not as different as this legal approach would appear to indicate. In considering harassment, then, bear in mind the question: how far does women's subordination in the workplace differ from their subordination in the home and family?

Most women have experienced some form of harassment. Whether it is being harangued in the street or harassed in the workplace, it is a common shared experience amongst women. However, harassment is only a relatively recent legal concept. Sexual harassment was brought into the public conciousness by Catherine MacKinnon's book: *Sexual Harassment of Working Women*, Yale University Press (1979). She argues that all harassment is about power. It can have a devastating effect on those who suffer it, ranging from health problems to loss of a career. It must not be tolerated either by the law or by society.

Current law

The law governing sexual harassment at work can be found in the SDA 1975. We have already seen that s1 defines discrimination as less favourable treatment on the ground of sex. Thus, to be successful in a claim for sexual harassment the applicant must show that:

1. they have been harassed; and
2. that the harassment was done on the ground of their sex.

The landmark ruling on this issue was *Strathclyde Regional Council* v *Porcelli* [1986] IRLR 135. For the first time it was held that sexual harassment was less favourable treatment and therefore amounted to sex discrimination. A school laboratory technician had been subjected to sexual harassment by her male colleagues, who wanted her to leave. They made suggestive remarks to her and often brushed up against her. Their defence was that they would have been equally unpleasant to a male colleague. This was accepted by the Industrial Tribunal, but rejected by the Employment Appeal Tribunal who said that part of the campaign was plainly adopted because she was a woman, and it was used as a weapon which could not have been used against a man.

This case raises an important point concerning sexual harassment. It frequently arises not from the harasser's sexual attraction to a woman, but from a desire to subordinate her (in this case, by forcing her out of her job). In other words, *Porcelli* illustrates MacKinnon's argument that sexual harassment is about power.

Definition

The SDA 1975 provides no legal definition of sexual harassment, but European law does in s2(2) Equal Treatment Amendment Directive (2002/73/EC): harassment occurs where, on grounds of sex, A engages in unwanted conduct which has the purpose or effect of either:

1. violating B's dignity; or
2. creating an intimidating, hostile, degrading, humiliating or offensive environment for B.

History

Since *Porcelli*, a number of cases have followed clarifying specific issues raised by the principle that sexual harassment is a form of sexual discrimination.

One incident is enough

While, as we will see below, outside the workplace harassment is required to involve a course of conduct, this is not true for employment claims. According to *Bracebridge Engineering* v *Darby* [1990] IRLR 3 and *Insitu Cleaning Co Ltd* v *Heads* [1995] IRLR 4, one incident is sufficient for a claim of sexual harassment to succeed.

Applicant's attitude towards sex

In *Snowball* v *Gardner Merchant Ltd* [1987] IRLR 397 a woman claimed that she had been harassed by her district manager. He had requested sex, sent her sexual material and pestered her by phone. The Employment Appeal Tribunal held that cross-examination about her sexual attitudes (on the basis that she apparently had black satin sheets and had referred to her bed as a 'playpen') was permissible to show how upset she was by this behaviour. This decision brings to employment tribunals some of the problems inherent in the rape trial, in particular the change of focus onto the victim's behaviour rather than that of their harasser.

Applicant's dress and behaviour

A similar approach has been taken in relation to women's non-sexual behaviour. In *Wileman* v *Minilec Engineering Ltd* [1988] IRLR 144, Employment Appeal Tribunal, a director of a firm made salacious remarks to the applicant and physically harassed her. The Employment Appeal Tribunal held that the test to be applied is a subjective test, eg not what the reasonable person would have found offensive, but rather what that particular individual would have found offensive. In this case her damages were limited to a token £50 because the tribunal held that she wore provocative clothes and flaunted herself.

Offensive pictures

Stewart v *Cleveland Guest (Engineering) Ltd* [1994] IRLR 440 held that a woman was not discriminated against where her colleagues displayed nude pin-ups that she found offensive. The Employment Appeal Tribunal held that a man might have found the pictures as offensive as the applicant did, and would not have been treated more favourably in the same circumstances. Mummery J did state that this case was not setting a precedent that pictures of this kind would never amount to sexual harassment. Nonetheless, it has been heavily criticised for its failure to understand the reality that women may experience pornography in the workplace very differently from men.

Offensive comments

In *Insitu Cleaning Co Ltd* v *Heads* [1995] IRLR 4, the woman applicant's manager (and son of the two directors of the company) greeted her with 'Hiya, big tits'. This was a sexual comment made to a woman nearly twice his age and was quite clearly meant to be offensive. It was found to constitute sexual harassment.

Must be 'behaviour' not atmosphere

In *British Telecommunications plc* v *Williams* [1997] IRLR 668 the case involved a woman who had attended her manager's office to be appraised. She maintained that during the appraisal he was sexually aroused, arranged the room in such a way as to ensure close proximity with her and made the meeting last for a long time. The tribunal rejected the allegations that he was aroused and had stared at her, but held that he had conducted the interview in a sexually intimidating manner, and so there had been sex discrimination. The Employment Appeal Tribunal allowed the company's appeal, arguing that no company was expected to have female chaperones to meetings or for female staff to have female managers. Once the tribunal had accepted that the manager was not sexually aroused, they had rejected the basis of the allegation since the issue was whether he was behaving inappropriately towards the applicant for sexual reasons. As with *Stewart* v *Cleveland Guest*, they took a narrow view of sexual harassment which failed to take account either of the woman's experience of such behaviour or of MacKinnon's insight that sexual harassment is about power rather than sexual desire.

Why is this a feminist issue?

As a result of the fact that harassment concerns power (and it's abuse), even if the harasser is not the woman's boss that harassment still affects the relative power positions of the women and men in the workplace. Often the aim of such harassment is to intimidate the woman, as in *Porcelli*. More senior managers are often implicated through failing to take the harassment seriously or to take effective steps against the harasser. Ultimately, the harassed person may feel that they have to leave their employment.

Most harassment is carried out by men on women. Catherine MacKinnon has stated that this is power-based as there is still a gender hierarchy. Sexual harassment concerns women's continued subordination and exclusion from the workplace. It is degrading and perpetuates the myths and stereotypes that surround women.

Sandra Freeman (*Women and the Law*, Oxford University Press (1997)) argues that sexual harassment in the workplace strips away the woman's identity and reduces her to a sexual object. We have seen in this chapter that not only the process of harassment itself, but also the tribunal procedure which may follow, concentrates upon the woman's sexual behaviour. Courts and tribunals are still influenced by stereotypes of women as in the *Snowball* and *Wileman* cases, with the outcome depending upon the woman appearing chaste and modest: stereotypes which also feature in many rape trials.

11.5 Harassment outside the workplace

Introduction

Unfortunately, harassment is not confined to only to the public sphere of women's lives. Women are vulnerable to domestic violence and harassment as well as workplace harassment. The harm is gendered because it is differentially distributed – it affects more women than men – and because the subjective experience of that harm is different for women, due to social perceptions of gender (Joanne Conaghan, 'Tort Litigation in the Context of Intra-Familial Abuse' (1993) 61 MLR 132).

Women are vulnerable to harassment because they have traditionally been confined to the private sphere and reliant on men. Although women are now entering the public sphere, they remain vulnerable because they earn significantly less than men, especially if bearing or rearing children. Women are also vulnerable to male harassment since they are (for whatever reason: see Germaine Greer, *The Female Eunuch*, Flamingo (1993)) physically less strong and less aggressive than men. This section will examine the law that protects women from such harassment.

The Protection from Harassment Act (PfHA) 1997 provides the framework for cases involving violence and stalking. This 1997 Act contains public and private law remedies for adult victims of domestic violence or stalking.

Current law

Protection from Harassment Act 1997

Harassment covers situations from 'stalking' by a stranger to domestic violence. The 1997 Act is known as the 'stalking' legislation, although this word is never mentioned in the Act.

Harassment is not defined in the 1997 PfHA: it is merely described in s1(1) as 'a course of conduct' which must have happened, as a result of s7(3), on at least two occasions. The Act creates two criminal offences (noted in detail in Chapter 7):

1. harassment; and
2. harassment putting another in fear of violence.

The legislation and the civil law

In addition to creating these criminal offences, the PfHA 1997 creates a civil remedy. Section 3 provides:

> 'An actual or apprehended breach of s1 may be the subject of a claim in civil proceedings by the person who is or may the victim of the course of conduct in question.
>
> On such a claim, damages may be awarded for (among other things) any anxiety caused by the harassment and any financial loss resulting from the harassment.'

This creates a statutory tort of harassment. As Lord Hoffmann in *Hunter* v *Canary Wharf Ltd* [1997] 2 All ER 426 stated:

> '[A] tort of harassment has now received statutory recognition (see Protection from Harassment Act 1997). We are therefore no longer troubled by the question whether the common law should be developed to provide such a remedy.'

In deciding whether the tort has been committed, the court must consider what a reasonable person in possession of the same information as the alleged harasser would know to be harassment. Thus the emphasis is on how the harasser perceives the situation, not how the victim feels. The victim's perception is ignored. This has a gendered dimension as men and women differ in their response to, and interpretation of, sexually aggressive conduct (Joanne Conaghan and Wade Mansell, *The Wrongs of Tort*, 2nd ed, Pluto (1990)).

This objective test, taken from the harasser's perspective, is shared by the civil and criminal provisions of the Act, and is arguably more appropriate to the criminal law. The problem with having both civil and criminal causes in one Act is that the legislation has been designed only working on a criminal standard (Joanne Conaghan, 'Enhancing Civil Remedies for (Sexual) Harassment: s3 of the Protection from Harassment Act 1997' (1999) 7(2) *Feminist Legal Studies* 203).

Although damages only are mentioned, the court has jurisdiction to grant an injunction as part of civil proceedings. However, because the injunction is granted under this inherent jurisdiction rather than under a statutory power, there is no provision for a power of arrest to be attached. If the defendant does anything that is prohibited under the injunction, the victim may apply to the court for a warrant of arrest under s3(3) PfHA 1997. Breach of such an injunction will amount to a criminal offence under s3(6).

The PfHA 1997 is a very positive piece of legislation for women, the persons most affected by stalking and domestic violence. Unlike the Family Law Act 1996, it does not require women to have a specific relationship to the defendant. It covers a wide range of offences against women. Yet there is ambiguity within the Act as to what constitutes harassment, leaving a great deal of discretion to the courts.

Conclusion

We have seen in this chapter that there have been significant developments in recent decades giving women rights to equal pay, to maternity and parental leave and providing some protection from sexual harassment. However, we have also seen the important limitations of those rights and protections, which go some way to explaining the discrimination which still exists in the workplace.

Sexual harassment has proved particularly problematic since the courts have not recognised the exercise of gendered power relations involved. This blindness to the particular perspectives of women – the way the courts have instead shared the perspective of the harassing man – is reflected in general civil remedies for harassment too. Again, this shortcoming can be seen in other areas of the law, such as rape.

The courts have proved willing to withdraw the protection women have been given by the law if they can be cast as having invited it in some way (as in *Wileman*). It is therefore unsurprising that women are particularly unprotected if the harassing behaviour can be construed as consensual, despite imbalances of power. Neither the SDA 1975 nor the PfHA 1997 are likely to avail a complainant in those circumstances. There are two possible answers to this problem: professional regulation and remedies in tort law.

First, in some circumstances, there may be a remedy through a profession's disciplinary proceedings. Many (but by no means all) professions state that it is unethical to have a relationship with a client or patient. However, the approach to such misconduct is variable, even within professions: for example, we can contrast the cases of *Dare* v *General Medical Council* [2002] UKPC 54 and *Council for the Regulation of Healthcare Professionals (CRHC)* v *General Medical Council* [2004] EWHC 944. In *Dare*, the doctor was a consultant psychiatrist who provided counselling for depression to a woman, a senior registrar psychiatrist specialising in a similar area. She consulted him about three times every week for several years, until he kissed her during one session, telling her that this was acceptable and she should trust him. The sexual activity continued in other sessions, and he then went to her home and had sexual intercourse with her on one occasion, telling her that it would help her feelings towards men. She refused further sexual activity and went on to seek treatment for depression elsewhere. The General Medical Council (GMC) accepted that this was a 'serious breach of trust' and that although the risk of similar future behaviour was small, the public needed to be protected. They directed that the male doctor's name be erased from the register – he was no longer allowed to practice as a doctor.

By contrast, the Council for the Regulation of Healthcare Professionals (CRHC) case took a very different view of the appropriate penalty for sexual conduct with a patient in the other case. The High Court considered the issue of whether a three-month suspension was unduly lenient for serious professional misconduct relating to a relationship with a female patient as well as the falsification of a birth certificate and CV (to hide the doctor's true age). The facts of the relationship with the patient were limited, since the original hearing had not established how it began, but it involved a six-month relationship while the doctor was treating her for depression. The GMC accepted as powerful mitigation the doctor's remorse, an assumed low risk of repeating the conduct and the fact that he was separated from his wife at the time, and she had apparently denied him access to the children. It is notable that a woman's conduct (albeit the wife rather than the patient) was used to excuse the man's actions. The readiness by the High Court (and presumably the GMC) to assume that *Dare* was decided on very different facts suggests that, unfortunately, the weight given to the protection of female patients in *Dare* was not typical.

However, the shortcomings of professional regulation are by no means the only reason that it does not offer a general solution. The principal difficulty is that such regulation only applies where the perpetrator belongs to an appropriate professional body, and that body prohibits such relationships. A better form of protection is required, and one particular response which has been suggested is a tort of sexual exploitation in professional relationships. Should there be civil liability for sexual exploitation? Allen ((1996) 59 MLR) argues that there should be such liability in the following situations.

1. Where the victim's capacity is impaired (by youth, physical, mental health, stress). Even where the victim has chosen to enter into the relationship, that

relationship may become so important that they are unable to express or make an independent choice.

2. Where the sexual exploitation puts the applicant at greater risk of harm than would an ordinary relationship.

3. Where there is a professional breach of trust. Power and dependency come from the institutional and social framework in which the relationship operates. Individuals are encouraged to put their trust in professionals.

The Canadian case *Norberg* v *Wynrib* (1992) 92 DLR (4th) 449 discussed circumstances of sexual exploitation. The applicant was addicted to a particular kind of painkiller. The painkiller she needed was only available by prescription: she saw a doctor who agreed to give her a prescription on the basis that she had sex with him. She brought a threefold claim:

1. for battery;
2. for negligence or breach of contract (he failed to cure her of her addiction);
3. in equity for breach of fiduciary duty.

She received substantial damages for her claim although the judges were divided on the grounds. One judge believed that she had consented and that there was never any violence threatened. Three found a breach of fiduciary duty. Three found that she had been battered: there was no true consent, this was a case of power dependency and she had been exploited. Clearly a new tort such as this could benefit women, as they are traditionally the party exploited by this kind of situation because this type of harm is gendered. However, any such legislation would need to be carefully worded so as not to deny a woman's autonomy: one might freely choose to enter a relationship with someone met originally in a professional context. Allen's proposal would seem to strike this important balance.

There are still further legal reforms which could improve women's position when discriminated against or harassed. However, as we have said in a number of other contexts too, the law can only do so much. While attitudes in the workplace and elsewhere fail to condemn (or even condone) sexual discrimination, women will continue to suffer: any form of legal recompense can often be too little, too late.

Index

Equity and Good Conscience

Second Edition

Margaret Halliwell, AIPM, LLB, ILTHE, TEP, Reader in Law at the Department of Law, City University, London

Since publication of the first edition, the principle of unconscionability in English law has developed considerably. It is now firmly recognised as the basis of proprietary estoppel, has been accepted as the basis of a change of position to personal restitutionary claims and is the current basis of liability for a third party who receives property in breach of trust. This timely opportunity has been taken to incorporate these developments in this second edition, as well as other developments in respect of illegality, undue influence and home ownership.

In *Equity and Good Conscience* Margaret Halliwell provides a critical analysis of the mass of English law concerning the remedying of unconscionable conduct. As well as considering new developments, the author undertakes comparisons with the relevant law in other Commonwealth countries. Detailed analysis covers the law of equity in the family and commercial context, which are seen as difficult and opaque. The author considers the various substantive areas of the law in the more general context of the jurisprudence of equity and, in particular, in assessing both the impact of the principle of unconscionability and the impact of the principle of unjust enrichment.

The first edition received very favourable reviews, and the author's aim has been to produce an even better second edition. *Equity and Good Conscience* will be of interest to all students of law and to practitioners, both in the area of equity and trusts and in other areas in which remedies for unconscionable conduct exist. An essential addition to any law library.

For further information on contents or to place an order, please contact:

Customer Services
Old Bailey Press
at Holborn College
Woolwich Road
Charlton
London
SE7 8LN

Telephone: 020 8317 6039
Fax: 020 8317 6004
Website: www.oldbaileypress.co.uk
E-Mail: customerservices@oldbaileypress.co.uk

ISBN 1 85836 572 4
Soft cover 246 x 175 mm
176 pages
£19.95
Published December 2004

Old Bailey Press

The Old Bailey Press Integrated Student Law Library is tailor-made to help you at every stage of your studies, from the preliminaries of each subject through to the final examination. The series of Textbooks, Revision WorkBooks, 150 Leading Cases and Cracknell's Statutes are interrelated to provide you with a comprehensive set of study materials.

You can buy Old Bailey Press books from your University Bookshop, your local Bookshop, directly using this form, or you can order a free catalogue of our titles from the address shown overleaf.

The following subjects each have a Textbook, 150 Leading Cases, Revision WorkBook and Cracknell's Statutes unless otherwise stated.

Administrative Law
Commercial Law
Company Law
Conflict of Laws
Constitutional Law
Conveyancing (Textbook and 150 Leading Cases)
Criminal Law
Criminology (Textbook and Sourcebook)
Employment Law (Textbook and Cracknell's Statutes)
English and European Legal Systems
Equity and Trusts
Evidence
Family Law
Jurisprudence: The Philosophy of Law (Textbook, Sourcebook and
    Revision WorkBook)
Land: The Law of Real Property
Law of International Trade
Law of the European Union
Legal Skills and System
    (Textbook)
Obligations: Contract Law
Obligations: The Law of Tort
Public International Law
Revenue Law (Textbook,
    Revision WorkBook and
    Cracknell's Statutes)
Succession (Textbook, Revision
    WorkBook and Cracknell's
    Statutes)

Mail order prices:	
Textbook	£15.95
150 Leading Cases	£12.95
Revision WorkBook	£10.95
Cracknell's Statutes	£11.95
Suggested Solutions 1999–2000	£6.95
Suggested Solutions 2000–2001	£6.95
Suggested Solutions 2001–2002	£6.95
101 Questions and Answers	£7.95
Law Update 2004	£10.95
Law Update 2005	£10.95

Please note details and prices are subject to alteration.

To complete your order, please fill in the form below:

Module	Books required	Quantity	Price	Cost
		Postage		
		TOTAL		

For the UK and Europe, add £4.95 for the first book ordered, then add £1.00 for each subsequent book ordered for postage and packing.

For the rest of the world, add 50% for airmail.

ORDERING

By telephone to Customer Services at 020 8317 6039, with your credit card to hand.

By fax to 020 8317 6004 (giving your credit card details).

Website: www.oldbaileypress.co.uk

E-Mail: customerservices@oldbaileypress.co.uk

By post to: Customer Services, Old Bailey Press at Holborn College, Woolwich Road, Charlton, London, SE7 8LN.

When ordering by post, please enclose full payment by cheque or banker's draft, or complete the credit card details below. You may also order a free catalogue of our complete range of titles from this address.

We aim to despatch your books within 3 working days of receiving your order. All parts of the form must be completed.

Name

Address

E-Mail

Postcode   Telephone

Total value of order, including postage: £

I enclose a cheque/banker's draft for the above sum, or

charge my   ☐ Access/Mastercard   ☐ Visa   ☐ American Express

Cardholder: ....

Card number

☐☐☐☐ ☐☐☐☐ ☐☐☐☐ ☐☐☐☐

Expiry date   ☐☐☐☐

Signature: ....Date: ....